Innovation Support in Latin America and Europe

Innovation Support in Latin America and Europe

Edited by

MARK ANDERSON

DAVID EDGAR

KEVIN GRANT

KEITH HALCRO

JULIO MARIO RODRIGUEZ DEVIS

and

LAUTARO GUERA GENSKOWSKY

Routledge
Taylor & Francis Group

LONDON AND NEW YORK

First published 2014 by Gower Publishing

2 Park Square, Milton Park, Abingdon, Oxfordshire OX14 4RN
52 Vanderbilt Avenue, New York, NY 10017

Routledge is an imprint of the Taylor & Francis Group, an informa business

First issued in paperback 2020

Gower Applied Business Research
Our programme provides leaders, practitioners, scholars and researchers with thought provoking, cutting edge books that combine conceptual insights, interdisciplinary rigour and practical relevance in key areas of business and management.

British Library Cataloguing in Publication Data
A catalogue record for this book is available from the British Library.

Library of Congress Cataloging-in-Publication Data
Anderson, Mark, 1952-
  Innovation support in Latin America and Europe : theory, practice and policy in
  innovation and innovation systems / by Mark Anderson, David Edgar, Kevin Grant, Keith
  Halcro, Julio Mario Rodriguez Devis, and Lautaro Guerra.
    pages cm
  Includes bibliographical references and index.
  ISBN 978-1-4094-1901-3 (hbk) -- ISBN 978-1-4094-1902-0 (ebook) --
  ISBN 978-1-4094-6032-9 (epub) 1. Technological innovations--Europe--Management.
  2. Technological innovations--Latin America--Management. 3. Knowledge management-
  -Europe. 4. Knowledge management--Latin America. 5. Creative ability in business--
  Management. 6. Organizational change. I. Title.
  HC79.T4.A5293 2013
  658.4'063094--dc23

                                                                                    2013020032

ISBN 13 : 978-1-4094-1901-3 (hbk)
ISBN 13 : 978-0-367-60619-0 (pbk)

Contents

List of Figures

List of Tables

About the Editors

Mark Anderson is International Projects Manager at Glasgow Caledonian University and Coordinator of the KICKSTART project, an EU-funded project that aims to create systems for innovation teaching and support in Latin America. Previously he was in charge of European Knowledge Transfer at Salamanca University. He has coordinated and worked on a number of other EC Innovation projects, most notably GLOBALSTART and SPINNOVA, both part of the programme Pilot Action of Excellence in Innovative Start-ups. He has edited and contributed to a number of books in English and Spanish, including *New Strategies for Innovation Support* (edited Peter van der Sijde, Alfredo Mateos and Mark Anderson, Edicones Amarau) and *Key Initiatives for the Commercialisation of Knowledge* (edited Alfredo Mateos, Mark Anderson, Ediciones Amarau).

Dr David Edgar is Professor of Strategy and Business Transformation at Glasgow School for Business and Society. His main areas of research and teaching are in the field of strategic management, specifically dynamic capabilities, business uncertainty and complexity, and innovation. He has worked with a range of organizations on Business Transformation projects in particular relating to e-Business strategies, innovation and knowledge or talent management. David's interest in innovation relates to innovation as an element of dynamic capabilities.

Dr Kevin Grant is Head of Department of Informatics at London South Bank University. Kevin is an active researcher with over 55 publications, a teacher of all levels of higher education and adviser to both the private and public sector in the areas of the management of innovation, technology enabled innovation and strategic IT/IS alignment.

Dr Keith Halcro is Head of Subject (Management: Innovation, Operations and Strategy) at Glasgow Caledonian University. He consults and researches within the field of innovation, particularly the interface between strategy and innovation. He has been involved in a number of international projects in Europe and Asia.

Julio Mario Rodriguez Devis is Dean of the Faculty of Engineering at the Universidad Central, Colombia. He is a researcher and expert in innovation and creativity management capacity-building in organisations using a complex systemic approach, as well as in the formulation and evaluation of innovation projects. He is a member on the Member' Commission Professional Body and coordinator of the Community of Thinking on Innovation for the ACIEM (Colombian Association of Electronic and Mechanical Engineering). Member of the Board of Directors of the Centre for Technological Development (CIGRAF). Academic Coordinator of the ALFA project, Founder and President of the Colombian Association of Technological Management (Acoltec).

Lautaro Guerra Genskowsky is Professor at the Informatics Department at Universidad Técnica Federico Santa María (UTFSM), Valparaíso, Chile, and has a Master of Sciences Industrial Engineering degree, LSU, USA, with postgraduate studies in Psychology at UAI and IFTI, Chile. Currently he is the Director of Modeling and Simulation of Mining Processes Center at UTFSM. He has published books and papers in the areas of systems, technological processes and innovation.

About the Contributors

Alexandra Mayr (Mag(FH)), is a Senior Project Manager at the University of Alicante (Spain). Ms Mayr was the main coordinator of the PILA-Network Project which promoted Intellectual Property Rights Management in Latin American Universities, and has participated in a number of projects, seminars, conferences and publications on R&D and innovation.

Aliandra Barlete has a degree in Communications from the Federal University of Santa Maria, Masters in Higher Education (2008) from the Erasmus Mundus programme at the University of Oslo (Norway), Tampere (Finland), and Aveiro (Portugal). She has worked with internationalisation of higher education in several countries and currently works for the British Council in Brazil.

Anne Smith lectures in entrepreneurship and innovation at Glasgow Caledonian University. Her research focuses on rural entrepreneurship and enterprise education. Research partnerships include CSIRN Complex Service Innovation Research Network, University of Glasgow and with CRLL Centre for research in Lifelong learning as a research associate.

Dr Bryan Temple has worked as an engineering designer for most of his life. Working in the glass, microfilm and electronic industries, he has considerable experience of company direction. Now retired, he has spent the last 20 years within academia where he has specialized in cross-discipline teaching.

Davide Diamantini is Associate Professor of Sociology of Innovation at the University of Milan – Bicocca. He is also vice-director of the Interdepartmental Center QUA_SI (Quality of Life in the Information Society). His research interests include companies' and schools' education and training, mobile learning, cyber bullying, business innovation, local development and technological innovation applied to the didactics.

Guillermo Solano Fuentes is Managing Director of Centro de Innovacion in Colombia (www.centrodeinnovacion.com) and founder of the Red de Innovaciòn initiative (www.reddeinnovacion.org). He runs the Taller de Ideas blog (www.tallerideas.blogspot.com). He is co-creator of the WakeUpBrain game (www.wakeupbrain.com) and author of the *Empresa Sapiens* and *From Idea to Product* books.

Jaime Parada-Avila has 35 years-plus experience in the fields of research, science and technology development, innovation and business management. He currently holds the position of CEO of the Institute for Innovation and Technology Transfer of Nuevo Leon, the agency in charge of driving the state policy towards a knowledge economy and society.

Julia Gottwald (Dipl.-Ing., MSc) works at the Hamburg University of Applied Science in Germany in the Research and Transfer Centre 'Applications of Life Sciences'. She is coordinating several EU-funded projects on technology transfer and development cooperation in the renewable energy sector in Latin America as well as African, Pacific and Caribbean small island development states.

Laura Meagher (PhD), Senior Partner of Technology Development Group, Scotland, has worked in innovation since co-founding and serving as first Vice President of the North Carolina Biotechnology Center, the first statewide biotech centre for economic development. She also conducts formal evaluations of Knowledge Exchange processes and non-academic impacts of research.

Lorena Alemán De La Garza is the coordinator of extension and special projects, most notably the Teacher Education Program for Higher Secondary Education (PROFORDEMS), and the New Teaching Profile Program. She is also a distance education teacher for Tecnológico de Monterrey's Graduate School of Education.

Lorena is also a member of Tecnológico de Monterrey's Senate, and is an associate researcher for the Network for Research and Innovation in Education from Northeastern Mexico (REDIIEN) and the 'KickStart' Network for the ALFA III Programme of the European Commission.

Lorena Rivera León was a research assistant in the London School of Economics and Political Science, Department of Media and Communications between 2008 and 2010. She is currently a consultant in the evaluation of innovation and research policies in Technopolis Group, and a PhD research fellow at UNU-MERIT in the Netherlands.

Marcel Georgina Gómez Zermeño is a member of the National System of Researchers (SNI 1). Currently, she is the director of the Educational Research Center at Tecnológico de Monterrey's Graduate School of Education. She is a professor for Tecnológico de Monterrey's Graduate School of Education, in the graduate programmes of Education, Educational Technology and Educational Institution Management.

Maria Cruz Barluenga works as an enterprise educator at the University of Sheffield. Previously Maria worked in corporate, non-profit and public administration institutions. She has participated in educational and economic development projects and programmes in the EU, USA, Latin America, eastern Europe, central Asia and northern Africa. Her postgraduate education includes a Master of International Affairs from Columbia University in New York and a Master in Financial Analysis from Universidad Carlos III de Madrid.

Mariangela Tommasone (PhD), is a research fellow at the Faculty of Education at the University of Milan – Bicocca. Her research interests deal with innovation and local development, with a focus on relations between the university and the various players of a territory. She also works on projects and training activities for companies and schools within the Higher Education and Advanced Research Center QUA_SI (Quality of Life in the Information Society).

Martha Leal-González has worked for over 30 years in private industry, federal and state government at director levels in the fields of science and technology policies, strategies and programmes. She has specialized in the role of functional leader in strategic analysis and in project, knowledge and technology management.

Paolo Dini (PhD, MS: Penn State; BS: UC Davis) is a Senior Research Fellow with the Media and Communications Department at LSE. Coming from an engineering background, in social science he works on the epistemologies of interdisciplinary research, social and economic theory, and sustainable socio-economic development catalysed by ICTs.

Rodrigo Kataishi is currently an advanced PhD Candidate at the University of Turín (Italy). He took a master on Management of Science, Technology and Innovation (Argentina), and worked at the Industry Institute – Universidad Nacional de General Sarmiento (Argentina) as Research Assistant. His research interests are related to new technologies, innovation and technological change in developing countries.

Professor Walter Leal Filho (BSc, PhD, DSc, DPhil, DL, DLitt, DEd) is a Senior Professor and Head of the Research and Transfer Centre 'Applications of Life Sciences' at the Hamburg University of Applied Sciences in Germany and at the London Metropolitan University Business School. He is a member of Working Group II (Climate Change Adaptation) at the Intergovernmental Panel on Climate Change (IPCC), founding editor of the *International Journal of Sustainability in Higher Education* and serves on the editorial board of various journals.

Dr Youssef Ahmad Youssef is a Professor at the School of Business, Humber Institute of Technology and Applied Learning, Toronto Canada. Youssef holds a PhD in Management and MSc in Production Engineering from the Federal University of Santa Catharina, Brazil and a BSc Electrical Engineering from Lins School of Engineering, Brazil

Introduction

Innovation in Latin America and the Role of KICKSTART

MARK ANDERSON, DAVID EDGAR, KEVIN GRANT, KEITH HALCRO, JULIO MARIO RODRIGUEZ DEVIS and LAUTARO GUERRA GENSKOWSKY

This book considers the idea of innovation within a setting that intrigues many, but has yet to be fully explored: Latin America. The book draws together a series of chapters written by policy makers, academics and practitioners on their observations and interpretations of innovation. The material is designed for both practitioners and scholars interested in this complex but increasingly relevant issue; however, it is hoped that anyone with an interest in innovation and/or Latin America will also enjoy this book. The discussion focuses on innovation, an idea that is widely discussed but frequently poorly understood. The writers seek to explore and clarify ideas and thinking behind the concept of innovation within a region that is rapidly developing economically and socially. The chapters' contents were outlined originally at the first Innovation Support in Latin America and Europe (ISLAE) conference. The conference aimed to bring together academics, practitioners and policy makers to explore current thinking and practice surrounding innovation, especially in relation to Latin America.

Innovation has become key to policy-making at all levels, not only within governmental and intergovernmental bodies, but also within companies and public institutions, such as universities. Unfortunately innovation can be defined in an infinite variety of ways and as such can be used as a blanket term to describe (and disguise) complex concepts and processes that are difficult to comprehend. In essence, innovation is about harnessing knowledge and applying it in a practical way. It is assumed that there is something implicitly novel about innovation either in the knowledge itself or the way that it is applied. In contrast to an invention, which does not necessarily need to be applied to anything, innovation must serve a purpose. So, for example, the wheel in itself is an invention, but using it as means of transportation is an innovation. It has been said that 'invention turns cash into ideas while innovation turns ideas into cash', in other words, that innovation is synonymous with commercialization. But, although the application of knowledge clearly adds value, this does not necessarily have to be commercial; it may be of social value. It is also increasingly recognized that innovation is not just about new products; it may also be about new processes, new forms of marketing or communication, new organizational structures, etc. This is why innovation has become important at so many different levels, but it also begs the question, what can we do to encourage people and organizations to innovate? How can we teach innovation effectively? It is about a whole range of skills: it is about entrepreneurship, about creativity and the ability to identify problems, it is about leadership and teambuilding, but it is also about strategy, networks and communication. It is about personal development but also about creating the right ecosystems to encourage and optimize innovation. It is about the relationship, not only between local and regional governments, university and business (often referred to as the triple helix relationship) but also with civil society organizations and international networks. This discussion within the context of Latin America is rapidly gaining traction, as the region seeks to harness more effectively, its human capital to create a more equitable and sustainable society.

Latin America stretches from Mexico in the north to Chile and Argentina in the south and encompasses all those countries, whose first language is either Spanish or Portuguese. Home to nearly 550 million people, it is an area projected in the coming years to experience some of the world's fastest rates of economic growth fuelled by its rich natural resources. However, there is a rising belief that Latin America must move beyond its role as a supplier of low-knowledge mineral and agrarian produce to a more knowledge-based society, particularly if it wishes to create more sustainable and equal societies. The ideas found in this book examine innovation in relation to a number of topics: systems, turbulence, knowledge exchange, commercialization, capacity building and practice. Innovation's role in a society's economic fortune has come to be widely accepted, but although our understanding of the dynamics involved in creating and sustaining innovation within a society has improved; practitioners, policy makers and researchers still confront gaps in their knowledge. This is evident in relation to Latin America, where researchers have sought to link the region's economic development to ideas associated with innovation. Politicians, business leaders and others frequently pronounce their belief in innovation and almost assume that uttering the expression will instil innovation, but the reality is that to develop innovation at micro and macro levels requires an understanding of the drivers operating within these settings. It is argued that various drivers encourage innovation: economic opportunities, government policy and availability of support agencies to name but a few, but one driver that occurs is the creation of effective networks of practitioners, policy makers and academics within and between societies. This should arguably be easier in a region characterized as sharing cultural, economic, geographical and historic DNA (Bulmer-Thomas 2003). However, to understand innovation within a Latin American context it is necessary to examine its history.

History of Innovation in Latin America

Historically Latin America has scored poorly in terms of innovation (Schneider 2009). Critics argue this problem reflects cultural forces rooted in the region's history. Centuries of indiscriminate exploitation of human and natural resources have characterized Latin America's economic, social, cultural and political development. The wealth plundered from the Aztecs, Incas and other Amerindian people by the first Conquistadores created a mythology which encouraged other adventurers and colonists to view the region as a treasure trove ripe for exploitation, often one worked by slave labour, whether Amerindians or Africans. This fascination reflected and engendered the idea of El Dorado, a city of fabulous wealth, exemplified by the belief that the king bathed in gold dust. It is argued that these notions of inexhaustible mineral wealth and cheap labour nurtured colonial economic development and came to characterize the region's subsequent economic model: extractive, primary industries.

The late eighteenth century saw ideas of the Enlightenment and the colonialists' success in the American Revolution inspire growing disillusionment with Spanish and Portuguese colonial rule. The disruption caused by the Napoleonic wars led to further disillusionment between the Iberian colonial powers and their colonies, culminating in a series of rebellions throughout the decades of the 1810s and 1820s. The result was the emergence of numerous independent countries, including Argentina (1816) Brazil (1822), Colombia (1819), Mexico (1821) and Peru (1821). Over the next 30 to 40 years Spain would try to re-establish its colonial empire, but was frustrated by other powers, notably Britain, France and the United States. The commercial opportunities afforded by these newly independent countries tempted many European and American businessmen to Latin America. The original fascination of gold and silver now gave way to economic possibilities afforded by other minerals, for example copper in Chile, or agriculture in Brazil and Argentina. This focus on primary resources continued unabated, often driven by outside capital, initially from the UK, although by the 1920s the United States of America had supplanted the UK to become the largest investor.

The emphasis on primary industries may have offered a degree of continuity pre- and post-independence, but political instability dogged these societies post-independence. Frequent bloody civil and/or inter-state wars racked the region, for example Uruguay (1839–1851) or Peru's war with Chile (1879–1883). This political turmoil and violent undercurrent persisted throughout much of the twentieth century. Even within living memory countries such as Argentina, Brazil and Chile have experienced bloody internal conflicts. Intriguingly though, these events did not deter waves of European and Asian immigration; however, Latin American societies continued to be controlled by landed elites whose ancestors had migrated during the colonial period. This elite developed and perpetuated systems and processes designed to maintain their economic and political status, ones that invariably rested on an ideology focused on raw material production, since this elite controlled the majority of the land. Although industrialization did occur in the mid to late nineteenth century, the evidence suggests it was patchy and centred around Buenos Aires and Sao Paolo where immigrants played the pivotal role of innovators (Barbero 2008). Latin America's countries never fully encouraged or attained the levels of industrialization enjoyed by other societies, such as France, Germany, the United Kingdom and the United States, or more latterly Japan.

The explanation for this reluctance to fully industrialize is inevitably complex, since it both reflected and perpetuated a focus on raw material production at the expense of a more widespread innovation. Certain sectors were noted for their innovation, notably mining, but development invariably rested in the hands of foreigners or foreign companies. Where Latin American innovators emerged, their ideas and companies often were bought over by Europeans or North Americans and the knowledge in time drifted to the parent company's home country. This stunted economic development; a feature which mirrored the political landscape. Latin American failed to develop more equitable, meritocratic societies and instead its political make-up in the nineteenth and twentieth centuries was blighted by gross inequality and repeated bouts of instability, as conservatives and liberals wrestled for political control. The incessant power struggles and instability that accrued, consequently encouraged a desire amongst many for strong military leaders or *caudillos*, e.g. Peron in Argentina.

It is suggested that these *caudillos* behaved like medieval European kings dispensing patronage to followers in exchange for their support, therefore power came to be held by those whose fortunes were based on social patronage, rather than ability. This thwarted political development, but societies arguably acquiesced in this arrangement, because they believed it created stability and avoided conflict. It is argued this lack of meritocracy or any form of constructive criticism stifled innovation and the emergence of entrepreneurs. Instead, political expedience and economic reality encouraged the elite to maintain Latin America's role in the world economy as a provider of raw materials. The concept of patronage extended to the idea of state intervention and the belief that successful enterprises needed to align themselves to the political elite, rather than trying to innovate to satisfy customer needs and expectations.

This observation explains Schneider's (2009) comment that writers in the 1960s had summarized that Latin American entrepreneurs were insufficiently entrepreneurial, a view that still persisted into the 1980s, but by then the explanation had morphed into the idea that state intervention, rather than innovation, was the solution to economic prosperity. Sutz (2003) posits that these experiences resulted in flawed, inadequate structures unable to stimulate or support innovation, consequently models were imported from abroad. These tended to be poorly implemented or realized, because key players in politics, business and education lacked the drive or enthusiasm to ensure its success. Therefore innovation emerged only fitfully and often lacked a champion.

Universities exist to research and transfer knowledge, yet the evidence suggests Latin American universities have failed to often engage in this activity, because of political and cultural factors. Whilst numerous writers have criticized the universities for a lack of intellectual leadership, they are also critical of politicians and business leaders for failing to engage and interact with the academic community role in stimulating and supporting innovation (Moguillansky 2006, Raffo et al. 2008, Sutz 2003). In fact, it is further argued that having started from a position of comparative advantage relative to east Asian countries, Latin American governments have been slow in developing institutions and infrastructure able to stimulate innovation or establish links between national and global innovation systems. Moguillansky (2006) argues that where linkage has occurred in Latin America, it has been driven by multinationals, although often for their benefit. He contends that these companies have failed to develop deep links to local suppliers, such as universities, partly because they believe universities lack an innovative culture; thus, in a bitter irony perpetuating the region's lack of innovation. Raffo et al. (2008) believe governments have to introduce policies that will stimulate innovation, but academic communities similarly have a role to engage in this process, both for the betterment of society, but also to reflect a key principle of a university's existence.

Innovation in Latin America

If innovation is important for countries within Europe, it is doubly important for low- and middle-income countries which do not have easy access to developed markets. Many of the obstacles to innovation in Latin America are at a macroeconomic level: governmental policies do not sufficiently address research and technology; as a consequence of this and due to social problems, there is a brain-drain whereby the best researchers emigrate (primarily to the US); there is a small scientific community with low publication and patenting rate. Most significantly, there is very little interaction between the university, government and business, and also with civil society and international networks. As a result any innovation that takes place in the region tends to focus on the adaptation of existing products, processes and services to the local social and economic realities, without a strong knowledge base, which means that expansion into other more developed markets is practically impossible. Paradoxically, in Latin America the level of early stage entrepreneurship is among the highest in the world according to the Global Entrepreneurship Monitor (Bosma and Levie 2009). However, these figures are largely due to the fact that in Latin America there is little social welfare to cushion the unemployed from poverty and as such most entrepreneurship that takes place is through need rather than choice. Nevertheless, it highlights an interesting question: if the communities in Latin America and individuals could become more aware of innovation, if the relationships between government, universities, business and civil society became more effective and, furthermore, if their networks became more internationalized, allowing them to access knowledge, markets and even funding more directly, the innate entrepreneurial spirit within the region could prove a powerful force.

KICKSTART (www.alfa-kickstart.org)

The KICKSTART (www.alfa-kickstart.org) project tackles the multifaceted but increasingly pertinent issue of international innovation by developing a network for academic entrepreneurship and knowledge transfer through a consortium of nine higher education institutions, from Latin America (Colombia, Mexico, Peru, Bolivia, Chile and Argentina) and Europe (Spain, Germany and the UK). The project also recognizes the importance of involving other key players within the innovation process and has designated a number of associated partners within each region, including chambers of commerce, ministerial departments and companies directly contributing to regional innovation support.

The project has been partially funded by the European Commission's ALFA programme for cooperation between Higher Education Institutions of the European Union and Latin America which aims to promote Higher Education in Latin America as a means to contribute to the economic and social development of the region. The first phase of the project, funded under ALFA II culminated in a series of web-streamed workshops, a business-plan competition, researcher-exchange programme and textbook. While the original project largely focused on knowledge transfer and commercialization (the acronym derives from Key Initiatives in the Commercialization of Knowledge) the second phase places a greater emphasis on *Ways to Teach Innovation* in its widest sense. The second phase of the project – funded under ALFA III – has strengthened and expanded the network, involving local stakeholders setting up three one-year innovation support programmes in Bolivia, Colombia and Peru, as well as designing an international master's programme in innovation. To accompany its activities the consortium has produced a number of books and tools, a web portal and a series of conferences under the title *Innovation Support in Latin America and Europe*.

From the outset, it was clear that the project could not be implemented in isolation within the universities. By its very nature, innovation needs to involve a range of different collaborators. The universities are ostensibly knowledge factories and in order for them to engage with the innovation process they must involve businesses and governmental organizations. It is all very well to promote entrepreneurship and creativity within the university but we must also arm academics with the means to externalize their activities. For this reason, each of the university partners has involved at least one of these external collaborators as an associated partner of the project. They have been vital in an advisory capacity and have helped to shape the activities of the project. Some of the associated partners are governmental organizations, others are SMEs but all of them are actively engaged in innovation and give added value to the project. What has become increasingly clear during the course of the project is that innovation is intrinsically linked to social cohesion. On the one hand, innovation increases wealth which in turn improves the quality of life, but innovation can also lead directly to social benefits since many of the ideas that are harnessed and applied have a direct impact on society in the fields of health, education, the environment etc. This aspect, of what is known as *Social Innovation*, is clearly of special relevance to the project as a whole.

Given the complexity of the subject, it comes as no surprise that innovation is extremely difficult to teach. At a personal level it may be about creativity, problem-solving, leadership or entrepreneurship, but institutionally it must also involve an understanding of the concepts and structures that need to be in place in order to develop an innovation ecosystem. Innovation can be taught as part of the curriculum or as part of an extracurricular activity, it might be about individual mentoring or the institutional development of a master's degree. The activities of the project aim to address all these areas.

In order to understand the realities of each participating region more comprehensively, a diagnostic study was made of all nine institutions within the consortium and an analysis made of the needs and best practices of their existing innovation ecosystems. As a continued part of this preparation process we have also developed a strategic tool which can be used to help institutions assess the support they are offering to optimize their innovation activities both in terms of the innovation process itself and the nurturing of innovative talent. A number areas were identified: business creation/strategic management; design and product development; project management; knowledge management; market intelligence; process improvement; creativity; human resources; interface management; collaboration and networking; decision-making; problem-solving. The tool has been validated by the Instituto Tecnológico de Monterrey (Mexico) and will be available online shortly.

In terms of implementation, a major deliverable is the establishment of institutional innovation centres or programmes in three of the partner universities in Colombia, Bolivia and Peru. The consortium organized a series of visits, initially as a diagnostic in order to characterize the innovation environment of each of the three universities through meetings and workshops with students, academics and local stakeholders including companies, chambers of commerce, governmental bodies etc. As a result, a blueprint for innovation teaching and support was developed and subsequently specialized trainers sent out to each institution in order to equip them with the skills necessary to deliver the programmes. We are pleased to report that in all three cases the programmes are now fully operational and leading to impressive results:

- *Colombia*: With the support of the University of Münster (Germany) the Universidad Central in Bogotá has trained 20 facilitators to deliver a series of workshops based on the ideas mining methodology (an innovation programme developed by the German university) for both students and business leaders. Furthermore, a university network will be built up in Bogotá, inspired by the Germans' POWeR network. The name of this new network will be *RUBI* (the Spanish word for 'ruby') – an acronym standing for *Red de Universidades Bogotanas Innovativas* (Network of Innovative Universities in Bogotá).

- *Bolivia*: With the support of the Universidad Técnica Federico Santa María (Chile), the Universidad Privada de Santa Cruz de la Sierra has established its *Centro de Innovación Internacional*. The centre has programmed a series of short courses, workshops and events related to innovation (elevator pitches, business plans, leadership, ideas mining, etc.) and has promoted the resulting projects at local entrepreneurship events as well as developing an incubation facility, innovation catalogues and an in-house website for the centre.
- *Peru*: With the support of the University of Buenos Aires (Argentina), the Pontificia Universidad Católica de Perú has established a *Programa de Emprendores* to promote entrepreneurship amongst its undergraduate students. The programme consists of a series of courses in Entrepreneurship, Design and Management of Enterprises and Innovation. There was also a masterclass in Intellectual Property Management, Licensing and Negotiation Contracts given by Javier Gómez, director of CONICET, Argentina. The university is also re-structuring its innovation processes as a direct result of the diagnostic visit by KICKSTART partners.

The MSc in International Innovation Management currently being developed by the Consortium will address the particular innovation challenges faced by managers, practitioners and policy makers from across Latin America and Europe (potentially, the world) who are tasked with ensuring that innovation is a central feature of their organization/company or countries culture. This attitude to innovation permeates all aspects of the business from its people to the development of new processes and products, to the global context within which the organization is operating. This programme will equip these 'players' in developing their current knowledge and skills and accessing new networks and clusters. The programme will be supported through a combination of online materials, web tutorials, learning groups and intensive block delivery (of flying faculty). This means that students must have regular access to email and to the Internet and that each centre where the MSc is offered will provide a module contextualized to their own countries innovation system. This is shown in the philosophy and structure of the programme.

The following chapters explain various practices and thinking designed to stimulate innovation within Latin America. These themes underpin the larger European Union project, KICKSTART (www.alfa-kickstart.org). This book is an expression of this initiative, but it is also designed to be a tool to encourage innovation and knowledge transfer between and within Europe and Latin America.

The KICKSTART project is partially funded by the European Union. However, the contents of this document are the sole responsibility of the authors and can under no circumstances be regarded as reflecting the position of the EU.

References

Barbero, M.I. 2008. Business history in Latin America: A historiographical perspective. *Business History Review*, 82(3), 555–75.

Bulmer-Thomas, V. 2003. *The Economic History of Latin America since Independence*. Cambridge: Cambridge University Press.

Bosma, N. and Levie, J. 2009. *Global Enterprise Monitor*. Babson College, MA: GEM consortium.

Moguillansky, G. 2006. Innovation, the missing link in Latin American countries. *Journal of Economic Issues*, 40(2), 343–57.

Julio Raffo, J., Lhuillery, S. and Luis Miotti, L. 2008. Northern and southern innovativity: A comparison across European and Latin American countries. *The European Journal of Development Research*, 20(2), 219–39.

Schneider, B.R. 2009. Hierarchical market economies and varieties of capitalism in Latin America. *Journal of Latin American Studies*, 41, 553–75.

Sutz, J. 2003. Inequality and university research agendas in Latin America. *Science, Technology, and Human Values*, 28(1), 52–68.

1

Innovation in Practice and Practising Innovation: Making Sense of a Contested Area – A Conceptual Framework for Educators

DAVID EDGAR, KEVIN GRANT, PETER DUNCAN, ANNE SMITH and KEITH HALCRO

Introduction

Innovation, the management of innovation and innovation in practice have been widely explored, debated, conceptualized and contested. The result is a plethora of tools, techniques and theories all claiming to encapsulate the essence of innovation and provide normative frameworks that allow anyone, anytime and anywhere to become more innovative. Indeed, some claim that from reading them one will become an expert in, and of, innovation. As such, the area of innovation, while still in a relatively embryonic stage of development (since the 1960s) has become disjointed, fragmented and cloudy – its landscape can be seen more as a messy swampland, piecemeal and lacking 'wholeness', rather than providing a clear, panoramic and uninterrupted view of practice, theory and development.

The aim of this chapter is to posit an informed conceptual framework (of innovation) that allows academics and practitioners of innovation to navigate the 'swamp like landscape' that currently exists. The process of developing the framework will unpick the basic premise that innovation can be considered and developed from two alternative, yet potentially interacting and interconnecting, perspectives. The result is the production of a conceptual understanding of innovation that allows academics, practitioners and policy makers to better understand and stimulate innovation practice and theory through recognizing the interplay and collision between systems, process and talent.

The chapter unpacks what is expected from the application of innovation, before identifying the range of tools and techniques that can be used to systematically and prescriptively develop 'innovation'. This is followed by a discussion of whether innovative capacity and its development is a craft or a science, before overlaying the need to integrate both processes and talent into how one conceptualizes and enacts innovation. A conceptual framework is then proposed, which attempts to make sense of the current innovation landscape from a systemic, process orientated vantage point. In this respect, the authors highlight a conceptual framework that binds together the 'management of and for innovation' as a process, with the 'management of innovative talent'; in effect, recognizing the interplay between innovation systems, processes and people. In support, the authors provide an extensive bibliography of further reading in the field to help consolidate thinking and attempt to move the field forward and allow others to find different and differing navigation routes through the current complex 'innovation landscape'.

Background

To understand innovation, it is useful to clarify the need for innovation, what is meant by 'innovation' and what various perspectives of innovation exist. Having established this, it will then be possible to explore the various tools and techniques used to stimulate innovation and capture innovative ideas, processes and concepts.

The OECD Innovation Strategy 2007 states:

> *In 2007, with productivity losing momentum, OECD ministers agreed on the need to improve the framework conditions for innovation. A worsening economic climate has increased that imperative. The analytical challenge of the OECD Innovation Strategy is to understand better how innovation works in a global market for science and technology. The goal is to help policy makers improve framework conditions for innovation and trigger a virtuous circle driving growth. (See www.oecd.org/innovation/strategy)*

The appreciation of a connection between the ability to innovate and economic growth means that governments and academia should challenge the image that is the current landscape of innovation and innovative practice.

Governments across the globe are setting and driving policies and initiatives to stimulate creativity and innovation, none more so than in the United Kingdom (UK) and the Scottish Parliament. The UK and Scottish Parliament are committed to the development of innovation and enterprise as a means for growth and future economic prosperity. So, innovation is needed as part of strategy to transform organizations and compete in a knowledge economy. What is vitally significant is that the drive for growth of such economies is seen to be achievable through innovation and the knowledge economy and its associated knowledge transfer mechanisms, and the need to reduce barriers to entrepreneurship to enable the creation and growth of new technology based firms and fast growing markets.

THE TROUBLESOME CONCEPT OF INNOVATION

In reviewing the literature on innovation, various definitions emerged highlighting different dimensions and domains of innovation or innovativeness. Schumpeter (1942) constructed the concept of the 'entrepreneur with innovation' in order to present it as a process of 'creative destruction' essential to the economic growth of a country. However, innovation extends beyond this view: it can be incremental or radical in nature; it can be across product (Oslo 2005), process (Edquist 1997), position (Pedersen and Dalum 2004), users (Von Hippel 1978, 1998, 1986, 2005), social networks (Rogers 1959, 1983), environments (Tushman et al. 1997, Tushman 1997, Tushman and O'Reilly 1996, Tushman and Nadler 1986, 1996) or even paradigms (Popadiuk and Choo 2006). These perspectives are based on concepts or sources of discontinuity, e.g. new markets, new technologies, new rules, new business models, unthinkable events, etc. In essence, the architecture of innovation is 'knowledge', knowledge about the components of the business, its market and industry, and how the components can and do fit together. In this regard, separating invention or creation from innovation and emphasizing that innovation is relative as a pursuit for 'novelty'. Also, innovation is part of a continuous process composed of a range of innovations. Categorizing innovation has received considerable debate, but it is clear there is a need to distinguishing between product innovation and process innovation.

The argument as how to categorize and distinguish between product innovation and process innovation has received considerable historical attention and debate (Abernathy and Clark 1988, Hollenstein 1996, 2003, Kraft 1990, Tidd et al. 1997). Product innovation represents the development of new technologies and products as well as new uses for existing products, while process innovation reflects more of an attempt to re-engineer or design the flow of work activity in the organization. In addition to the nature of the innovation, it is widely recognized that such innovation needs to impact on business performance in order to have any degree of significance. Indeed several studies have examined the impact of different innovation forms and innovation dimensions on business performance (Yamin et al. 1997, Subramanian and Nilakanta 1996, Gallouj and Weinstein 1997) and shown that positive relationships do exist between business performance and innovations (see Deshpande et al. 1993, Dwyer and Mellor 1993).

Therefore, it can be seen that innovation includes product, process and service development at its core, and in the workplace, it tends to be about examining the way things are currently done with a view to finding new and better ways of doing them. It can be applied to any element of the business/organization, throughout the value chain and does not have to be original or groundbreaking in nature. Innovation can simply be the extension, modification, or combination of already existing ideas in a way that improves existing functions. Indeed, in many ways innovation is relative.

MECHANISMS FOR INNOVATION

Given the former, it is clear innovation as a process is both important and 'manageable' (i.e. capable of being proactively managed). This section highlights briefly some of the key mechanisms used for fostering innovation and encouraging invention or creativity, i.e. 'seeking novelty' before the next section explores the tools and techniques available.

In this context, mechanisms represent the vehicles (including tools and techniques, processes, and perspectives) used to stimulate creativity and deliver innovation. The mechanisms for innovation include the following:

- novelty in product and service;
- novelty in process;
- management of complexity;

- protection of innovation, i.e. intellectual property;
- extending the range of competitive factors;
- effective and strategic use of timing;
- robust design platforms;
- rewriting the rules of the industry or changing the rules of the game;
- reconfiguring the process (all or parts);
- transferring across different contexts, applications and domains.

The above mechanisms are often supported by sets of processes or systems facilitated by what Etzkowitz (2003) terms the 'Triple Helix' of government (enterprise schemes, companies, policy, initiatives, university funding, research grants), private industry (incubators, prizes, specific units) and universities (enterprise funding, specific knowledge transfer departments, knowledge exchanges, research and innovation services).

Tools and Techniques to Stimulate Innovation

Innovation can be developed from two perspectives: either a prescriptive, systematic attempt to harness innovation; or from an emergent, systemic, eco approach to innovation and understanding innovation practices. This section explores the tools and techniques, which can be applied to adopt a prescriptive/systematic approach to innovation.

Systematic or prescriptive innovation is 'the purposeful and organized search for changes, and the systematic analysis of the opportunities such changes might offer for economic or social innovation' (Drucker 1994: 11). The following table (Table 1.1) provides an overview of the key tools and techniques used for this purpose. These tools and techniques are distinct from innovation models (e.g. Rothwell's five generations of innovation model) or the basic systemic steps of investigation; preparation; incubation; illumination; verification and application, but should be considered in conjunction with such models.

Table 1.1   Tools and techniques for systematic or prescriptive innovation

Area	Tools/Techniques
Business creation/strategic management	Business planning
	Business simulations
	Knowledge trees
	Market tracking study
	Parametric analysis
	PEST analysis
	Problem abstraction
	Product development risk analysis
	Product life cycle analysis
	Risk analysis matrix
	Spin-offs from research to market
	SWOT analysis
	Technology roadmaps
	Visual mapping

Table 1.1   Continued

Area	Tools/Techniques
Design and product development	CAD systems Card post-it systems Delphi techniques FAST (function analysis systematic technique) FMEA (failure mode effect analysis) Function and feature analysis Knowledge trees Market needs research Opportunity specification Product function analysis Quality function deployment Rapid prototyping Usability approaches Value analysis VAVE (value analysis value engineering) Visual mapping
Project management	Project appraisal Project management Project portfolio management
Knowledge management	Document management IPR management Knowledge audits Knowledge mapping Storytelling
Market intelligence	Business intelligence CRM Geo-marketing Patents analysis Technology search Technology watch
Process improvement	Benchmarking BPR JiT Workflow
Creativity	Analogies Brainstorming (catalogue technique) Brainstorming (Osborne) Brainwriting – trigger and cascade Card post-it systems Clichés and proverbs Evaluation – phases of integrated problem-solving Excursive techniques Ideas book Knowledge trees Lateral thinking Mind mapping Orthographic analysis

Table 1.1   Continued

Area	Tools/Techniques
Creativity (continued)	Parametric analysis Problem abstraction SCAMPER – stretch matrix Semantic processes – idea search matrix Semantic processes – random matching TRIZ
Human resources	Competence management Corporate intranets e-learning Online recruitment Tele-working
Interface management	Concurrent engineering R&D-marketing interface management
Cooperative and networking	Groupware Industrial clustering Supply chain management Team-building
Decision-making	Paired elimination analysis (PEA) Priorities analysis matrix Risk analysis matrix SWOT analysis
Problem-solving	Brainstorming – Osbourne Fishbone Force field analysis Pareto chart Problem abstraction Search and re-apply TRIZ

Source: Adapted and extensively developed from Hidalgo and Albors 2008.

Variations of the tools and techniques in Table 1.1 are often used in the overall generic process of the innovation cycle.

What is clear from the myriad of tools and techniques is that innovation spans not only the interdisciplinary domains but also a variety of perspectives. As such, and with such an array of approaches, we need to step back from the 'operationalizing' of tools and techniques, and rethink the 'bigger' picture in terms of the overall process of innovation, that is, the connections that hold innovation as a phenomenon together. Our conceptual framework will attempt to provide such connections.

Underlying the application of tools and techniques is the generic innovation cycle. In short, the cycle outlines linkages and connections between individual users, the organization and the environment. These linkages and connections can be viewed as more the 'spaghetti model' (often referred to in open source innovation), of innovation where the extensiveness and density of connections is evident in the practice of innovation, which piles things on top, without finding the centre or the essence. However, current understanding of these connections is that 'the complex interaction is all about knowledge and the ways it flows and is combined and deployed to make innovation happen' (Tidd and Bessant 2009: 83), which focuses on the centre and the collision of the elements, in a form a plexus rather than looking at individual strands (of spaghetti).

Unpacking the tools and techniques and considering the innovation cycle as forms of how to 'do' innovation, is a start. However, it is still no explanation as to the 'interplay' of elements of innovation. For this, we need a new conceptual framework, but first, we consider the emergent approach to the field of innovation. The next section explores the emergent, systemic nature of innovation practice, and asks 'can innovation be managed?'

Can Innovation be Managed? The Need for Talent and Talent Process Management

This section explores the skills and attributes needed to adopt an emergent perspective on innovation.

As noted earlier, to be competitive in the global market, organizations must continuously develop innovative and high-quality products and services, and deliver them on time and at a lower cost than their competitors. As such, actors are required to look for new opportunities and ways of doing things, i.e. to be creative. At the same time, they are required to be professional, understand the boundaries of their responsibilities and authority, and to work within the rules and standards of their profession. Defining the skill set of the corporate professional is becoming ever more informed and taking more prominence in the education sector and recruitment agendas. A white paper by the University of Cambridge and IBM (2008) highlights the need to nurture an interdisciplinary individual who encompasses all the skills required for innovative practice. The enabling skills stimulate opportunities in organizations through interactions and relationships, creating service innovations, which are the reconfigurations of organization, people and groups (to some extent reflecting much of the MIT90s work and associated impacts of IT on Business Transformation). It is these relationships and reconfigurations that often underpin creativity and innovation process in the organization and where organizational boundaries are crossed and the status quo is challenged. Such developments at an organizational level require management and indeed creative management. It is therefore necessary to unpack further what is meant by creativity or inventions, and the detailed architecture of individual creativity in relation to the organization.

Creativity is often perceived to be essential, yet creativity is not synonymous with innovation (Kirton 1976, 1980, 1994, Kirton and De Ciantis 1986, Levitt 2002, Rogers 1959, Hayes and Allinson 1988, 1994, 1998), rather 'innovation is the successful implementation of creative ideas by an organization' (Amabile 2000: 332). This perspective is useful for us, as it distinguishes between the generation of new ideas and their implementation (West 2002) and poses questions as to the skills sets and knowledge required to support and generate 'innovation.' In other words, the innovative 'talent'.

Creativity is undoubtedly the dominant factor that brings a new idea to the implementation stage (Amabile 2000). Amabile (1983, 1988, 1996) suggests creativity as being the production of novel ideas that are useful and appropriate to a given situation, but creativity is also often defined as a personal characteristic. So what are the personal characteristics required for creativity or being creative? A large body of literature has focused on identifying the personal characteristics, cognitive styles, and other attributes associated with creative achievement (see Scott and Bruce 1994, Amabile 1983, 1996, 2000). Overall, cognitive styles are recognized as core characteristics of employee creativity (Kirton 1976, Scott and Bruce 1994), where cognitive style is a person's preferred way of gathering, processing and evaluating information. As such the style influences how people scan their environment, organize and interpret information, and how they 'integrate their interpretations into the mental model and subjective theories that guide their actions' (Hayes and Allinson 1998: 850).

Often innovators are seen as doing things differently and preferring breakthrough to incremental improvement. As such, they seem to be ill disciplined, impractical and incapable of adhering to detailed work and are differentiated from the 'norm' by three personal characteristics: originality and idea creation; lack of conformity to rules and group norms; and limited concern for efficiency (i.e. not paying attention to detail, and lacking thoroughness (Kirton 1976, Janssen et al. 1998)).

The combination of creativity and its implementation leads to innovation. The implementation of a 'new' idea often implies taking the initiative to execute the idea (Amabile 2000, Kanter 1988). Creative people have many ideas, but sometimes have little business-like follow-through, and no initiative to make the right kind of effort to help their ideas get heard and tried (Levitt 2002). Implementing new ideas may often encounter obstacles and resistance from others, however, initiative means that one deals with these obstacles actively and persistently (Frese et al. 1997). This implies a need to manage context as well as, or as part of process. Thus, in a similar fashion to the execution of leadership, the creation of innovation is about the 'person' and the process. Perhaps it is the expression/enactment of creativity that contributes to innovation? This means that how creativity is applied in an organization could be functionalized which in turn can affect individual ability to be creative. This of course creates a distinction between style and capacity.

Nonetheless, innovative capabilities go beyond creativity. Creativity is the membrane that surrounds the process and holds it together. To be innovative therefore requires a set of abilities or capabilities to recognize an opportunity, align, acquire, generate, choose, execute, implement, learn and develop the organization. It then needs processes to help realize the opportunity.

Therefore, it would appear that the tools and techniques that exist can help support and structure the innovation process, in effect providing for the efficiency dimensions required and the sharing of ideas in a systematic and methodologically 'comfortable' way to allow buy in and ultimately implementation but at the heart of innovation is the talent base and the related behaviours that are associated with innovation such as professionalization, ethics, citizenship, venturing and talent. As such a conceptual approach is required that combines both of the important philosophical aspects to draw out the 'benefits' of each.

Having explored both the product and the process of innovation practice, we now turn our attention to present a conceptual framework, which seeks to act as practitioner's navigation aid to this area of business activity and hopefully enhance the practitioners approach to innovation.

A Conceptual Framework of Innovation in Practice and Practising Innovation

From the earlier discussion it is clear that innovation is at the heart of future business in terms of competitive advantage, knowledge based processes and core business processes. As such, innovation should form an implicit and pervasive dimension to any business and management, and thus form a core part of business and management research, study and practice. However, while innovation, the management of innovation, and innovation in practice have been widely explored, investigated and conceptualized, the result has been a plethora of tools, techniques and theories and a lack of cohesiveness or 'glue' to hold it all together. All of these claim to encapsulate the 'essence' of innovation and provide normative frameworks to allow students or practitioner to be more innovative. Ultimately, the area of innovation, while still evolving, has thus become disjointed and confused and the essence of prescriptive vs emergent approaches to innovation lost. A danger therefore exists that the practitioner may disengage unless sense can be made of how the various components fit, collide and are held in place.

The conceptual framework below offers a schematic designed to provide a plexus of both the descriptive and systematic perspective (management of and for innovative process) along with the emergent and systemic perspective (management of and for innovative talent) in the form of experimental theorizing. The informed framework seeks to spark debate with the various communities of practices connected to (and with) innovation and the practices of innovation. The inclusive nature of the conceptual framework attempts to enable sight of the bigger picture of innovative practice as well as the detail that constructs the whole image.

For the purposes of this chapter, the authors posit an informed conceptual framework which is a description of a set of integrated ideas and concepts about what innovation practice (as a systemic whole) should be, should do, and should behave like. The framework would be understood by various stakeholders who have a covert and overt interest in the study of innovation and innovation practices. One of the ideologies behind this is to request interested parties not to move to a solution of 'how to do' and 'how to improve' innovation and innovation practices too quickly, but to allow stakeholders to iterate and re-iterate, considering alternatives as to what is the essence of innovative practice and its associated intertwined elements and attributes.

The challenge for any modelling based approach is to deal with the practical aspects of modelling, the level of complexity and the constantly changing reality. Trying to capture and 'picture' innovation and innovation practices is difficult and complex, as different stakeholders will have different views as to what they see innovation to be and mean, given their intellectual, experience and ideological baggage. It is hard for individuals to separate what is actually being done from what should be done. The solution is to take the value judgements that they have, which are usually implicit, and make these explicit. As such, a framework is a representation of reality from the modeller's perspective. A number of frameworks help with explicit analysis by enabling a 'standard' to be determined, based on the 'vision' of a more future orientated landscape of innovation and innovation practice, to allow a comparison with the current position and understanding and as such will necessitate a change in the subjectivity of innovation and innovation practices. Such an ontological and epistemological shift involves an engagement with, and navigation of, innovation and innovative practices and it will entail a degree of unlearning and reconstitution of innovation and innovation practice.

Unpacking the Framework

Figure 1.1 presents our conceptual framework that binds together the 'management of and for innovation' as a process, with the 'management of innovative talent'. This framework recognizes the interplay between innovation systems, processes and people, and we believe, makes a significant contribution to the field. Innovation is about talent and processes, and this requires a combination of the two perspectives. The conceptual framework attempts to consolidate both views in a workable framework to assist in understanding a more holistic view of innovation.

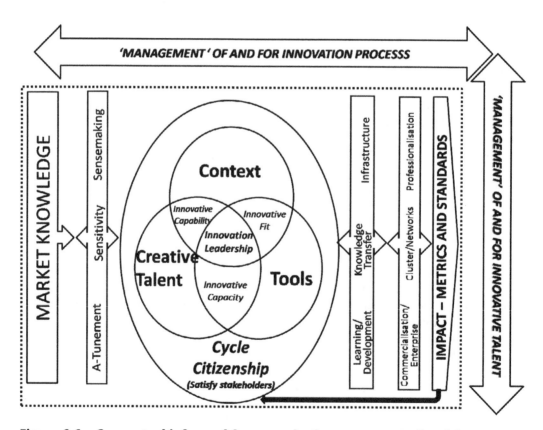

Figure 1.1   Conceptual informed framework of management of and for innovation

Taking each element of the framework and working from left (market knowledge (1)) to right (impacts (6)) we contend that the framework combines both elements of process and talent that allow for a richer understanding of innovation, and therefore 'foreground' the key components or elements that allow for a degree of effective innovation management.

Table 1.2 unpacks components 1 to 6 of the framework above.

Table 1.2   Key elements of the 'Management of and for the innovation process'

Management of and for the innovation process	
(1) Market knowledge	The changes to the external general and specific environments as reflected in economic, social, political and technological change.
(2) The market filter	This filter between the external/specific environments of market knowledge and the cycle citizenship is comprises of three elements:
	A-tunement: awareness of the interconnections in the market and the potential knock-on effects of change.
	Sensitivity: The degree to which changes can be sensed and the timeliness of such awareness/sensing.
	Sense-making: Synthesis of the changes in the market and awareness as to potential impacts and opportunities.
(3) Talent (cycle citizenship)	Cycle citizenship refers to the collective ownership, identity and sense of belonging that aligns the stakeholders in relation to the innovation process. The cycle comprises three interacting elements (creative talent, context and tools) – discussed in Table 1.3 on the following page.
(4) Transition processes	Learning and development: Part of the process that supports, develops and nurtures innovative talent through learning, reflection and reflexive activity.
	Knowledge transfer: Components of knowledge management to share, refine, develop and adapt ideas, knowledge and learning.
	Infrastructure: Physical resources and facilitating processes and policies adopted by organizations.
(5) Governance processes	Commercialization/Enterprise: Taking innovation to market for either profit or 'the common good'.
	Clusters/Networks: Sustainability of innovation through the maturity phases through the development and operation of groups of complementary (sometimes similar) innovators and/or implementers.
	Professionalization: Management and professional skills and knowledge required to support commercialization, roll out and expansion of ideas through growth and maturity phases.
(6) Impact: metrics and standards	The impact of the innovation may be measured against metrics and standards. These provide feedback, which informs the cycle citizenship. There are two elements:
	Metrics: A set of measures to measure the impact and contributions of innovations.
	Standards: The standard to be achieved for professional recognition of innovative capability and ultimate benchmark.

Table 1.2 identified the key process elements of the framework. The following table (Table 1.3) unpacks the key elements of the cycle citizenship ('Talent'; element 3 in the framework) domain of the framework. Cycle citizenship comprises three interlocking elements (creative talent, context and tools) and focuses on the management of, and for, innovative talent.

Table 1.3   Key elements of the 'cycle citizenship' domain

Management of and for innovative talent	
(a) Creative Talent	The creativity of the individual.
(b) Context	Different industry, geographic, time and relative situations, which provide a set of differing (sometimes-unique) characteristics.
(c) Tools	The range of tools and techniques available to the individual or groups to help facilitates elements of the innovation process.

As can be seen from Figure 1.1, the three components of cycle citizenship (a–c; Table 1.3) provide four interstices where the three components interact (see Table 1.4; d–f).

Table 1.4   Key elements of the 'cycle citizenship' domain

Management of and for Innovative Talent	
(d) Innovative capability	The ability to align creative competencies to the contextual situation.
(e) Innovative fit	The appropriateness of the tools and techniques used and available to the particular circumstances or contextual situation.
(f) Innovative capacity	The ability of the individual or group to select appropriate tools and techniques to match their talent capabilities and the required outcomes.
(g) Innovation leadership	The combination all of elements that compose the core of the innovation cycle.

The former components (Figure 1.1 and Tables 1.2–1.4) make up, the authors believe, what is a comprehensive, understandable and formative means by which to understand and explore the process of innovation. It also provides a way in which to understand what elements contribute to how (and in what ways) innovation can be managed, coached or nurtured. The framework also highlights areas which are under-researched and establishes the need to better understand the interplay between process and talent components. In effect the framework provides for a further research agenda which will support and facilitate the practice of 'innovation'.

Conclusions

The management of, and for, innovation is crucial to economic growth. The key value adding of this chapter is the development of a conceptual framework, via experimental theorizing, that binds together the 'management of and for innovation' as a process and helps inform educators and practitioners alike. This is particularly timely, given the emerging trend that industry may be entering a new era of 'open innovation' and the need for practitioners to ensure some form of absorptive capacity concerning innovation. The proposed framework demonstrates strategic, intellectual and formal structural dimensions, but it is flexible enough to recognize (but does not make explicit) the informal dimension that is often ignored. This element recognizes that it is these informal relationships (which cut across the formal structural boundaries), that are often the source of innovative processes and products/services, in effect the ability to lead innovation and operate a cycle of innovation citizenship. Areas often neglected by educators.

The concepts of professionalization, talent and citizenship embedded in the framework also suggest that social and cultural dimensions associated to and with innovation and innovation practices are important. Given the macro and micro climates that characterize organizational life the framework demonstrates the need to measure innovation, innovation practices and the impact of such activity on organization, individuals and society. One major weakness of the framework is its inability to fully explain the differing and different levels of innovation and innovation practices that can be in the 'system' at any one time, particularly learning from failure, given the agents involved are not all homogeneous. Nor does it fully take into account the dimension of 'open innovation' and the role community at the local, regional, national and international area could play. However, the framework does go some way is suggesting the innovation 'interplay' is the key, not the individual parts, a proposition worthy of reflection by educators and practitioners alike. Future work might include validation of the framework through multiple case studies focusing on the reality of organizations innovation processes and practices. Based on the varied process/talent dimensions of the framework, developing metrics to capture the impact of innovation initiatives and their management may also be possible; perhaps based around a balanced scorecard type approach.

References

Abernathy, W.J. and Clark, K.B. 1988. Innovation: Mapping the Winds of Creative Destruction, in *Readings in the Management of Innovation*, edited by M.L. Tushman and W.L. Moore. New York, NY: Harper Business, 55–77.

Amabile, T.M. 1983. The social psychology of creativity: Detrimental effects of competition in a field setting. *Personality and Social Psychology*, 45, 357–76.

Amabile, T.M. 1988. A Model of Creativity and Innovation in Organizations, in *Research in Organizational Behaviour*, edited by B.M. Staw and L.L. Cummings. Greenwich, CT: JAI Press, 123–67.

Amabile, T.M. 1996. *Creativity in Context: Update to 'the Social Psychology of Creativity'*. Boulder, CO: Westview Press.

Amabile, T.M. 2000. Stimulate Creativity by Fueling Passion, in *Handbook of Principle of Organizational Behaviour*, edited by E. Locke. Malden, MA: Blackwell, 331–41.

Deshpande, R., Farley, J.U. and Webster, F.E., Jr. 1993. Corporate culture, customer orientation, and innovativeness in Japanese firms: A quadrad analysis. *Journal of Marketing*, 57(1), 23–7.

Drucker, P.F. 1994. *Innovation and Entrepreneurialship*. Oxford: Butterworth Heinemann.

Dwyer, L. and Mellor, R. 1993. Product innovation strategies and performance of Australian firms. *Australian Journal of Management*, 18(2), 159–80.

Edquist, C. 1997. *Systems of Innovation: Technologies, Institutions and Organizations*. London: Pinter.

Etzkowitz, H. 2003. Innovation in innovation: The triple helix of university-industry-government relations. *Social Science Information*, 42(3), 293–337.

Frese, M., Fay, D., Hilburger, T., Leng, K. and Tag, A. 1997. The concept of personal initiative: Operationalization, reliability and validity in two German samples. *Journal of Occupational and Organizational Psychology*, 70, 139–61.

Gallouj, F. and Weinstein, O. 1997. Innovation in services. *Research Policy*, 26(4/5), 537–56.

Hayes, J., Allinson, C.W. 1988. Cultural differences in the learning styles of managers. *Management International Review*, 28, 75–80.

Hayes, J. and Allinson, C.W. 1994. Cognitive style and its relevance for management practice. *British Journal of Management*, 5, 53–71.

Hayes, J. and Allinson, C.W. 1998. Cognitive style and the theory and practice of individual and collective learning in organization. *Human Relations*, 51(7), 847–71.

Hollenstein, H. 1996. A composite indicator of a firm's innovativeness: An empirical analysis based on survey data for Swiss manufacturing. *Research Policy*, 25(4), 633–45.

Hollenstein, H. 2003. Innovation modes in the Swiss service sector: A cluster analysis based on firm-level data. *Research Policy*, 32(5), 845–63.

Janssen, O., DeVries, T. and Cozijnsen, A.J. 1998. Voicing by adapting and innovating employees: An empirical study on how personality and environment interact to affect voice behavior. *Human Relations*, 51(7), 945–67.

Kanter, R. 1988. When a Thousand Flowers Bloom: Structural, Collective and Social Conditions for Innovation in Organizations, in *Research in Organizational Behaviour*, edited by B.M. Staw and L.L. Cummings. Greenwich, CT: JAI Press, 169–211.

Kirton, M. 1976. Adaptors and innovators: A description and measure. *Journal of Applied Psychology*, 61(5), 622–9.

Kirton, M.J. 1980. Adaptors and innovators in organizations. *Human Relations*, 3, 213–31.

Kirton, M.J. 1994. *Adaptors and Innovators: Styles of Creativity and Problem-Solving* (2nd edn). New York, NY: Routledge.

Kirton, M.J. and De Ciantis, S.M. 1986. Cognitive style and personality: The Kirton adaptation–innovation and Cattel's sixteen personality factor inventories. *Personality and Individual Differences*, 7(2), 141–6.

Kraft, K. 1990. Are product- and process-innovations independent of each other? *Applied Economics*, 22(8), 1029–38.

Levitt, T. 2002. Creativity is not enough. *Harvard Business Review*, August, 137–44.

OECD and Eurostat. 2005. 'Oslo Manual'. [Online]. Available at: http://epp.eurostat.ec.europa.eu/cache/ITY_PUBLIC/OSLO/EN/OSLO-EN.PDF.

Pedersen, C.R. and Dalum, B. 2004. 'Incremental versus radical change: The case of the digital north Denmark program'. International Schumpeter Society Conference, Italy. DRUID/IKE Group, Department of Business Studies, Aalborg University.

Popadiuk, S. and Choo, C.W. 2006. Innovation and knowledge creation: How are these concepts related? *International Journal of Information Management*, 26, 302–12.

Rogers, C.R. 1959. Towards a Theory of Creativity, in *Creativity and its Cultivation*, edited by H.H. Anderson. New York, NY: Harper.

Rogers, E.M. 1983. *Diffusions of Innovations*. New York, NY: Free Press.

Schumpeter, JA. 1942. *Capitalism, Socialism and Democracy*. London: Unwin.

Scott, S. and Bruce, R. 1994. Determinants of innovative behaviour: A path model of individual innovation. *Academy of Management Journal*, 37, 580–607.

Subramanian, A. and Nilakanta, S. 1996. Organizational innovativeness: Exploring the relationship between organizational determinants of innovation, types of innovations, and measures of organizational performance. *International Journal of Management Science*, 24(6), 631–47.

Tidd, J. and Bessant, J. 2009. *Managing Innovation: Integrating Technological, Market and Organizational Change* (4th edn). Chichester: John Wiley and Sons.

Tidd, J., Bessant, J. and Pavitt, K. 1997. *Managing Innovation: Integrating Technological, Market, and Organizational Change*. Chichester: John Wiley and Sons.

Tushman, M. 1997. Winning through Innovation. *Strategy and Leadership*, 25(4), 14–9.

Tushman, M. and Nadler, D. 1986. Organizing for innovation. *California Management Review*, 28(3), 74–92.

Tushman, M. and Nadler, D. 1996. Organizing for Innovation, in *New Product Development: A Reader*, edited by S. Hart. London: The Dryden Press.

Tushman, M.L. and O'Reilly, C.A. 1996. Ambidextrous organizations: Managing evolutionary and revolutionary change. *California Management Review*, 38(4), 8–30.

Tushman, M. and O'Reilly, C.A. 1997. *Winning through Innovation: A Practical Guide to Leading Organizational Change and Renewal*. Boston, MA: Harvard Business School Press.

Tushman, M.L., Anderson, P.C. and O'Reilly, C. 1997. Technology cycles, innovation streams, and ambidextrous organizations: Organization renewal through innovation streams and strategic change. *Managing Strategic Innovation and Change*, 3–23.

University of Cambridge and IBM. 2008. *Succeeding through Service Innovation: A Service Perspective for Education, Research, Business and Government*. University of Cambridge Institute for Manufacturing (IfM) and International Business Machines Corporation (IBM).

Von Hippel, E.A. 1978. Users as innovators. *Technology Review*, 3, 11.

Von Hippel, E.A. 1986. Lead users: A source of novel product concepts. *Management Science*, 32, 791–805.

Von Hippel, E.A. 1998. *The Sources of Innovation*. New York, NY: Oxford University Press.

Von Hippel, E.A. 2005. *Democratizing Innovation*. Cambridge MA: MIT Press.

West, M.A. 2002. Sparkling fountains or stagnant ponds: An integrative model of creativity and innovation implementation in work groups. *Applied Psychology: An International Review*, 51, 355–424.

Yamin, S., Mavondo, F., Gunasekaran, A. and Sarros, J. 1997. A study of competitive strategy, organizational innovation and organizational performance among Australian manufacturing companies. *International Journal of Production Economics*, 52(1/2), 161–72.

2 *Nuances in Entrepreneurial and Innovative Activity: Developing an Understanding through Regional Studies from Latin America and Europe*

ANNE SMITH, BRYAN TEMPLE and DAVID EDGAR

Introduction

The purpose of this chapter is to explore entrepreneurial activity involving innovation across nations, regions and sectors and argue for the importance of nuance in studies that underpin policy development. In this chapter we will discuss entrepreneurial and innovative activity firstly from a global perspective and then from a regional perspective. National data from the 2008 Global Entrepreneurship Monitor GEM (2008) in conjunction with reviews of empirical research papers from regional studies in Europe and Latin America will provide the platform for exploration and discussion. This will allow us to introduce the concept of nuance and the relationship with regional and local innovation systems. We will then discuss and explore nuance in different forms illustrating the possibilities of disconnectivity as well as connectivity with innovation systems. We conclude this chapter with a developed understanding of the concept of nuance for connectivity with regional innovation systems and the impact on policy development.

The Global Understanding of Entrepreneurial Activity with Innovation

The Global Entrepreneurship Monitor (GEM) analyses data across the globe. In order to provide a coherent analysis GEM uses a framework that adopts Porters work on competitive analysis; the three principal types of economic activity applied are factor-driven, efficiency driven, and innovation-driven. Thus, the framework allows for a consistent measurement over time of entrepreneurial activity. Therefore using GEM data, the activity of a cluster of countries can be considered by understanding their entrepreneurial activity through their economy type. Using this approach, a clear distinction can be made between Latin American countries with relatively high early stage entrepreneurial activity and Eastern European countries with relatively low rates of early stage entrepreneurial activity (GEM 2008). Understanding how a country in general performs entrepreneurially, can direct further research into culture, sector expertise and the drive to pursue change. This argument is supported by the 2008 results from Argentina where 'Argentina in particular has shown a significant reaction to its national economic crisis; in 2001–2003 the Argentinean rate of necessity early stage entrepreneurs rose from 3.9 to 7.4 per cent' (GEM 2008). Therefore, if the economic climate creates a basic need to change then the necessity entrepreneur is likely to be more active. Such activity will include the use of innovation on a variety of levels. The GEM results show that entrepreneurial activity varies across the framework and so different economic contexts. Therefore from a national perspective the overall economic conditions create expectations for particular types of entrepreneurial activity. The success of GEM means that, on a global level, there is a sound understanding of entrepreneurial activity in relation to national economic conditions. However, regional studies are necessary to contribute detail, subtleties and nuances to the understanding of national, regional and sector entrepreneurial and innovate activity.

A Regional Understanding of Entrepreneurial Activity with Innovation

In order to demonstrate the nuances in regional entrepreneurial and innovate activity, two empirically based papers have been selected for detailed consideration, one from Belgium and the other Argentina. The first study by Moreno, Castillo and Masere (2007) investigates the level of entrepreneurs' self-confidence in relation to sector, regional and national entrepreneurial activity. The study uses a two stage analysis to reveal statistical significances in terms of entrepreneurial typologies, sectors and regional economic health. The authors note that 'we find that the growth of the economy ... is negatively and significantly related with the entrepreneurs' self-confidence in their business activity'. However, they also report 'local dynamism' and regional exceptions in their findings. The study used factors such as entrepreneurial typologies, geographical region, sectors, and business size. GEM 2008 placed Argentina in the framework as an efficiency driven economy and to a greater extent Moreno et al. are able, in their analysis, to reveal the connections and disconnections of the economic situation at regional and sectoral levels, with the self-confidence of the entrepreneur.

The second study considers entrepreneurial activity in the context of food sector innovation in Belgium. Gellynck, Vermeire and Viane (2007) explore 'the role of regional networks' in innovation processes. The focus is on networking behaviour for entrepreneurial activity. The authors highlight the need to position a firm in context; social, cultural and regional, before satisfactorily summating. The authors hypothesize that innovation can be found more so in regional networks and that participation in regional networks improves innovative competence. Knowledge is a key variable in their analysis, along with market orientation. Their findings reveal 'low scores of innovators ... linked to the limited regional market orientation'. However, the study supports regional networking as part of a business internationalization strategy and promotes interconnectedness at regional level for innovation competence. The nuances surrounding this paper are important: at national level Belgium is an innovation-driven economy (GEM 2008), but paradoxically networking for innovation is a regional activity.

Nuance: A Concept

Nuance captures subtleties of difference in meaning, shape and form. It is the subtleties that create difference and difference in a marketplace can mean a successful or unsuccessful innovation. Nuance as a concept means that what can exist is a very high level of difference and variation across business activity. Difference and variation offer advantages and disadvantages; difference can be considered detrimental to a product or service for example, difference is not what we expect as consumers of cars or electronic products; we expect standardization. What we are standardizing is output, inputs and the human management of knowledge and information (Gray 2006, Dalley and Hamilton 2000). However, the interaction between market, consumer and producer often requires subtle differences depending where in the world you live. For example, chocolate has different cocoa content, according to which continent it is produced for. The same standard global product can be branded with a different name according to the marketing strategy created for each country and continent. In order to protect difference and variation the European Union recognizes regional foods and protects them under the regional association and so from being produced elsewhere, for example Champagne.

Difference and its creator nuance occupy a space concerning dynamic interactions associated with entrepreneurial activity and innovation. This space is at a human level and involves the capacity for multiple computations of variables during the creativity and opportunity identification processes. The process of opportunity identification demands relevant market knowledge and a human ability to adapt and embed. The entrepreneur shapes and crafts the product, process or service with a selected set of market conditions to achieve the most favourable economic outcome (Baron 2006, Bhowmick 2007). Timmons' (2003) concept of opportunity identification might offer insight to sources of nuance; markets, economics and people. This suggests that as the concept of nuance can be developed by adapting economics, markets and people and then viewing the human interactions. Developing this idea means we need to consider how nuance is formed. Essentially it is the multiple computations of knowledge and information through human interaction that is nuance. The probability of many potential outcomes that could result from the three sources of nuance through multiple interactions during the innovation process is infinite. This means that nuance offers the entrepreneur and innovator the ability to be creative on a unique level by understanding and applying nuance in their entrepreneurial and innovation processes. The following sections consider nuance in light of the three sources – economics, people and markets.

Nuance: The Economics

Nuance can be created by what might be considered as favourable or unfavourable economic conditions. An entrepreneur and innovator will adapt and craft what they intend to do by understanding the economics of their intention and moving towards a positive economic outcome. Firstly, the geography of the region can make distribution either more or less favourable as a result of basic economics. An example can be found in an engineering and die-casting case study (Smith and Temple 2007). This company, located in Scotland, was importing raw materials from Eastern Europe, manufacturing and processing before exporting and selling to domestic markets. Two clear problems emerge: firstly, the strength of the pound meant that the gross margins were squeezed at various times during economic cycles; secondly, the cost of labour in Scotland meant that the competitiveness on a global level was compromised. Eventually this business was economically unsustainable and it is now located in a manufacturing region of Romania near airport links where the economics of the business are far more favourable. Existence of favourable and unfavourable conditions suggests that regions are wholly susceptible to economic nuance from an entrepreneur and innovator. Unfortunately this often results in the disconnnectivity by entrepreneurs and innovators from a regional innovation system. Policy over various economic cycles has attempted to promote innovation and entrepreneurial capability encouraging regional development but also in education and learning (IFM and IBM 2007, Sainsbury 2007, DTI 2007, Scottish Executive 2006). In Europe the importance of driving innovation is highly visible:

> The analytical challenge of the OECD Innovation Strategy is to better understand how innovation works in a global market for science and technology. The goal is to help policy makers improve framework conditions for innovation and trigger a virtuous circle driving growth. (OECD 2010)

The dynamics of policy means that actions based on policy will have a life span resulting in entrepreneurial or innovative activity that is transient and the economic nuance of that region is once again revealed as strategy adapts.

Nuance: People and their Behavioural Characteristics

At a human level, individual and group, nuance is prolific. People have a capability to see things differently the source of which is creativity. Creativity is being able to see things differently, being able to create something different (REF< REF< REF). Creativity precedes innovation and is the assembly of previously unrelated ideas. Technology hubs, research and development units and innovation centres have often been created by a national clustering policy to encourage creativity and knowledge sharing. Gellynck et al. (2007) highlight the advantages of clusters and hubs especially for regional networking which they found improved innovation capability. In the study by Moreno, Castillo and Masere (2007) the notion of self-confidence is fixed as an important factor on the successes of economic development at a regional level. Interesting then, that Gellynck et al. (2007) suggest regional networking is also critical; perhaps the idea of regional information and knowledge sharing builds a self-confidence. Self-confidence has been explored extensively in entrepreneurship literature and is evident in work by Cooper and Lucas (2007) where self-efficacy was a significant monitor for entrepreneurial capability. Self-efficacy and a self-confidence can be traced back in literature to social learning theory and the work of Bandura (1977). Importantly learning from social interaction is what develops the individual. It cannot be ignored that social learning is contributing to the underpinning of this argument for the existence of nuance. People will organize themselves socially for a number of different reasons. This social organization leads to networks sharing, collaboration and collectiveness demonstrating that entrepreneurial and innovative behaviours in business are indeed grounded in social learning. The multiple social interactions that create organizations and networks of people are the root of nuance. It should be minded that social interactions extend to the creation of markets. The infinite possibilities surrounding people and social interaction might contribute to an explanation of the existence of complexity in global markets.

Nuance: Complex Markets

The study by Gellynck, Vermeire and Viane (2007) highlighted that a firm with a regional market orientation was more likely to have a less developed innovation capability than that of a firm who internationalized their markets. The importance of this finding reveals an idea that infinite nuance exists in the market place; in other words an entrepreneur can keep changing and adding difference to what is delivered in the market place using the many variables. However, their study also revealed that regional networking was important to the innovative capability of the internationalizing firm. A regional orientation is a localized supplier and customer interface. It is a local embeddedness that is often constrained by market size. By dissembedding from a local structure or market the firm might create a new entrepreneurial opportunity and enter larger markets thus scaling up the business and maximizing any entrepreneurial and innovative opportunity. Scalability is often a measurement of profit potential but risk exists in the disembedding process from a local marketplace and the subsequent reembedding process in a more extensive marketplace. This is a process of development which involves relationships around socioeconomic and cultural vectors. Complex markets exist because of the extensiveness of these vectors and the nuances created by them. The study by Smith and Temple (2007) demonstrated how a construction firm can grow extensively within a regional location and with a market orientation. Key to growth in this case and the scaling up process was the firm's ability to adopt innovations but not originate. This case study revealed that strategic alliances and the use of the regional network was critical to strategic growth. In the main this supports the findings from the Gellynck et al. (2007) study but shows that there are possibilities to achieve scalability albeit with a regional market orientation. Nuance can explain this, the very fact that so many differences exist in any one situation means that a study with larger populations is less likely to trace nuance. Another example can be found in a study by McElwee, Anderson and Vesala (2006) where an English farmer approached a diversification venture as a cheese producer by entering into new markets, dealing with new customers and suppliers. The farmer struggled with the embedding process and the opportunity to venture and achieve stability was not achieved. The embedding process in a new market and with a new supply chain was too uncomfortable. Such case work is a rich source of nuance evidence, showing the importance of difference and effects of nuance in complex market situations.

Connections in Innovation Systems

Nuance in a dynamic form is entrepreneurial crafting of an idea or innovation to optimize favourable market conditions; subtle changes in how the idea is presented or shaped for the market, subtle differences in target markets, and subtle differences in how people interact during the entrepreneurial process. Together the nuances that have been discussed can enhance the competitive position in the market place. Bessant and Tidd (2007) refer to 'proactive Linkages' as the connections that set off an innovation process. These proactive linkages are the multiple interactions where information and knowledge is shared. The triple helix exemplifies the potential from managed proactive linkages specifically between academia, business and government. The triple helix provides architecture for connections with the innovation systems whether they are regional or national. Business clubs can provide a local architecture for knowledge and information sharing again potentially linking individuals and firms into an innovation system. The interaction, however, requires communication and language. This complex situation has been considered using network theory (Conway and Steward 2009, Gellynck 2007, Requier-Desjardins 2003, Blundel 2002, Erenius and De Clercq 2005, Sharp, Agnitsch and Flora 2002)). Conway and Steward (2009: 63) view innovation from a network perspective in a chapter with that title and define:

- Actors: the individuals that are members of a network.
- Links: the relationships between those actors.
- Flows: the content of interaction and exchanges.
- Mechanisms: the modes of interaction and exchanges.

These network perspective definitions are particularly useful in terms of complementing the understanding of the sources of nuance previously described; markets, people,

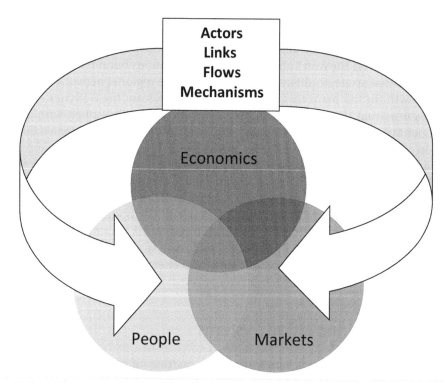

Figure 2.1   Showing relationships between sources of nuance with innovation from a network perspective

economics. Therefore from these two domains, i.e. sources and network definitions we can see an interplay that functions on nuances; nuance in a network members, nuance in their strength of participation including social and economic ties, nuance in the interactions and exchanges and finally nuance in mode, e.g. virtual, physical and so on. Subtlety, variation and difference at all these levels are an integral element in the entrepreneur's landscape. The study by Gellynck et al. (2007) demonstrated that the regional network cluster is not contradictory to an international market orientation; this suggests that the actors, links, flows and mechanisms were of such a variation that allowed them to develop beyond regional networking. The maintenance of a regional network but with an international strategy might mean that the three sources of nuance specifically people and behaviours were maintaining a social tie between actors beyond the benefits of an economic tie. Nuance in every scenario means that the differences created through the lens of the three sources of nuance and the network perspective definitions are extensive. Equally, in the Argentine study by Moreno, Castillo and Masere (2007) the impact of the economic source on the other sources and the network perspective means that a whole sector and region can be positively or negatively affected. Figure 2.1 on the opposite page views the three sources absorbed into in a network perspective bringing together the idea that through interplay nuance exists.

Identifying Disconnections in Innovation Systems

The previous section argued that nuance capitalizes on three sources and a network perspective and ultimately exists through the interplay. In any summation of findings nuance takes a role in the outcome. However, regional market orientation, localization, socially unembedded, over-embeddedment, closed operating systems all potentially negatively impact on an ability to connect with national innovation systems (Granovetter 1985). This means that although GEM presents a collective western Europe as being innovation-driven economies there is evidence from regional studies to show that there are as many disconnected enterprises and individuals from innovation. The nature of firms means that case by case there is evidence of broken supply chains (REF), controlled economic systems, e.g. European farm subsidies (Smith 2008), and over-embeddedment (McElwee et al. 2006) all resulting in non-adaptive strategic practices. Dynamic markets, succession and technological development means that national innovation systems cannot neglect regional or individual nuance.

Conclusion

In conclusion, this chapter presents the idea that understanding nuance in national, regional entrepreneurial activity is an important dimension to summations of innovative performance. Nuance in some cases might be inexplicable but equally some are as a result of geography, sector, networking activity, regional wealth, embeddedment and so on. Further reviews of studies can serve to offer a mosaic of nuance that ultimately might affect how entrepreneurial and innovative activity can be better understood.

References

Bandura, A. 1977. Self-efficacy: Toward a unifying theory of behavior change. *Psychological Review*, 84(2), 191–215.

Baron, R.A. 2006. Opportunity recognition as pattern recognition: How entrepreneurs 'connect the dots' to identify new business opportunities. *Academy of Management Perspective*, February, 104–19.

Bessant, J. and Tidd, J. 2007. *Innovation and Entrepreneurship* (2nd edn). Chichester: John Wiley and Sons.

Bhowmick, S. 2007. Opportunity creation as structuration: Illustrations from three technology entrepreneurial initiatives. *International Journal of Technoentrepreneurship*, 1(2), 129–45.

Blundel, R. 2002. Network evolution and the growth of artisanal firms: A tale of two regional cheese makers. *Entrepreneurship and Regional Development*, 14, 1–30.

Conway, S. and Steward, F. 2009. *Managing and Shaping Innovation*. Oxford: Oxford University Press.

Cooper, S.Y. and Lucas, W.A. 2007. 'Building entrepreneurial self-efficacy and intent through education and experience'. Institute for Small Business and Entrepreneurship Conference, 7–9 November, Glasgow.

Dalley, J. and Hamilton, B. 2000. Knowledge, context and learning in the small business. *International Small Business Journal*, 18(3), 51–9.

DTI. 2007. *Innovation in Services*, DTI Occasional Paper no. 9, June. London: HMSO.

Erenius, P. and De Clercq, D. 2005. A network-based approach on opportunity recognition. *Small Business Economics*, 24(3), 249–65.

GEM. 2008. *Global Entrepreneurship Monitor*. [Online]. Available at: http://www.gemconsortium.org/download/1255094564561/GEM_Global_08.pdf.

Gellynck, X., Vermeire, B. and Viaene, J. 2007. Innovation in food firms: Contribution of regional networks within the international business context. *Entrepreneurship and Regional Development*, 19(3), 209–26.

Granovetter, M. 1985. Economic action and social structure: The problem of embeddedness. *The American Journal of Sociology*, 91(3), 481–510.

Gray, C. 2006. Absorptive capacity, knowledge management and innovation in entrepreneurial small firms. *International Journal of Entrepreneurial Behaviour and Research*, 12(6), 345–60.

IfM and IBM. 2007. *Succeeding through Services Innovation: A Discussion Paper*. Cambridge: University of Cambridge Institute for Manufacturing.

McElwee, G., Anderson, A. and Vesala, K. 2006. The strategic farmer: A cheese producer with cold feet? *Journal of Business Strategy*, 27(6), 65–72.

Moreno, J., Castillo, L. and Masere, E. 2007. Influence of entrepreneur type, region and sector effects on business self-confidence: Empirical evidence from Argentine firms. *Entrepreneurship and Regional Development*, 19(1), 25–48.

OECD. 2010. [Online]. Available at: www.oecd.org/innovation/strategy [accessed: 6 May 2010].

Requier-Desjardins, D., Boucher, F. and Cerdan, C. 2003. Globalisation, competitive advantages and the evolution of production systems: Rural food processing and localised agri-food systems in Latin American countries. *Entrepreneurship and Regional Development*, 15, 49–67.

Sainsbury, Lord. 2007. *Race to the Top: A Review of the Government's Science and Innovation Policies*, Independent HM Treasury Report. London: HMSO.

Scottish Executive. 2006. *The Scottish Innovation System: Actors, Roles and Actions*. Report prepared by Stephen Roper and Jim Love (Aston Business School, Birmingham) and Phil Cooke and Nick Clifton (Cardiff University).

Sharp, J.S., Agnitsch, K. and Flora, J. 2002. Social infrastructure and community economic development strategies: The case of self-development and industrial recruitment in rural Iowa. *Journal of Rural Studies*, 8(4), 405–17.

Smith, A.M.J. 2008. Blots, bovines, buildings, businesses and brands: Monitoring the landscape of rural assets. *International Journal of Entrepreneurship and Small Business*, 5(6), 437–49.

Smith, A. and Temple, B.K. 2007. Growing and developing old economy firms. *Journal of International Business and Economy*, 8(1), 143–61.

Timmons, J. 2003. *New Venture Creation* (6th edn). Boston, MA: McGraw-Hill.

3

Generating Innovation Through Knowledge Exchange: Capturing Lessons Learned

LAURA MEAGHER

Introduction

All governments seek a return on their investment in research. While traditionally this has often taken the form of advancement of basic understanding, increasingly attempts are made to support innovation that will lead to impacts on the economy and society. Along with this, governments are more and more frequently requesting evidence that such impacts have occurred. Yet, significant challenges exist both in generating impacts from research and in identifying such impacts, While sometimes a technological breakthrough leads neatly to a commercialized innovative product, more often the picture is less clear. Sometimes interaction between researchers and users is targeted to a particular innovation but many times it is open-ended. Different protagonists and different external factors will play key roles at various times. Perhaps especially when the 'hard cases' of policymaking and professional practice are considered, impacts can be diffuse and take place over a protracted time frame, with attribution of causality to a particular research effort very difficult if not impossible. (Imagine, for example, the difficulty of identifying a one-to-one causal relationship between a specific research project and an innovative modification of a nation's educational policies.)

To address the increased desire for impacts, there is a need for enhanced understanding of effectiveness in 'Knowledge Exchange', the term used here as covering a spectrum of two-way communication between researchers and users. This can occur in interactions between researchers and companies commissioning their research, iterative dialogue over time between researchers and prospective users, or a set of multiple actors sharing different sorts of knowledge or even co-producing new knowledge. Focused attention on Knowledge Exchange *processes* can contribute to both generation and evaluation of impacts. Understanding dynamics, factors and roles will improve capacity to make the most of Knowledge Exchange processes, so that they generate innovation impacts.

One way of gaining such understanding is to view different funding schemes, large-scale initiatives or individual projects as 'experiments' in fostering Knowledge Exchange and generating impacts. Through these experiments, lessons can be learned about good practice by involved researchers, knowledge intermediaries, users/stakeholders and funders. Tapping into the reservoir of tacit knowledge gained by participants in many different projects can enrich understanding of the subtleties of Knowledge Exchange and the processes that generate positive impacts on the economy and society. Through sensitive evaluation, stepping back and analysing diverse innovative schemes or projects can: encourage organizational learning; inform Knowledge Exchange processes; and (therefore) increase the likelihood of future innovation and impact. If evaluation is to be appropriately sensitive to such processes, it is important to identify not only the conventional sorts of impacts from research (instrumental, conceptual and capacity-building), but also less tangible yet very important process-based impacts (attitude/culture change about Knowledge Exchange and enduring connectivity between academics and non-academics). In short, appropriate evaluation eliciting tacit knowledge as to flows and processes of Knowledge Exchange can contribute to a virtuous spiral, informing both generation of innovation impacts and their subsequent evaluation.

Key aspects of Knowledge Exchange are highlighted here with findings from three case studies: a learning review of Scottish projects developing mechanisms for Knowledge Exchange with policymakers and practitioners; a UK-wide initiative in ICT research aiming to have impact on a range of users; and a set of Knowledge Exchange workshops regarding the future of a biotechnology workforce in the Chilean fruit industry. Although these case studies are (deliberately) different in subject, sector and format, they nonetheless contribute lessons learned that illuminate a set of five key action steps offered here for consideration by those hoping to foster innovation and impact through Knowledge Exchange processes. This set of seemingly disparate case studies can contribute practical insights while also illustrating the value of capturing tacit knowledge into process.

Literature Review

Around the globe, governments seek to promote innovation as they aim for success in the Knowledge Economy. One key strategy lies in not only investing in research but also in making the most of research-generated knowledge. Increasing emphasis is put on effective Knowledge Exchange that can lead to beneficial innovation impacts (for example, Abreu et al. 2009, Academy of Social Sciences 2008).

Once investments in research have taken place, governments (or their research funding bodies) frequently seek to encourage return on these investments. So, for example, the UK saw the 2003 Lambert Review of Business–University Collaboration, the House of Commons Select Committee Enquiry into Knowledge Transfer and the External Challenge Report on Research Council Knowledge Transfer. The 'Warry Report' (Research Councils UK 2006) exhorted the UK's set of government funders of research, the Research Councils, to increase their economic impact ('economic' included policy, practice and other social dimensions). In response, Research Councils UK developed an action plan for Increasing the Economic Impact of the Research Councils (Research Councils UK 2007). With a key strand the development of 18 case studies (PA Consulting/SQA Consulting 2007), the RCUK's Excellence with Impact report documents 'progress in implementing the recommendations of the Warry Report on the Economic Impact of the Research Councils' – and called for yet more to be done to promote proactive knowledge transfer and connection with users. Impact has rapidly become embedded into the strategic plans of individual Research Councils (for example, ESRC 2009a) and is in the process of becoming incorporated into expectations of research initiatives and research projects, some but not all of which are explicitly targeted at promotion of Knowledge Exchange between researchers and users.

These expectations can lead to assessment of innovation impacts of particular research and schemes or initiatives. For example, the Rural Economy and Land Use (Relu) research initiative tracks and reports on its Knowledge Exchange activities with various stakeholders (Relu 2007, 2010). The author has conducted various evaluations of impacts of research and of schemes (for example, Meagher and Lyall 2007, Meagher et al. 2008, Meagher 2009, Meagher and Kettle 2009).

Weighting to be placed on effectiveness in generating research impacts beyond academia is a matter of live controversy today, as evidenced by the current heated debates over the United Kingdom's planned inclusion of 'impact' as an important review criterion in ranking departments of each discipline across the entire country (Jump 2011). With impact accounting for an expected 20 per cent of such ranking, this has very real implications for later financial allocations secured by departments and their universities.

The issue of weight placed by governments on research impacts is made even more fraught by the fact that effective approaches to identifying impacts are still being developed (CHSRF 2000, Davies et al. 2000, Lomas 2000, Molas-Gallart et al. 2000, Molas-Gallart et al. 2002, Hanney et al. 2002, Davies et al. 2005, Nutley et al. 2007, Boaz et al. 2009, Grant et al. 2009). Challenges to identification of impacts arising from research include: the difficulty of attributing causality when multiple causes may underlie any one impact, the subtlety of processes involved, and the long-term nature of most impact development, in the face of changing personnel and fading memories.

Particular challenges to impact identification arise when innovation impacts sought are in relatively intangible and elusive arenas such as policymaking, in which impacts may be even more difficult to trace than, for example, a new piece of equipment derived from engineering research. The UK's Economic and Social Science Research Council, for example, has held a series of workshops and invested in various assessments, periodically summarizing learning (for example, ESRC 2009b).

Two types of evaluation are 'summative' and 'formative'. The former comes at the end of an activity and assesses past performance with retrospective analysis aimed at some sort of accountability. The latter typically takes place during an activity, so that evaluation is 'live' and feeds into decision-making throughout the activity. Whereas assessment of research impacts might be seen automatically as a summative evaluation exercise, the author suggests that elucidation of impacts can also be viewed as part of 'formative evaluation' and that taking this view can lead to organizational learning and continuous improvement. Deep analysis of the connection between research and innovation impacts can go further than impact identification, to enhance understanding of how Knowledge Exchange actually does or could occur (for example, Davies et al. 2000, Lomas 2000). Not only does this approach have to potential to contribute to future behaviours, but it may also be a pragmatic choice. Nutley et al. (2007), for instance, suggest that learning about processes of research impact may be more readily attainable as an objective than marshalling solid evidence of impact.

It is possible to see each funding scheme, set of projects or initiative as an experiment in the generation of innovation, from which it is possible to learn. Viewed in this way, results of assessments can go beyond identification of impacts to elucidation of the processes involved in Knowledge Exchange (Meagher et al. 2008). It may be just this understanding of impact-generating processes that will actually increase innovation impacts; thus sensitive evaluation has an important contribution to make.

Methodology

The approach taken in this chapter is to present three empirical case studies, deliberately diverse in nature and focus, and examine them in light of key elements of a conceptual framework developed through the author's previous research into generation of research impacts. The focus is on eliciting, analysing, distilling and sharing tacit knowledge concerning processes involved in the generation of impacts. Thus primarily qualitative methods (semi-structured interviews, learning visits, workshops, surveys, document analysis and in one case participation/observation) were used to capture and convey practical insights in the three case studies, each based on work. Davies et al. (2005) encourage the use of case studies and suggest that greater prominence may need to be placed on mapping different research impact processes and learning about how to support and enhance future research impact. The case studies will be described in more detail below, as they illustrate key lessons learned relative to a conceptual framework for the generation of impacts from research.

It is widely suggested (for example, Nutley et al. 2007) that analyses into use of research knowledge employ a conceptual framework. The one provided here was developed from a study of 134 individual 'response-mode' research grants in psychology, funded by the UK's Economic and Social Science Research Council (Meagher et al. 2008, Meagher and Lyall 2007), and also drew upon literature on research impact which highlights the importance of interactions and multiple flows of knowledge (for example, Molas-Gallart et al. 2000, Hanney et al. 2002, Lavis et al. 2003, Davies et al. 2005) and the 'linkage and exchange model' developed by the Canadian Health Services Research Foundation to capture the research-policy relationship (CHSRF 2000, Lomas 2000). The UK Economic and Social Science Research Council now employs a not dissimilar conceptual framework.

A CONCEPTUAL FRAMEWORK: FLOWS OF KNOWLEDGE

The conceptual framework in Figure 3.1 provides a view of how knowledge flows in processes of innovation, depicting as an integrated whole various interrelationships among knowledge producers (researchers), users and others, within the context of benefiting society. When considering key processes and roles, highlighted findings captured in this framework include three key points:

- The sheer heterogeneity present in all facets – researchers, projects, relevance, users and needs.
- The vital importance of two-way communication, and the dynamic relationship-building that brings this about.
- The often unsung but important role of a wide range of 'knowledge intermediaries' occupying spaces in between researchers and users.

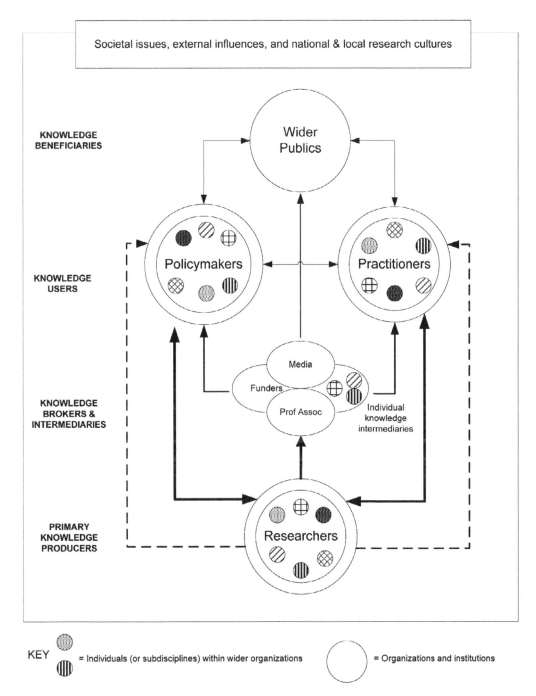

Figure 3.1   A conceptual framework: Flows of knowledge

THREE CASE STUDIES

Three case studies are discussed here as they may shed some useful light on processes and roles generating innovation and impact:

* A Learning Review, or formative evaluation study of a new Scottish funding scheme (SPIRIT) for projects developing innovative mechanisms of Knowledge Exchange with policymakers and practitioners.
* An Impact Evaluation of a large UK research initiative (PACCIT) composed of multiple projects, with many having a mandate for Knowledge Exchange.
* Investigation (by IDEA Consultora) of biotechnology workforce needs for the future Chilean agricultural industry.

Methods employed in the development of the case studies are summarized briefly here. One of the three case studies, the SPIRIT Learning Review was itself an innovative approach, funded by the Scottish Funding Council, to ensure that learning took place throughout the pilot scheme, 2008–2009. Focused on arenas ranging as widely as justice, health, the environment and other subjects, selected projects were each aimed at the development of KE mechanisms. As the Learning Review team, the author and a colleague guided self-reflection and sharing across the projects, capturing key learning. This involved iterations of semi-structured interviews (with project leaders and involved stakeholders), surveys (project leaders, stakeholders, other researchers), learning visits/focus groups with project steering committees, and two workshops devoted to sharing issues and lessons learned across projects. In addition, document analysis was enhanced by developing and providing to project leaders a guide to self-reflection and related templates for interim and final reports. Nine projects were in the scheme; views of over 50 individuals were gathered by at least one method each. Products of the Learning Review included both a report to the Scottish Funding Council and a set of Briefing Notes on Knowledge Exchange in Public Policy and Practice, now shared even beyond the original projects (Meagher and Kettle 2009).

The second case study, the 2008 evaluation of non-academic impacts arising from the large-scale initiative, People at the Centre of Computers and Information Technology (PACCIT), was commissioned by one of its three funders, the UK Economic and Social Science Research Council, at the close of funding. (Other funders were the UK Engineering and Physical Science Research Council and what was then the UK Department of Trade and Industry.) The remit was to identify impacts arising beyond academia from the 30 projects involved, the latter half of which had been explicitly encouraged to engage in Knowledge Exchange, and to reflect both on good practice/lessons learned about Knowledge Exchange and on effectiveness of methods being developed to capture impacts. A portfolio of quantitative and qualitative methods was employed, including: surveys (50), semi-structured interviews (23), document and media analysis, observation of a concluding workshop, and development of (5) in-depth case studies of particular projects illustrating Knowledge Exchange (Meagher 2009).

The third case study represents a different approach: participation and observation. In May of 2008, as a speaker and discussant at a set of three workshops held in three different regions of Chile (Santiago, Talca, Valparaiso), the author was able to observe the preparation, actions and (later) reporting of IDEA Consultora Ltda., a consulting company funded by CONICYT for 'Formacion de Capital Humano Avanzado en Biotecnologia

Fruticola' to disseminate innovation efforts from the central government to the regions while also stimulating within the regions cross-sector examination of needs, barriers and opportunities for innovation in Chile's fruit industry, as related to an agricultural biotechnology workforce (IDEA Consultora 2009). These workshops involved individuals from academia, government and industry, joining together to consider ways in which to optimize the future impact of research and training, particularly through communication and scientific workforce development. Observation of the consulting company's catalysis of these discussions sheds light on the important role of 'knowledge intermediary' in Knowledge Exchange.

Thus, insights into Knowledge Exchange processes are drawn here from a set of case studies deliberately chosen as varying in terms of sector, subject and format.

Case Study	Country	Sector	Subject	Format
PACCIT	UK	IT	Human-oriented computer technology	Large multi-project programme, KE-oriented
SPIRIT	Scotland	Policy and practice	Range from environment to health	Small pilots, learning about KE
IDEA Consultora	Chile	Biotech	Agricultural fruit biotech	Consultative workshops, strategic analysis

Findings and Discussion

As underscored in the Literature Review, a priority for those seeking innovation impacts is increased understanding of Knowledge Exchange processes that generate innovation impacts. Each of the three case studies will be used below to explore and illustrate one of the three key highlighted findings as to important processes and roles that generate innovation impacts, as noted above in relation to previous work and the conceptual framework diagram. Each highlighted finding will be illustrated by one of the three case studies. (Of course each case study incorporated more than one of these roles or processes.)

Case Study	Key Finding
1) PACCIT	The sheer heterogeneity present in all facets, researchers, projects, relevance, users and needs
2) SPIRIT	The vital importance of two-way communication, and the dynamic relationship-building that brings this about
3) IDEA Consultora	The often unsung but important role of a wide range of 'knowledge intermediaries' occupying spaces in between researchers and users

Following exploration of these three case studies will be a discussion of capturing, sharing and utilizing lessons learned as to how innovation can be fostered through effective Knowledge Exchange processes.

One) The sheer heterogeneity present in all facets, researchers, projects, relevance, users and needs – Illustrated by finding non-academic impacts of research funded to promote KE: PACCIT in the UK

Knowledge Exchange processes occur in relation to a nearly infinite range of subjects, within a variety of settings, between diverse researchers with varying interests and diverse stakeholders with varying needs ... and they give rise to a spectrum of types of impacts. Getting to the core of Knowledge Exchange entails appreciating this heterogeneity without being blinded by it. The case study of impact evaluation of the PACCIT programme illustrates heterogeneity but also the drawing of useful commonalities in terms of process understanding. Projects within PACCIT all related to People at the Centre of Computers and Information Technology, but involved various disciplines, foci, users and approaches. From the 17 projects having Knowledge Exchange as one of their explicit aims, we developed five within-PACCIT cases tracing impacts from PACCIT research projects; heterogeneity is visible even in this subset, as highlighted here:

- *MAKING GAMES – Developing games authoring software for educational and creative use*: Close working with a small high-tech company led to a tool allowing teenagers to design computer games in school; also, the company became more interested in working with researchers to explore possible products. Stakeholders also included over 200 schools using the software and some policymakers that revised policy for ICT in schools. Academics and a teacher continued dissemination to diverse users after the project.
- *E-ADVICE – The cognitive science of financial E-Advice*: Research into decision-making was blended with research into applications helpful for individuals wanting to use their money effectively. The academic work into decision-making under risk won an award, while the prototype developed for an online financial system supporting advice led to a spinout company. Stakeholders included the company, its clients, and also various policymakers and others in financial and retail sectors, education and health boards.
- *E-DRAMA – Enhancement of people, technology and their interaction*: Artificial intelligence research enhanced improvisational interaction of avatars in e-drama, working with a charity's e-drama software, a large company's R&D group, a television company and schools. Although the system remains as a prototype, it did allow demonstration of what this approach could do, particularly as it was tested in schools. Various participants became more willing to participate in Knowledge Exchange collaborations in the future.
- *ROLLOUT – Innovative representations for scheduling for quality and training*: Working with a consortium of 10 companies including commercial bakeries and supermarkets, and a private sector research and technology organization as knowledge intermediary, researchers applied principles of representational design of systems to the complex, real-time scheduling issues faced by commercial bakers. The knowledge intermediary secured funding for further collaboration with the researchers and a major supermarket established a production planning programme based on similar principles. Many of the other companies achieved a new appreciation of computer human interaction.

- *HOMEWORK – Home and school linked via divergent technology in a pedagogic framework:* Academics and non-academic collaborators worked with teachers, learners and parents to develop a system using a tablet PC to teach maths. The research on this personal learning device drew on educational technology, TV production and artificial intelligence. Stakeholders included an SME specializing in technology-based educational products, a television company, and pilot school teachers, children and parents, and policymakers, with the Principal Investigator placed on a key committee.

Each of these five within-PACCIT cases led to multiple categories of impact, as seen in the figure below.

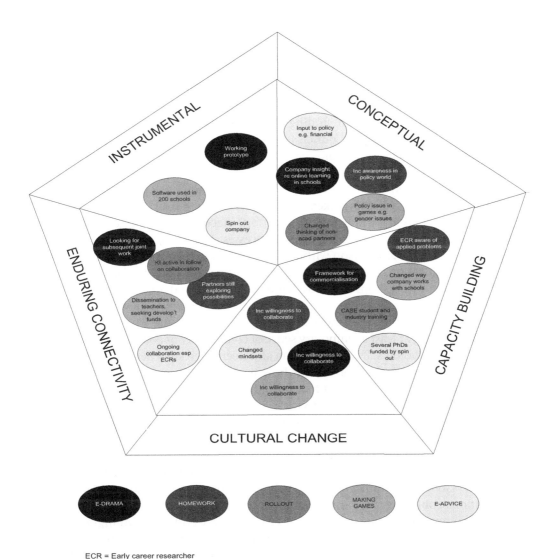

ECR = Early career researcher

Figure 3.2   From Meagher 2009

Together, the projects illustrated heterogeneity in Knowledge Exchange processes. As an example of common learning across diverse projects, we found that – not surprisingly – individuals made a difference. Knowledge Exchange is fostered by individuals who are by nature or effort open to building relationships and also to acting as 'champions' for projects within their own organizations. Learning as to impact evaluation was rich, as the PACCIT projects underscored the existence of a range of impacts and the protracted time frame over which many impacts are generated.

Two) The vital importance of two-way communication, and the dynamic relationship-building that brings this about – Illustrated by reflection on Knowledge Exchange for policy and practice: Scotland's SPIRIT

Knowledge Exchange between academics and policymakers or practitioners can seem subtle and intangible, perhaps giving rise to impacts such as slightly altered legislation or services, compared to Knowledge Exchange between, for example, engineers and manufacturing companies giving rise to innovative widgets. Yet, the essence of the process appears to be the same in that two-way communication between researchers and potential 'users' of research finding is critical. The experiences of the projects funded by the Scottish Funding Council's pilot scheme on Knowledge Exchange in this arena illustrate challenges of bringing about and sustaining such communication and relationship-building.

One challenge faced by all nine of the projects is that it is critical but often very difficult to engage busy policymakers/practitioners with research. Almost all project members were surprised by the time (and effort) necessary to engage non-academic partners and develop Knowledge Exchange processes. For some, it was difficult simply reach and engage the 'right' person within an organization with whom to try to establish two-way communication. Project members often put a great deal of effort into attempts such as multi-sector workshops (the most common mechanism), in hopes of encouraging prospective non-academic partners to: a) articulate the problems they needed help on or b) see the potential value of research to their problems. Some workshops were very successful in creating at least a temporary sense of community or common cause between academics and stakeholders. Event evaluation and steering group reflection helped project members to learn practical lessons about how to make such engagement mechanisms effective – so that the tone, format or focus could be improved. Two-way communication sometimes took place within such activities; other times it took place on a one-to-one basis between a researcher and a stakeholder, or in small groups such as advisory/steering committees which included non-academics.

A number of issues can arise during Knowledge Exchange that can be resolved more readily within the context of a positive relationship of mutual understanding, trust and respect. Good communication can help in many ways, including identification of motivational objectives and appreciation of each other's constraints. For example, enthusiastic researchers in one project had to try to convey both their willingness to work with 'hungry' stakeholders and also the constraints placed upon them by their university such that they had to teach, do research and bring in research income; they simply could not give all their time to Knowledge Exchange. Equally, many stakeholders had to meet a vast array of Key Performance Indicators that did not relate at all to research; this was a new insight for some researchers. To set a tone of mutual respect, some projects deliberately incorporated both research knowledge and stakeholder knowledge into dissemination products. It was clear that Knowledge Exchange calls for 'people skills' as well as communication skills.

An important challenge encountered by the projects was that of moving beyond occasional communication into long-term relationship-building. Close working, whether actual co-production of knowledge or through steering committees (for example), contributed to several projects' sense of building a lasting relationship. However, frequent turnover in posts (perhaps especially in the case of government partners) meant that carefully cultivated 'champions' were sometimes lost, along with institutional memory even as to how research might be helpful. Projects coped with this challenge in different ways; one shifted its sights from policymakers to practitioners when a key government post was abolished.

Sustaining academic/stakeholder relationships is a real challenge. Yet, as we have argued elsewhere, 'enduring connectivity' after a project's end may be an indicator of enhanced likelihood that future more tangible impacts may arise. Continuing interaction may increase the chance of uptake and embedding of research findings. Although constrained by brief duration (primarily 12–18 months), many of the projects made deliberate attempts to put knowledge-sharing onto a continuing basis, with a few developing joint proposals for other funding and several developing a website or adding to a website already frequented by their targeted stakeholders. It was hoped that such websites would contribute both to dissemination of understanding and to cohesiveness of early stage multi-sector networks formed during the projects.

The nature of the Learning Review was such that academic and non-academic project members were able to step back and reflect on challenges such as those described here, to share experiences in tackling issues and to generate advice, captured and discussed below as 'lessons learned'.

Three) The often unsung but important role of a wide range of 'knowledge intermediaries' occupying spaces in between researchers and users – Illustrated by consultation, strategic change and a knowledge intermediary: IDEA Consultora, Chile

Whether referred to as 'knowledge intermediaries', 'knowledge brokers', 'research brokers' or some other term, those individuals and organizations who act as bridges between researchers and established or potential stakeholders play a critical role in Knowledge Exchange. Acting at the interface between researchers and, for example, policymakers, knowledge intermediaries can facilitate the two-way flow of questions or problems, and understanding, that is at the heart of Knowledge Exchange. Knowledge intermediaries can play a variety of roles, it should be noted. For example, in guidance provided for maximizing impact of research, the UK Economic and Social Science Research Council lists as among the key factors: 'Where appropriate, the involvement of intermediaries and knowledge brokers as translators, amplifiers, network providers' (ESRC 2011). Sometimes knowledge intermediaries play a catalytic role, as well. The case used here to illustrate the proactive role of knowledge intermediaries included a set of workshops as a key strand of the knowledge intermediaries' work.

With funding from CONICYT (La Comisión Nacional de Investigación Científica y Tecnológica), the consultancy IDEA Consultora worked as a knowledge intermediary to develop a strategic road map for human capital development in fruit agricultural biotechnology. Through their overall project, IDEA Consultora synthesized input for government, while at the same time stimulating interactions and a shared vision for a culture of innovation among a variety of organizations. As 'brokers' of a developing new strategy, IDEA Consultora were able to 'translate' back and forth between government aspirations and the knowledge of academics and industry individuals who would be crucial to implementation.

IDEA Consultora's 'linkage programme' consisted of Diagnosis analysing international experience and also strengths, needs and gaps in Chile, the joint workshops discussed here, and development of recommended Continuing Actions. An essential component of the whole effort was bringing together scientists, technologists, technology managers, business representatives and the public sector in interactive, consultative joint workshops. A range of potential opinion leaders from the various sectors were invited to each full-day workshop. To foster effective networking among multi-sector attendees within each of the three regions of Chile, the workshops were held in three different regions of Chile. Each was contributed to by a Regional Work Committee and was hosted by a local university (the Universidad de Chile in Santiago, the Pontificia Universidad Catolica de Valparaiso and the Universidad de Talca). The workshops were designed to help the mixed groups of participants move toward a shared vision and strategy for future innovation. Talks by international panellists were used to inform and to spark open discussion. This was complemented by structured, professionally facilitated discussion which gathered input to be incorporated into the subsequent report.

Participants and others were able to see a result of their input in the form of IDEA Consultora's report on a National Strategy for 'Capacity-building for Human Resources in Biotechnology Applied to Fruit Production in Chile' (IDEA Consultora 2009). The process begun during the workshops is continuing through the work of a subsequently established Public-Private Committee to implement recommendations. Thus IDEA Consultora's proactive knowledge intermediary role not only led to the exchange of particular elements of knowledge, but also to a process of ongoing Knowledge Exchange.

Capturing, sharing and utilizing lessons learned: How to foster innovation through Knowledge Exchange processes

Both formally, through interviews and surveys, and informally, through observation (in the Chilean case study), it has been possible to capture lessons learned by participants as to good practice. These are consonant with wider literature on research use processes (for example, Nutley et al. 2007) and findings from the author's other evaluations; in fact they echo the five factors identified in earlier work (Meagher et al. 2008) as influencing processes that appear to lead to non-academic research impacts:

1. Value placed upon/incentives provided for generation of impact.
2. Two-way interactions between researchers and users.
3. Injections of financial support, dedicated staff, infrastructure.
4. Facilitating role(s) of knowledge intermediaries.
5. Communication/increasing accessibility of research.

So, for example, the very framing of the PACCIT programme meant that it incorporated two of these factors:

- value placed upon/incentives provided for generation of impact;
- injections of financial support, dedicated staff, infrastructure.

And, particularly in its second funding phase which emphasized Knowledge Exchange, the programme provided explicit encouragement for the other three:

- two-way interactions between researchers and users;
- facilitating role(s) of knowledge intermediaries;
- communication/increasing accessibility of research.

When PACCIT survey respondents were asked to select facilitating factors that helped the generation of impacts in their case, the most often-cited factor (by far) was the straightforward 'injection of financial support'. This was followed by 'two-way interactions between researchers and non-academics'. Interviewees noted the value of the many joint academic/non-academic meetings and networking opportunities created by the programme, along with coaching by the director and others. Case studies developed within the PACCIT study illustrated the importance of mutually respecting two-way interactions, trust-building and continuing dialogue.

The reservoir of tacit knowledge accumulated by those involved in programmes such as the three case studies described in this paper is deep, but it often goes unrecognized. It can be useful to condense from this reservoir a finite set of insights and advice. Doing so within a particular endeavour facilitates self-reflection and thus mid-course corrections and learning among participants. When disseminated beyond the participants, particularly when considered across endeavours, learning can be taken up by those directly involved in future endeavours and/or by those who shape the contexts for future Knowledge Exchange, such as government funders/drivers or institutional leaders. Thus organizational learning can be captured, shared, and used to lead to improvement of Knowledge Exchange processes so that they generate innovation impacts effectively.

So, for example, the SPIRIT study explicitly incorporated self-reflection, including but not limited to identification of issues identified by participants: several issues were clustered under each of the two overarching issues of Engagement of Non-academic Partners and Sustainability (including impacts). Points of 'promising practice' identified included: two-way Knowledge Exchange, taking extra effort, optimization/tailoring of workshops and dissemination, willingness to adapt and evolve, and self-reflection/discussion. Implications for evaluation of Knowledge Exchange projects were drawn out of the learning as well. In addition to the SPIRIT study's analytical report, a *Briefing Note: Knowledge Exchange in Public Policy and Practice* (Meagher and Kettle 2009) was developed; it has been shared by the study's commissioner, a funding body, with leaders of other projects involving Knowledge Exchange. The *Briefing Note* offered a 'broad-brush map' to Knowledge Exchange territory, with 'Travel Tips' addressing two key issues of engagement and sustainability.

'Travel tips' for Knowledge Exchange processes leading to impacts (Meagher and Kettle 2009)

Addressing Engagement:

- making the most of two-way Knowledge Exchange
- taking the time and effort for relationship-building
- identifying objectives
- fostering mutual understanding
- understanding each other's constraints
- identifying/reaching the right partners
- building in resilience
- designing effective KE activities
- *addressing sustainability*
- evolution and self-reflection
- embedding motivation for KE and research
- creating lasting connections
- meaningful dissemination
- finding funding
- managing expectations after a project ends
- fostering and identifying impacts

Such frameworks of lessons learned can be used to examine and illuminate processes of Knowledge Exchange. In their role as proactive knowledge intermediary, IDEA Consultora visibly enacted such points related to engagement through their workshops, for instance by:

- Serving as facilitators making the most of Knowledge Exchange between researchers, industry and government.
- Dedicating a set of high-level workshops (and follow-on activity) to relationship-building.
- Developing analyses (such as international benchmarking) and selecting both national and international speakers to identify objectives, foster mutual understanding and understanding of constraints.
- Inviting participants based in three different regions, to help bring together the right (potential) partners.
- Embedding the fruits of the study involving the workshops into follow-on activity, an ongoing Committee dedicated to implementation.
- Taking great care that the workshops, as Knowledge Exchange activities, were professionally and appropriately designed and conducted, with a mix of selected speakers and adeptly facilitated discussion to stimulate engagement and early community-building.

Conclusions

Despite differences in formats, subject matter, sectors and countries, tacit knowledge from all these cases reinforce similar learning about Knowledge Exchange leading to innovation impacts. In different ways, all three of the case studies involve proactive efforts in communication, gathering of input across different perspectives and relationship-building – labour-intensive activities that are critical in fostering innovation. Generation of innovation and impacts is a dynamic process which takes effort and time but which can be learned about and thus improved. Suggestive points from three case studies are presented here in hopes that consideration of their implications will be helpful to those hoping to foster innovation and impact. Facilitated self-reflection and formative evaluation (as well as later summative evaluation) can help participants in Knowledge Exchange processes recognize, test, debate and share the tacit understanding they are developing as to how best to generate innovation and impacts.

Ongoing organizational learning – by researchers, stakeholders and government funders – can in this way continue to improve these processes and enhance the likelihood of non-academic as well as academic return on investment in research. Appropriate evaluation can be a useful mechanism for organizational learning. Based on growing understanding of these processes, evaluation of such return should be sensitive to the dynamics and time frames involved. Impacts can be subtle and elusive, and take place over protracted timelines, with causality infamously difficult to attribute. Conventional sorts of impacts need to be captured, e.g. instrumental impacts, conceptual or enlightenment impact, and capacity-building (for example, Nutley et al. 2007). However, a strong recommendation is to also capture process-based impacts that can be identified shortly after the end of a research investment and that may even serve as 'proxy indicators' that viable Knowledge Exchange processes are in train with an enhanced likelihood of leading to later, more tangible impacts. The authors (Meagher et al. 2008) have called these 'Attitude or Culture change' (when individuals within or outside academia become more positive toward Knowledge Exchange goals) and 'Enduring Connectivity' (when researchers and stakeholders continue to interact after project funding ceases, perhaps visiting, placing students, holding joint workshops or writing joint proposals for follow-on funding). Schemes and initiatives promoting (and evaluating) innovation can be informed by appreciation of the full portfolio of types of possible impacts and the processes that give rise to them.

A further recommendation is that, if practice and evaluation draw upon deep understanding of Knowledge Exchange processes, more innovation and impacts are likely to be generated and also captured. If each funding scheme or initiative supporting innovation can be reflected upon and evaluated sensitively as an 'experiment', cumulatively, rich tacit knowledge and lessons learned can benefit everyone. Through continuous sharing of good practice and organizational learning (by researchers, stakeholders, university leaders and funders), improved understanding of key processes, factors and roles leading toward impacts can enhance subsequent generation of those impacts, building Knowledge Exchange capacity. In short:

- Sensitive evaluation can uncover participants' 'tacit knowledge' – lessons learned, insights and advice as to good practice in the generation of innovation impacts.
- It is possible to understand and share subtleties of Knowledge Exchange processes leading toward innovation and impacts on society and the economy.
- Individuals and organizations can learn and continue to improve.

Questions to Consider

1. To promote Knowledge Exchange, what support and what incentives could most effectively ensure that sufficient time and proactive effort are put into communication, gathering of input across different perspectives and relationship-building?
2. How can knowledge intermediaries be identified, supported and utilized?
3. During Knowledge Exchange processes, how can participants be encouraged to reflect upon what is working and what is not, to improve the process before it ends? How can formative evaluation play a helpful role?
4. What sorts of innovation impacts can arise from interactions between stakeholders and researchers?
5. How could such innovation impacts be tracked or identified?
6. What short-term indicators might be feasibly found to suggest that innovation impacts are at an early stage of developing?

Acknowledgements

*   UK/PACCIT: Dr Catherine Lyall, Information Browser Ltd; Professor Sandra Nutley, University of Edinburgh; Dr Heather Alexander, Clearsight Consulting Ltd.
*   Scotland/SPIRIT: Ann J. Kettle, OBE.
*   Chile/IDEA Consultora: Margarita d'Etigny Lira, Macarena Vio Gana, Maria Jose Etchegaray. [Online]. Available at: http://www.ideaconsultora.cl/ and Fernando Quezada, Massachusetts Biotechnology Center of Excellence Corporation.
*   All those participants who contributed their insights to each case study.

References

Abreu, M., Grinevich, V., Hughes, A. and Kitson, M. 2009. *Knowledge Exchange between Academics and the Business, Public and Third Sectors*. Centre for Business Research, University of Cambridge, Cambridge. [Online]. Available at: www.cbr.cam.ac.uk/pdf/AcademicSurveyReport.pdf [accessed: 30 March 2011].

Academy of Social Sciences. 2008. 'Developing Dialogue. Learned Societies in the Social Sciences: Developing Knowledge Transfer and Public Engagement'. Final Report from the AcSS and ESRC Project, *Journal of the Academy of Social Sciences*, 3, Supplement (December).

Boaz, A., Fitzpatrick, S. and Shaw, B. 2009. Assessing the impact of research on policy: A literature review. *Science and Public Policy*, 36(4), 255–70.

CHSRF. 2000. *Health Services Research and Evidence-Based Decision-Making*. Ottawa: Canadian Health Services Research Foundation (CHSRF).

Davies, H.T.O., Nutley, S.M. and Smith P.C. 2000. *What Works? Evidence-Based Policy and Practice in Public Services*. Bristol: Policy Press.

Davies, H.T.O., Nutley, S.M. and Walter, I. 2005. 'Approaches to assessing the non-academic impact of social science research'. Report of ESRC Symposium, on assessing the non-academic impact of research, 12–13 May 2005, Research Unit for Research Utilisation, University of St Andrews.

ESRC. 2009a. *ESRC Strategic Plan 2009–14. Delivering impact through Social Science*. [Online]. Available at: http://www.esrc.ac.uk/Image/Strategic_Plan_FINAL_tcm11–13164.pdf [accessed: 30 March 2011].

ESRC. 2009b. *Taking Stock: A Summary of ESRC's Work to Evaluate the Impact of Research on Policy and Practice*. [Online]. Available at: http://www.esrc.ac.uk/_images/Taking%20Stock_tcm8–4545.pdf [accessed: 30 March 2011].

ESRC. 2011. *Impact Toolkit*. [Online]. Available at: http://www.esrc.ac.uk/funding-and-guidance/tools-and-resources/impact-toolkit/ [accessed: 30 March 2011].

Grant, J., Brutscher, P.-B., Kirk, S., Butler, L. and Wooding, S. 2009. *Capturing Research Impacts: A Review of International Practice*. Prepared for HEFCE by RAND Europe, December 2009. [Online]. Available at: http://www.hefce.ac.uk/pubs/rdreports/2009/rd23_09/rd23_09.pdf [accessed: 30 March 2011].

Hanney, S.R., Gonzalez-Block, M.A., Buxton, M.J. and Kogan, M. 2002. 'The utilisation of health research in policy-making: Concepts, examples and methods of assessment'. A report to the World Health Organisation, Health Economics Research Group, Brunel University, Uxbridge.

IDEA Consultora. 2009. *Formación de capital humano avanzado en Biotecnología Frutícola*. [Online]. Available at: http://www.ideaconsultora.cl/proyecto13.htm [accessed: 30 March 2011].

Jump, P. 2011. 'Cushioning the impact (slightly)'. *Times Higher Education*, 3 March 2011. [Online]. Available at: http://www.timeshighereducation.co.uk/story.asp?sectioncode=26andstorycode=415360 [accessed: 30 March 2011].

Lavis, J., Ross, S., McLeod, C. and Gildiner, A. 2003. Measuring the impact of health research. *Journal of Health Services Research and Policy*, 8(3), 165–70.

Lomas, J. 2000. Using 'Linkage and Exchange' to move research into policy at a Canadian foundation. *Health Affairs*, 19(3), 236–40.

Meagher, L. 2009. 'Impact evaluation of people at the centre of communication and information technologies (PACCIT)'. Report to ESRC. [Online]. Available at: http://www.esrc.ac.uk/_images/PACCIT_Impact_Evaluation_Report_tcm8–3821.pdf [accessed: 30 March 2011].

Meagher, L. and Kettle, A. 2009. *Briefing Note: Knowledge Exchange in Public Policy and Practice*. [Online]. Available at: http://www.sfc.ac.uk/web/FILES/Our_Priorities_Knowledge_Exchange/KE_Public_Policy_Practice_-_Briefing_Note.pdf [accessed: 30 March 2011].

Meagher, L.M. and Lyall, C. 2007. *Policy and Practice Impact Case Study of ESRC Grants and Fellowships in Psychology*. Report to ESRC, June 2007. [Online]. Available at: http://www.esrc.ac.uk/_images/Policy_and_Practice_Impact_Case_Study_of_ESRC_Grants_and_Fellowships_in_Psychology__Report_tcm8–3828.pdf [accessed: 30 March 2011].

Meagher, L.M., Lyall, C. and Nutley, S. 2008. Flows of knowledge, expertise and influence: A method for assessing policy and practice impacts from social science research. *Research Evaluation*, 17(3), 163–73.

Molas-Gallart, J., Salter, A., Patel, P., Scott, A. and Duran, X. 2002. *Measuring Third Stream Activities*. Brighton: SPRU.

Molas-Gallart, J., Tang, P. and Morrow, S. 2000. Assessing the non-academic impact of grant-funded socioeconomic research: Results from a pilot study. *Research Evaluation*, 9(3), 171–82.

Nutley, S., Walter, I. and Davies, H. 2007. *Using Evidence: How Research Can Inform Public Services*. Bristol: Policy Press.

PA Consulting/SQW Consulting. 2007. *Research Councils UK. Study on the Economic Impact of the Research Councils*, October 2007.

Relu. 2007. Common knowledge? An exploration of knowledge transfer. RELU Briefing Series No. 6. [Online]. Available at: http://www.relu.ac.uk/news/briefings/RELUBrief6%20Common%20 Knowledge.pdf [accessed: 30 March 2011].

Relu. 2010. *Programme Briefing Series No. 10: Telling Stories: Accounting for Knowledge Exchange.* [Online]. Available at: http://www.relu.ac.uk/news/briefings/Brif10.pdf [accessed: 30 March 2011].

Research Councils UK. 2006. *Increasing the Economic Impact of Research Councils* ('The Warry Report'). [Online]. Available at: http://www.berr.gov.uk/files/file32802.pdf [accessed: 30 March 2011].

Research Councils UK. 2007. *Excellence with Impact: Progress in Implementing the Recommendations of the Warry Report on the Economic Impact of the Research Councils.* [Online]. Available at: http://www.rcuk.ac.uk/documents/economicimpact/excellenceimpact.pdf [accessed: 30 March 2011].

4 The Use of Intellectual Property in Latin American Higher Education Institutions

ALEXANDRA MAYR with MARIA CRUZ BARLUENGA and ALIANDRA BARLETE

Introduction

Innovation is key to competitiveness and wealth in the global and knowledge-based economy. Governments and policy makers in virtually all parts of the world have recognized and are actively promoting the university as a key tool to generating innovation and knowledge-based economic development. Striving to take up their role in the innovation process, and responding to government pressures, universities have engaged in various forms of technology transfer with a view to mobilize their research potential.

In Europe, a gap between world-class scientific research performed in the universities (measured for example by the number of publications/citations) and their limited role in innovation and technology development (in terms of commercialization of research results) has been emphasized, especially when comparing to other highly dynamic and innovative economies such as the United States and Japan. This situation has led to concrete initiatives promoting the entrepreneurial university model in the European Union (EU), and has in particular stimulated technology transfer and the adequate use of the intellectual property rights (IPR) system (European Commission 2006). In the case of Latin America, there is still a long way until its countries' economic growth will be based on their own produced knowledge and technology. One of the reasons is the low investment in research and development (R&D), as well as the insufficient expenditure in higher education, considering that most research and innovation in the region is developed at public universities.

Based on a review of relevant literature and international trends, this chapter points out that higher education institutions, in particular in Latin America, must not disregard the importance of the IPR system as one of several tools to promote innovation and entrepreneurship in the region. Moreover, the chapter points out that learning how to use the IP system to their advantage – based on their specific needs and without resigning the academic freedom – universities can make enhance the relevance of their research for society and promote entrepreneurship.

In showing that universities in Latin America are increasingly finding themselves confronted with IP issues, this article analyzes the level of awareness and use of intellectual property (IP) within Latin American higher education institutions (HEIs), while exploring the main constraints and inhibiting factors for HEIs in working with the IP system and integrating IP management. This is pursued by presenting empirical data generated through a study conducted among 147 Latin American HEIs in 18 different countries. The study was carried out in the framework of the PILA-Network project, an initiative coordinated by the General Foundation of the University of Alicante, Spain. The PILA-Network project is based on the assumption that Latin American HEIs have considerable research potential, and assuming that research and innovation are the core of economic prosperity, HEIs are a promising source for stimulating innovation and economic development in Latin America. Unlocking this potential should therefore be among the major objectives of the regional governments and policy makers.

Literature Review

INNOVATION AND THE CHANGING ROLE OF HIGHER EDUCATION INSTITUTIONS

Innovation is key to competitiveness in the global and knowledge-based economy. Numerous concepts have been developed to describe what is it that makes the innovation process work, such as cluster theories, the triple helix, network and stakeholder models. However, even though these various models are based on different approaches, they do have a common denominator. Innovation is a complex and interactive process of systematic nature, nurtured by relationships between actors and unexpected combinations. An essential ingredient for innovation is cooperation among different actors, including among others government, education, research, industry, service and financial sectors.

Governments and policy makers in virtually all parts of the world have recognized and are actively promoting the university as a key tool to generating innovation and economic development. The role of universities as knowledge-producing and disseminating institutions has increased exponentially, and especially the importance of universities in technological innovation has become a central element of economic development strategies in many countries all around the world. The university's "third mission," namely its active contribution to social and economic development, has been emphasized, and entrepreneurial universities which have taken up this challenge by developing new mechanisms to enhance their role in economic development gained momentum (Alänge et al. 2009).

Traditionally places for higher education and basic research, universities are increasingly pursuing applied research and industry needs, and adopting values from the corporate culture of industry. Globalization has fostered this process and 'forced universities to engage with the market' (Delanty 2001), cooperate with industry and compete with each other on national and international level (for students, staff and for funding).

As universities establish and intensify links with industry, they are at the same time responding to government pressures. Etzkowitz and Leydesdorff (1997) attempt to account for this new configuration of institutional forces emerging within innovation systems, with the "triple helix" model of university–industry–government relations (Etzkowitz et al. 2000). In the light of increasing enrolment numbers and diminishing state funding, cooperation with the industry sector intensified as universities are required to diversify their income streams to finance their research and teaching activities. In the industrialized world, the universities' need for extra funding is matched with the increasing importance of knowledge-(and innovation-)based economic development model – and the need of the industry/business sector for new products and innovations which require a significant input of scientific knowledge (Delanty 2001). A rise in cooperation activities among university and industry followed, by what can be observed for example in terms of increasing numbers of joint R&D projects, consultancy work for industry, and the development of joint research facilities, science and technology parks.

However, there is some skepticism with regards to the promotion of entrepreneurial university models in developing regions. Because growth is not based on knowledge-intensive products and national IPR systems are not well developed, the needs of the local society and industry in developing countries are often in no relation to the research interests of the international scientific community. Arocena and Sutz (2005) point out that this situation creates a conflict of interest for universities in these countries: there is a trade-off for researchers, who often work in isolation and with limited resources, to either conduct research which allows them to become integrated into the international community of scholars and publish their research in mainstream publications, or to pursue research that serves the local industry but entails lower potential for international reward and recognition. Therefore, the authors suggest that universities in developing countries need to make a special effort in promoting excellence in research while simultaneously focusing on the needs of local industry and society.

Empirical evidence shows that universities can enhance their role in the innovation process and act as regional innovation organizers. This can be done through promoting entrepreneurship among staff and students, offering consultancy and scientific analysis services to businesses, establishing joint research centers with industry, creating industry liaison and technology transfer offices and through organizing IP and making it available to local enterprises (Alänge et al. 2009). Striving to translate research into economic development, universities increasingly engage in various forms of technology transfer, including patenting, licensing and creating spin-off companies. According to Etzkowitz et al. (2000), empirical evidence shows that identification, creation and commercialization of IP have become institutional objectives in many academic systems. In recent years, many universities have addressed the issue of IPR at institutional level, implementing IP policies, organizing information events and providing training to faculty and students on IP issues, and not least by patenting and licensing out research results. The issue of IPR has created much debate within universities around the globe, especially in issues such as the extent to which universities or researchers shall claim IP rights over their research findings, also in whether and to what extent universities shall adopt business-focused research strategies, or in whether restrictions on publication of research can be accepted. In the midst of such heated topics, what would be the reason for universities to engage in IPR issues in the first place? Wouldn't it be better for universities to avoid such debates and focus on teaching, doing "open research" and publishing the results in journals, leaving IPR issues to the business sector?

Universities in both the developed and the developing world today should not and must not disregard the IPR system. The reasons therefore are numerous. It is a fact that the world is ever more based upon knowledge and intangible assets, which increasingly need to be captured and controlled in terms of IP to generate economic development and wealth. New technologies are developed increasingly by consortia consisting of many different actors, and IPR regulations rule the game. IP management furthermore is not only for the developed countries, but also a potentially strong tool for less-developed economies. And IP management, if pursued in the right way should not – and must not – interfere with academic freedom. Neither does it entail a conflict for universities in the developing world whose mission includes serving the local needs.

In a university setting, various activities and stakeholders are involved through their daily activities in IP issues. Therefore it is essential that institutions adopt a strategic approach to IP management. IP issues cannot be considered in isolation, but are interrelated with many other institutional strategies and policies. Some examples are (Auril 2002):

- human resource policy: the general framework of rewards within the institution and employment contracts should reflect the IP strategy, incentives for staff to engage in IP and entrepreneurship activities;
- research services: IP databases may be used to organize research activities; IP issues are important when organizing research projects;
- cooperation strategy: dealing with collaborators and sponsors, IP influences the terms of cooperation with other public or private entities;
- budget setting: an integrated IP approach may generate the need for additional sources of funding, for example for training of staff.

Integrating IP management capacities in HEIs involves processes and decisions on multiple levels. Even if some universities have built sophisticated competence, policies and systems to engage in IP and research commercialization which may at present not be appropriate for most universities Latin American countries, any university should consider to least starting to regulate IP and develop a policy and strategic statement. In function of context, ambition, structure, financing, and other factors, each institution then may decide how far to integrate IP in their organization and how much effort and resources to dedicate (Alänge et al. 2009).

THE BENEFITS OF INTELLECTUAL PROPERTY MANAGEMENT IN UNIVERSITIES

Higher education institutions are not always aware of the advantages of using the IPR system and the benefits which a strategic approach and integrated IP management may present for them. The following activities exemplify – in a non-exhaustive manner – how institutions may benefit from properly enforced IP management (WIPO 2004).

Use of patent databases as important source of information in R&D

Patent databases represent the single most comprehensive technical information source worldwide, conveying the most recent and detailed information on solving technical problems. Documents are presented in a uniform way, with respect to layout and bibliographical data, including also drawings and detailed explanations. IP databases are useful for monitoring trends in R&D activities, designing research agendas, setting priorities and allocating funds, identifying the patentability potential of R&D activities at early stages of development, or solving potential disputes involving patents. A proper use of IP databases can avoid duplicating efforts, or "reinventing the wheel," investing time and efforts in a research which has already been developed by others. Especially for developing countries, the use of patent databases presents a powerful tool to explore new business opportunities. As many inventions are not patented in these countries, patent databases contain knowledge and ideas that can be applied to solve problems of the local society, and commercially developed and exploited. Yet the use of patent databases to search for ideas is not commonly known or applied in universities.

Cooperation with other public or private entities

Institutions which have well-defined IPR rules and strategies will find it easier to find partners and cooperate with others in R&D projects. Any cooperation in R&D needs to be based on clear rules. According to a report from the European Research Advisory Board *International Research Cooperation* (2006), transparency and mutual understanding of IP issues are vital to establishing successful and sustainable cooperation activities and projects. Increasingly new technologies are developed by consortia that may include a variety of different entities such as corporate R&D units, university centers and government laboratories. Clear rules are thus crucial to assure that potential results will actually be used and assigned to the most adequate partner for further research or commercialization.

Staff recruitment and retention

The quality of IP management can strengthen recruitment and retention of highly qualified academic, research and management staff. This may occur due to the good reputation of the institution as a consequence of perceived effectiveness of IP management. On the other hand, IP management normally will influence the financial benefits that staff receives for commercially related work. In addition, the opportunity to supplement salaries through commercialization activities may inform the choices of qualified research staff.

Effective knowledge transfer

In return for public funding, institutions usually opt for open publication and making research results freely available, and often this might be the most effective form of knowledge transfer. In other cases, however, the protection of the underlying research results, or ensuring the knowledge is not disseminated too early (through non-disclosure agreements for example) is vital to encourage commercial investment and transfer the results to the market. According to Alänge (2009), the "patenting-licensing" approach requires excellence in science combined with the availability of resources to maintain and negotiate commercial contracts. In developing countries these factors are not always given, which is why alternative IP management strategies should be explored in addition.

Generation of income through technology transfer and commercialization

Technology transfer and commercialization initiatives are means by which ideas created in universities can be brought to the market and transformed into economic value, e.g. in the form of new products, production methods, or companies. The most suitable means of technology transfer will depend on each individual case and circumstances of the institution and environment. In general, expectations over economic benefits resulting directly from the sale or licensing of IP are too high and ambitious. There is, however, a strong need for realism over the scale of returns, and direct financial benefits. Experience shows that it requires an integrated approach to IP, qualified staff and years of experience to generate a stable flow of income from technology transfer.

It is important to highlight that the IPR system is not a mere tool to commercialize research results or potentially generate financial benefits – as often commonly and mistakenly perceived, and that an integrated IP management approach presents several direct and indirect benefits to any higher education institution. The following section aims to provide an overview on how IPR issues have been addressed in the European and Latin American higher education systems.

IPR AND INTERNATIONAL DEVELOPMENTS IN THE HIGHER EDUCATION SECTOR

International trends and policy initiatives

Assuming that universities hold significant unrealized potential for technology development, the mobilization of this potential became a central concern for policy makers and governments all around the world.

Aiming to provide the legal grounds to facilitate the flow of knowledge from universities into new sources of technological innovation, many countries established rules on the ownership of research results arising from public funded research.

In this regard, policy makers and academics often refer to the United States' Bayh–Dole Act (1980), which created a uniform patent policy, enabling universities, SMEs and non-profit organizations to retain title to inventions made under federally funded research programs. The Act encompassed that universities were encouraged to collaborate with commercial concerns to promote the utilization of inventions arising from public funding, and expected to give licensing preference to small businesses (Autum 2010). In the US, this had noticeable impacts on the number of patents owned by universities, and in fact, university involvement in innovation processes increased in a considerable way in the country since 1980. However, it has to be made clear that Bayh–Dole resolved a very specific, inefficient situation in the US, which is very different from the reality in Europe and Latin America. Nevertheless, the Bayh–Dole Act has influenced policy makers in other countries to make decisions to grant ownership rights to universities (Alänge 2009). A study carried out by the OECD (2003) confirmed that many countries had reconsidered their ownership regimes of public funded research. Many Asian economies reconsidered their legislations with the Science and Technology Basic Law (STBL) during the late 1990s, and countries like Austria, Denmark, Germany and Norway introduced changes in recent years. Today, most countries of the EU have granted ownership of IP-generated from public funds to universities.

Governments in Latin American countries have been encouraging innovation in general and the use of the IP system by universities in particular in recent years. For example, Venezuela recently introduced the "Law of Science, Technology and Innovation," Panama the "Law 35 for Intellectual Property," plus the Law 15 for Author's rights, and the "Law for Collective Rights of Indigenous people." In Brazil, IPR issues have been reconsidered recently by the Law 10.973 on Innovation, published on December 2, 2004.

Even if such laws may present a certain incentive for universities to mobilize their research capacities and results, it is clear that ownership rights alone do not guarantee that universities effectively change their traditional ways of working and integrate IP management in their functions. There are many factors that influence the success of universities in this regard, but primarily and most importantly, institutions need to build human, organizational and managerial competences allowing them to detect, evaluate, effectively manage and exploit research results.

In the EU, several concrete initiatives have been taken on policy and institutional levels to promote the use of the IP system, improving the management of IP by higher education and research institutions, and helping to address discrepancies among national knowledge transfer systems with view to facilitate knowledge transfer across sectors and countries. EU funding programs provide resources to create intermediary mechanisms and networks to market university research, such as the Enterprise Europe Network. Regarding Intellectual Property, the "Commission Recommendation on the management of Intellectual Property in knowledge transfer activities and Code of Practice for universities and other public research organisations" of 2008 calls universities to establish IP policies which guarantee that potentially valuable research results are being transferred to be market. A remarkable point about this communication is that it provides concrete recommendations to institutions and good practice examples.

IPR and Latin American HEIs in practice

This chapter will illustrate that Latin American HEIs have significant, but largely unrealized, knowledge-production and dissemination potential, part of which could be realized if universities used more actively the IPR system and build competences in IP management. When referring to "using the IPR system and managing IP" it embraces creating awareness and know-how on IP amongst university leaders, staff and students, and learning how to use the IPR system and the related tools in the most appropriate way, based on context and mission.

So far, economic growth in Latin America has not been based on its own produced science. One reason therefore may be the relatively low industrial capabilities of Latin American countries (Arocena et al. 2001), and low investments in R&D and innovation in general. Considering the scarcity of high-tech industry and low number of research centers, by far the largest part of the research pursued in this region is attributed to public universities. Assuming that knowledge and innovation are key elements of economic prosperity, Latin American universities are probably the most promising source of innovation and economic development in the region.

In recent years, shifting relations among industry and government has encouraged rapid and discontinuous change in Latin American universities. Nevertheless, most universities in the region have only recently started to explore or intensify cooperation with the industry sector, and engaged in applied research and technology transfer activities. In virtually all Latin American countries, universities have been building their own organizations to foster and manage their relations with industry, promoting research cooperation with the private sector, through technology transfer offices, technology and science parks for example, and have established IP policies. According to Arocena (2001) it is not clear whether IP issues were a true problem that needed to be solved in Latin America once contractual relationships between universities and firms became more common, or whether it was a response to the international trends, which have been mentioned above.

When analyzing higher education from a regional perspective, in this case Latin America, it must be underlined that the higher education and innovation systems differ considerably from one country to the other. For instance, Brazil has experienced a significant development of its higher education and research sector in recent years. Several Brazilian universities are conducting world-class research, with exceptional activity in publications, industry cooperation, patenting, licensing, and spin-off creation.

The higher education sector in some of the less-developed countries in Latin America, such as Bolivia, Honduras and Nicaragua, witnessed considerable changes and the growth of new institutions for learning, including a new breed of private universities and Internet-based educational institutions promoting distance-learning. Research, however, is still an activity predominantly conducted in traditional public universities, and only to a limited extent benefits industry and other parts of society. The reasons therefore may be attributed to the fact that academia was traditionally independent from private sector/industry. According to Alänge et al. (2009), another reason expressed both by industry representatives and academics may be mistrust between industry and university. During recent years a considerable research competence has been built up in several universities but according to Alänge (2009: 2), "this research does only to a limited extent reach the local industry." This situation may also be explained by the fact that the business sector in these countries does not have the capacity to benefit from innovations developed by researchers. With regards to the benefits of using IP in universities, critics argue that, considering the low innovation potential of the private sector in Latin America, the probability of reaping benefits from research conducted in HEIs is higher if the research results be protected and produced in the industrialized world, rather than in Latin America. Registering research results in industrialized countries, however, requires considerable organizational and budgetary efforts from the universities (Arocena 2001). This argument, however, centers primarily on the economic benefits that a university may obtain through IP management – which in fact should not be the primary objective of any HEI, as illustrated earlier. In this sense, universities should also take into account that the patenting-licensing approach is by far not the only process by which proper IP management can improve the rate at which knowledge developed in HEIs is used for the benefit of society.

Considering the differences within the Latin American region regarding research and technology development, and bearing in mind the similarities among the countries concerning history and language, countries and universities with very little experience could benefit considerably from the more experienced partners in the region if they cooperated in a network.

While analyzing the data on IP awareness, it was found that currently, awareness and trust about IP management opportunities are generally low in academics in Latin American HEIs. As a result, universities decide to disengage and avoid using the IPR system, and in consequence many valuable opportunities and much innovation potential are left unrealized in the region. Through actively promoting research, working closer with the business sector, and learning to use the IP system for their advantage, HEIs in Latin America have the potential to reap major benefits for society at large – improving the level and quality of higher education and research, contributing to the development of high-tech industries, generating employment and wealth.

Unlocking the development potential of Latin American universities may embrace further promoting elements of the entrepreneurial university model, motivating and incentivizing academics to perform research, modernizing research facilities/infrastructures, and exploring areas of cooperation with the local business sector, complemented by building awareness and competences in IP management. Universities and professionals working with IP and technology transfer in Europe and the USA have found support through working in networks, such as the network of technology transfer offices in Spain (Red OTRI), the Association of Science and Technology Professionals (ASTP) in Europe and AUTUM in the US (Alänge 2009). Therefore, networks facilitating HEIs to study successful examples of leading universities in the region while promoting mutual support for building awareness and competences within HEIs, could present a valuable tool for improving IP management in Latin American universities.

In this context the idea for the PILA-Network project was born.

The PILA-Network and the study on IP awareness and use in Latin American higher education institutions

PILA-Network is a project co-financed by the EU in the framework of the ALFA III program and is composed of HEIs from 18 different Latin American countries (Argentina, Bolivia, Brazil, Chile, Colombia, Costa Rica, Cuba, Ecuador, El Salvador, Guatemala, Honduras, Mexico, Nicaragua, Panama, Paraguay, Peru, Uruguay, Venezuela), and four European universities (University of Alicante (Spain) as co-coordinating institution, Chalmers University (Sweden), Jagiellonian University (Poland) and FH Joanneum (Austria)). Associated partners to the project are the respective national intellectual property offices from Latin America, as well as the European Patent Organisation (EPO), the Spanish Patent and Trademark Office, Universia Network and the World Intellectual Property Organization (WIPO).

The main objective of PILA is to promote the modernization of IP management practices in Latin American higher education systems with a view to contribute to economic and social development. The creation of an IP network of HEIs aims to pursue this objective through creating a platform for dialogue, promoting the exchange of experiences and creating a basis for strategic discussion between LA universities, political decision-makers and regional authorities.

Targeted training, fostering the dialogue among key stakeholders, creating web-based information services, networking and mutual support are the key principles of PILA. Accordingly the key action lines are analysis, tailored training measures, policy support actions and networking. One of the main concerns of the project is the development of human, organizational and managerial capacities within the participating universities in all aspects of IP management through targeted training actions. The trained personnel of the partner universities consequently organize workshops on IP management for other universities and interested individuals, creating thus a multiplier effect and spreading the know-how to other HEIs in the region. Moreover, the PILA-Network envisages a number of targeted policy support actions in the form of national round tables and international conferences with a view to stimulate strategic discussion on the design of universities' policies and procedures related to the protection of IP and involve relevant stakeholders from the government and private sectors. The policy support actions are expected to result in practical recommendations for the design and implementation of institutional IP policies within LA higher education institutions, which are responding to the particularities of each country's innovation system and structure. Given the complexity of the IPR system and the highly dynamic nature of the innovation process, the challenge for HEIs lies in the development of relevant human and organizational capacities to facilitate the information and management processes related to innovation and IP, and to offer competent advice and support to the academic/scientific communities. Through organizing workshops and conferences and establishing web-based information services, specialized databases and e-learning facilities the PILA-Network aims to constitute a powerful tool for Latin American HEIs concerned with IP issues.

Before commencing the core activities of the project, namely training and policy support actions, among the first objectives of the PILA project was to study in detail awareness and use of IP in Latin American higher education institutions, and examining the main challenges HEIs face with regards to IP management. The subsequent sections describe the methodology used for this study, and the data obtained

Methodology and Analysis

The aim of the analysis of the level of IP awareness and use in Latin American higher education institutions was to obtain the crucial information and data on the initial situation in this area which had not been revealed so far. Besides, the study should help to generate awareness on IP issues among the target group, establish contacts and helped to tailor the network to the needs of the regional HEIs.

Therefore, a questionnaire was designed, presenting three different sections:

1. general data on the institutions, especially regarding research (such as number of researchers, R&D budgets, R&D projects, patents);
2. AIDA[1] questionnaire to measure the level of IP awareness and use of IP in the institutions (consistent of some 80 questions in total regarding all aspects of IP);
3. questions on the main reasons and barriers perceived for IP in HEIs.

The methodology underlying part (2) of the analysis was based on a special adaption of the AIDA methodology for the measurement of Intellectual Property awareness, where the AIDA level quantifies the maturity level of a higher education institutions, with respect to its IP practices and /or knowledge on IP. The methodology was developed by "Le Centre du Recherche Publique Henri Tudor" (Luxembourg) in the framework of the IPeuropAware Project,[2] as a tool to measure IP awareness among European small

---

1   The AIDA methodology finds its origin in the simplistic marketing/sales concept (E.K. Strong, 1925, Theories of selling. *Journal of Applied Psychology* 9, 75–86).

2   The project website is available at: www.ipeuropaware.eu/.

and medium sized enterprises (SMEs). With the consent of CRP Henri Tudor, the AIDA methodology was adapted by the General Foundation of the University of Alicante for the PILA project to measure IP awareness in higher education and research institutions in Latin America.

The AIDA methodology is based on the assumption that, schematically, an optimal integration of IP in an organization is pursued successively, following a linear process that starts with (1) awareness and knowledge on IP issues, which leads to (2) increased use of the IP system and tools (including formal registration and protection of results when necessary), which when developed further will lead to (3) active management of research results and IP of an organization, and ultimately enabling (4) enhanced exploitation of the research results through various channels of technology transfer and commercialization. The AIDA scale can be visualized as in Figure 4.1 below.

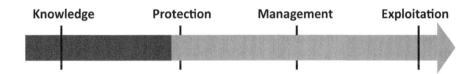

Figure 4.1   Graphical representation of the AIDA scale

The AIDA scale is categorized following an increasing level of IP integration in the university structure, which can be described as shown in Table 4.1.

Table 4.1   Summary of the main characteristics of the AIDA scale, own depiction

A	A (Attention): The HEI is aware of IP
	Knowledge and awareness: this first level deals with the overall knowledge and awareness of the institutions concerning IP: general knowledge on intangible assets, different IP titles, trade secrets, non-disclosure agreements.
I	I (Interest): The HEI is protecting IP on a more or less regular and systematic basis
	Protection: this second level deals with the means used by the institutions to find the value in their research, internally take account of the results, valorize and disseminate them (e.g. awareness and protection of registered and non-registered IP, confidentiality, risks of information disclosures).
D	D (Desire): The HEI possesses an IP portfolio and is managing its IP rights
	Management: the third level deals with the administrative and operational management of IP in the institutions (measures taken to mobilize IPR – protected or not) and the respect of third-party IPR.
A	A (Action): The HEI is exploiting its IP rights
	Exploitation: this last level represents the most advanced practices of IP that could exist in a university. It is related to the IP strategy and policy developed by universities to transfer and/or commercialize their research results, enforcement of IP rights (in relation with third parties), as well as the exploitation of IP information.

The AIDA questionnaire starts with a general and global evaluation of the IP knowledge to end with questions related to a high level of IP practices (exploitation of IP). It progresses with questions of greater technicality and complexity. Furthermore, the AIDA methodology was complemented by a general set of questions designed to obtain data on the research activity of the institutions as well as to analyze in more detail the reasons for high or low integration of IP in the organization.

The data collection was carried out through personal and telephone interviews between February and July 2009. The PILA-Network partners contacted a total of 260 HEIs in 18 different Latin American countries: Argentina, Bolivia, Brazil, Chile, Colombia, Costa Rica, Cuba, Ecuador, El Salvador, Guatemala,[3] Honduras, Mexico, Nicaragua, Panama, Paraguay, Peru, Uruguay, Venezuela. The target number of HEIs interviewed per country was established in relation to size of its population, ranging from four in Uruguay to 18 in Mexico and Brazil. Based on the interest in the interview's subject and the availability of personnel capable to answer the questionnaires, in-depth interviews were conducted in 147 of the 260 institutions. The target group within the HEIs was top management staff from technology transfer offices, IP units, vice presidents of research and/or scientific coordination, depending on the organizational structure of each HEI.

The main difficulties faced when carrying out the interviews were: resistance on the part of university staff to share the information requested, difficulties to locate the right persons to be interviewed and answer the questions, the information requested was not always available (due to a lack of internal documentation for example), and a lack of time of the interviewees to respond to the large and relatively time-consuming questionnaire.

The AIDA methodology as it was applied in this study entails a number of limitations. The questions had to be answered through assigning values to the answers between 0 and 10. As no specific responses can be assigned to these values, the results have been influenced through several factors, such as the interviewee, the knowledge and attitude of the interviewer, cultural issues, etc. Different persons conducted the interviews in the different countries. They may have interpreted questions and results in a slightly different manner. Moreover, the means of data collection differed depending on geographical circumstances and time constraints. Interviews were conducted mostly via personal face-to-face meetings; however, some were conducted via telephone, and others via email.

The data collected from the 147 HEIs have been analyzed by country, and detailed country reports have been published on the PILA-Network website.[4] For the purpose of the present book chapter, some data have been selected, analyzed and interpreted to make regional comparisons. The detailed results for each AIDA level are not presented here, as the data would lose validity if analyzed and interpreted as regional averages. For detailed results it is recommend to consult the individual country reports.

---

3   The data for Guatemala are not available. Only one interview was conducted, thus the data is not representative for the country and has not been included in the analysis.

4   The country reports are available at the following website: www.pila-network.org.

Findings of the Study on IP Awareness and Use in Latin American Higher Education Institutions

INTRODUCTION

This section discusses selected data and findings drawn from the study on IP awareness and use among Latin American HEIs.

First, some selected indicators on the research activities of the interviewed Latin American HEIs will be presented what will allow observing dissimilarities among the different countries participating in the study. Secondly, a global analysis of the AIDA level by country and for the region as a whole is offered. Some indicators have been selected to cross data and interpret the regional differences. Lastly, the principal perceived barriers and challenges for HEIs on national, institutional, cultural, strategic, operational, financial and human levels will be discussed.

The comparisons and interpretations of the data are based on aggregated national averages. Consequently, it will not be taken into account the differences among the individual universities interviewed in a country, which are in some cases very significant.

INDICATORS ON RESEARCH ACTIVITY

Selected basic indicators describing the sample of HEIs who participated in the study and indicators concerning research and IP of are shown in Table 4.2 on the next page. Focus is given here on the number of researchers, projects with enterprises and registered patents, whereas the original analysis and country reports contain further data such as the different IP titles and prevailing country of registration, research budgets and more.

The data shown in Table 4.2 reveals significant differences among Latin American countries regarding engagement in research cooperation and personnel devoted to research, as well as in the generation of patents (selected here as an approximation of the IP activity). According to the data, based on the number of patents registered by the participating HEIs, including those registered nationally, in Europe and in the USA, it can be observed that Brazil is at the forefront in Latin America, followed by Mexico, Uruguay and Argentina. Furthermore, it can be observed that patent registration by HEIs in Central American HEIs is very limited or non-existent in many institutions. Cuba shows a high level of protection of intangible assets; however, registration is carried out mostly only at the national level in Cuba.

Another interesting trend is that Argentinian universities appear to have strong links to the industry sector, measured in terms of number of research cooperation projects, where Argentina leads the field with an outstanding number of research projects with enterprises (a weighted average of 1,774 per institution). At the same time it can be observed that the number of patents registered by Argentinean universities is rather low in comparison. The reason therefore could be that the enterprise partner, and not the university, is usually the owner of the IPR in contract and collaborative research projects. As a result, Argentinean universities may be enforcing their role in technology development without pursuing extensive institutional patenting.

Table 4.2   Basic data and research and IP indicators of the HEIs included in the sample

Countries	HEIs interviewed	Total no. of researchers	Total no. of research projects with enterprises	Total no. of patents (1)	Average no. of projects with enterprises per HEI	Average no. of patents per HEI	Weighted average no. of projects with enterprises per HEI (2)	Weighted average no. of patents per HEI (2)
Argentina	10	13,281	11,148	85	1,115	9	1,774	12
Bolivia	8	427	51	NA	6	NA	15	NA
Brazil	10	15,620	1,470	1,324	147	132	101	208
Chile	11	1,797	771	81	70	7	211	14
Colombia	11	2,145	286	11	26	1	25	1
Costa Rica	4	1,815	119	5	30	1	55	2
Cuba	8	1,049	73	85	9	11	13	15
Ecuador	10	902	43	2	4	0.2	4	0.56
El Salvador	8	362	12	2	1.5	0.25	5.26	5.78
Guatemala (3)	1	7	NA	NA	NA	NA	NA	NA
Honduras	7	135	33	2	5	0.3	9	1.35
Mexico	15	2,378	387	153	26	10	78	35
Nicaragua	5	449	8	NA	1.6	NA	1.23	NA
Panama	10	442	29	2	3	0.2	9	0.8
Paraguay	8	564	23	3	3	0.38	17	2.66
Peru	10	4,133	31	15	3	1.5	3	1.6
Uruguay	4	672	30	45	8	11	14	29.3
Venezuela	7	3,320	86	21	12	3	5.3	2.4
TOTAL	147	49,498	14,600	1,836				

1. Includes patents registered nationally, in Europe and in the USA.
2. The weights were calculated on the basis of the total number of researchers in a given country.
3. Only one interview was conducted in Guatemala. Therefore the data from Guatemala have not been considered in the analysis.

OVERVIEW OF THE RESULTS OF THE AIDA QUESTIONNAIRE

The results presented in this following section are based on the AIDA methodology, where the HEIs consulted in this study answered a number of specific questions regarding knowledge of IP rights, level of protection, management, and exploitation. Each of the four AIDA levels consists of four sub-levels. The questionnaire embraced some 20 questions for each AIDA level, the answers being assigned a value between 0 for very low and 10 for very high.

Global analysis of IP awareness and use in Latin American HEIs

With the average responses from the institutions in each country's sample, a national value for each AIDA level was calculated and is presented by AIDA level in Table 4.3.

Table 4.3   AIDA values per level of analysis and per country

Countries	AIDA Level				
	Knowledge	Protection	Management	Exploitation	Average
Argentina	8.33	4.19	5.15	3.54	5.30
Bolivia	2.44	0.96	1.26	1.15	1.45
Brazil	8.81	6.19	6.58	4.45	6.51
Chile	6.06	4.45	4.31	3.47	4.57
Colombia	8.06	3.89	3.68	2.91	4.63
Costa Rica	7.71	4.59	4.34	3.65	5.08
Cuba	7.01	4.48	3.56	2.99	4.51
Ecuador	7.00	4.43	4.52	3.26	4.80
El Salvador	5.08	1.62	1.40	1.58	2.42
Honduras	5.02	1.54	0.77	1.14	2.12
Mexico	6.18	4.84	4.94	3.90	4.96
Nicaragua	5.50	3.01	3.15	2.53	3.55
Panama	7.68	4.05	3.98	3.96	4.91
Paraguay	1.87	0.45	0.46	0.33	0.78
Peru	6.58	4.16	3.05	2.94	4.18
Uruguay	7.18	3.60	2.78	1.88	3.86
Venezuela	6.79	3.01	2.82	2.22	3.71
Average	6.31	3.50	3.34	2.76	3.96

The data in Table 4.3 can be interpreted as follows:

Level 1: "knowledge" consists of 4 sub-levels, this is:

a) general knowledge on IP;
b) confidence in IP;

c) information search and knowledge improvement in IP (including knowledge regarding the benefits of using IP databases as a source of information);

d) awareness concerning confidentiality measures and IP protection tools.

In general the data reveal that Argentina, Brazil and Colombia show, on average, the highest level of IP awareness in their universities. In the Central American region, Costa Rica and Panama are clearly leading the field. On the other hand, Bolivia and Paraguay show remarkably low levels of knowledge and awareness of the basic components IP system. HEIs in Bolivia and Paraguay demonstrate a very limited awareness of IP issues within their institutions.

Level 2: "protection" is to measure the use the interviewed HEIs make of the IP system and is characterized by the sub-levels:

a) use of registered IP rights (including how registration is pursued and for what purpose);

b) use of other IP tools (such as non-registered IP);

c) use of other means of IP protection (such as secret information, know-how);

d) contractual procedures and sanctions (for example staff contracts, non-disclosure agreements).

At this level it was also evaluated if the HEI has a clear and well disseminated IP policy in place. When comparing the average results for all countries in the column "knowledge", to the column "protection" it can be observed that the AIDA values dramatically decrease. This proves that besides good knowledge on IP issues among specific actors within the institutions, the interviewed HEIs do not use in practice the IP system in a regular way and their IP policies, if they exist, are not well implemented. An exception here is Brazil (with an average level of 6.19 out of 10), where the use of IP seems to be more widespread and regular than in any other country in the region. Considerably lower levels of IP use and protection, but higher than on regional average, can be observed in Mexico, Costa Rica, Cuba, Chile, Ecuador, Argentina, Peru, Panama, and Colombia. El Salvador, Honduras, Bolivia and Paraguay seem to come in last in comparison.

Level 3: "management" deals with the procedures in place to manage IP in the university, embracing issues such as:

a) organization and administration of IP (who is managing IP and how);

b) operational management of IP (effectively implemented protection-means);

c) time management of IP aspects (for example IP aspects are taken into account at the beginning and during a project);

d) third-party IP rights (e.g. if the IP owned by third parties is taken into account).

The data show that the values in this column are generally very close to the values concerning IP protection and use (in some cases they are slightly higher, in others slightly lower). This suggests that by and large, depending on how much an institution uses the different IP tools, it has adequate structure and processes in place to manage IP. It seems to confirm that with increasing use and protection of IP, the organizational efforts for IP management increase too (for example in Brazil).

Level 4: "exploitation" is the last and highest level on the AIDA scale. Here the objective is to evaluate aspects related to:

a)   the integration of IP in the broader institutional strategy;
b)   commercialization and valorization of IP by transfer (this is how the HEI exploits or would like to exploit its IP – e.g. licensing, selling IP, spin-off creation);
c)   the defense policy of IP in the university in case of infringement;
d)   IP information monitoring (how to use, understand, monitor IP information).

In this regard the study revealed that across the sample, most universities do not have global IP strategies in place, and IP management is not integrated in the wider strategy of the HEIs. While there is awareness on the existing ways of exploiting research results, the practical aspects related to evaluating exploitation options, contracts and negotiation are widely considered by HEIs as a weakness. The data confirm that overall exploitation of IP owned by universities is low in Latin America. In fact, when going back to the original data it can be observed that activities related to the commercialization of IP appear to be completely non-existent in many HEIs consulted in the study. When contrasting the regional results, Brazil seems to lead the field also in exploitation issues, but is closely followed by Panama, Mexico, Costa Rica, Argentina and Chile.

Overall, when considering the average global level of IP integration on the AIDA scale by country (see last column in Table 4.3), Brazil, Argentina and Costa Rica stand out as the countries in Latin America with relatively higher levels of IP integration in their institutions, closely followed by Mexico and Panamá. Ecuador, Colombia, Chile, Cuba, Peru, Uruguay, Venezuela, and Nicaragua show low levels (between 4.8 and 3.5) and are performing around the regional average, while El Salvador, Honduras, Bolivia and Paraguay show low levels of IP integration (between 2.42 and 0.78). When aggregating the average AIDA values of all 17 countries considered in this study, the results can be visualized in Figure 4.2 on the next page.

In summary, the main conclusions that may be drawn on a regional level from the study are:

•   Knowledge about the IP system in general and the different IP tools and rights is considerably high in university and department-level management staff among the HEIs consulted in the study. However, specific awareness on IP information sources, databases and organizations dealing with IP issues is low. It was revealed furthermore that academic/research staff and students are not offered training or practical information on IP issues. With this regard, most of the institutions in the analysis indicated lack of professionals to act as trainers, training materials, top-level support

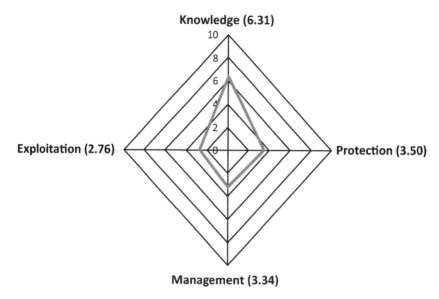

Figure 4.2   Global values in the AIDA analysis in Latin American HEIs

and financial resources as the main barriers to disseminate knowledge on IP to all levels at their institution.

As it was shown before, the levels of protection, management and exploitation of IP in Latin American HEIs are very low in general all over the region. The study confirms that although university leaders seem to be aware of the importance of managing their research results in the best possible manner, fully integrating IP within their institutions is not among their priorities. The promotion of research as such is, however, becoming ever more important it seems, as the interviews revealed that considerable efforts are underway throughout the region to increase the quality and size of PhD programs.

Most of the interviewed HEIs lack formal IP management units/structures and qualified personnel with relevant experience. IP protection and commercialization, if pursued at all, is often subcontracted with third parties.

Maturity level on the AIDA scale

With a global position of 3.96 (out of 10), Figure 4.3 visualizes the average maturity level on the AIDA scale of the 147 Latin American HEIs interviewed. The result suggests that

Figure 4.3   Global level of IP integration

Latin American HEIs are still in the preliminary phases of IP integration at the institutional levels and that, IP policies and aspects regarding IP management and exploitation have not been developed broadly.

It is, however, important to complement this result with information gathered from the individual interviews, observations and indicators provided by the HEIs throughout the study. Overall the following general patterns can be observed:

- With regards to the awareness and use of IP, there is a significant heterogeneity among countries, but also among different institutions within each country based on their public or private status, focus on research, fields of specialization, and other factors.
- While many HEIs pursue increasing institutional IP knowledge and awareness initiatives, they do not reach all levels of the institutions, not even those that are directly involved with the production of patentable results. Communication channels and procedures between IP offices (or staff in charge of IP) and researchers are not clear and organized.
- IP is not part of most Latin American HEIs institutional strategies yet. Consequently, there are limited and weak IP policies, practices and supporting structures.
- There is an evident confidence in IP tools as powerful instruments to bring research results to the market; however, there is not a systematic use of them.
- Training programs in IP are increasingly offered in Latin America, but they often do not include acquiring practical experience and are focused on legal issues. At the same time there is evidence that there are not enough experts with practical know-how in the field yet. Commercialization is the least developed area of IP management and where most.
- Most institutions interviewed demonstrated a lively interest in enhancing IP integration in their institutions. In general HEIs confirmed that they are interested in participating in any conferences and training events related to IP to learn what other universities with respect.

INTEGRATION OF INTELLECTUAL PROPERTY MANAGEMENT IN LATIN AMERICAN HIGHER EDUCATION INSTITUTIONS: MAIN BARRIERS

Besides looking at the current situation, the PILA study also asked for the main observed barriers and factors that determine the integration of IP management practices and policies in Latin American HEIs. The factors most commonly perceived throughout the region have been aggregated and structured in different categories which are presented herein.

National level factors

The PILA study shows that despite the various national initiatives on innovation, there is still a perceived limited development of national innovation and IP systems. Respondents find that there is often a lack of information and support from national IP offices, despite the high level of bureaucracy involved. There is also a perceived lack of clarity in the requirements for a research result to constitute a novelty or an invention qualifying for an IP title. These factors could imply that while there is political support for innovation, the *capacity* to support innovation and strengthen links among all relevant stakeholders is still weak. Identifying novelty or invention in research is a complicated task normally undertaken by patent lawyers alongside technologists. The perceived lack of clarity raised here shows that there is a great need to have trained professionals to support the implementation of national innovation and IP policies, and especially to support researchers. The results suggest that effort has to be made to effectively communicate the policies and detailed regulations to the relevant stakeholders.

Institutional level factors

At an institutional level, results point to a perceived absence of institutional IP regulation and structure. Several other factors could contribute to this weak IP culture institutionally – HEI decision-makers are seen to have insufficient commitment to the full integration of IP. IP is also perceived as conflicting with traditional institutional values. The study also points out that there is low diffusion of IP issues at all institutional levels including staff and stakeholders. IP policies, if in place, are perceived to be too weak, or not well implemented, and not tackling all stakeholders and aspects involved. Clearly, while HEIs do have access to basic training on IP, there is a strong need for training in practical issues of IP management.

Cultural factors

Given the level of IP barriers at institutional level, it is telling that at a cultural one, respondents strongly identified that there is mistrust amongst researchers regarding IP systems, and that there is a perception of a trade-off in publishing and IP. This confirms the findings presented by Arocena and Sutz (2005) who perceive a trade-off for researchers to either conduct research which allows them to become integrated into the international community of scholars and publish their research in mainstream publications, or conduct applied research potentially generating IP titles. Furthermore, the PILA study identifies that amongst researchers and students, there is low awareness and knowledge of fundamental IP issues such as rights, obligations and benefits, as well as a lack of know-how on how to use IP information systems as a basis for the formulation of research strategies and projects. This consequently explains why there is a perceived view that there is little tradition of research and intellectual production amongst academics. Staff are not informed of the benefits and rewards of research as well as the role IP can play.

Strategy level factors

Results of perceptions at strategy level show that many view generation and exploitation of IP does not form a part of institutional strategies. Another barrier perceived is that research is not aligned with socioeconomic problems and market needs. Respondents also view that there is limited cooperation with the industry and potential partners in order to fully exploit any research results. Additionally, there is limited technical knowledge to properly exploit IP-generated within institutions. These barriers identified not only point to low capacity of institutions to conceptualize IP strategies and policies, but also to the capacity of actually implementing any consequent IP strategies.

Operational level factors

The barriers identified at strategy level subsequently relate to those at operational level. Results of the study indicated that another formidable barrier is the lack of a systematic approach, and proper processes for IP management, specifically regarding disclosure of results, technology vigilance and state-of-the-art search. There is also lack of communication and coordination among different department/stakeholders involved. Another barrier at operational level is that IP units or technology transfer offices lack financial resources and qualified staff with know-how, especially with regards to valorization and exploitation. These barriers effectively demonstrate Alänge (2009)'s idea that the "patenting-licensing" approach requires a broader approach to IP management than simply setting up an office. It entails linking science and legal capacity, supported by committed resources to translate scientific discovery into viable commercial contracts.

Financial factors

Financially, the study identified barriers in limitation of funds to support research and IP management. Firstly, there are limited financial resources to support the creation and maintenance of IP units. IP units also have insufficient funds to finance professional training of their IP staff. Further, IP protection's high cost act as a barrier to the integration of IP practices in HEIs. The barriers identified here strongly support Arocena's argument that registering research results requires considerable organizational and budgetary efforts from the universities (Arocena 2001).

Human factors

At the human level, within research institutions, the study points out there is effectively a lack of basic awareness and training for researchers in IP. Others point to the barrier of lack of qualified staff in IP management and exploitation with practical experience as well as lack of human technical capacity for IP monitoring. Unsurprisingly, these barriers stem from the financial and strategic barriers raised above. Another perceived barrier at human level is the absence of incentives for intellectual production, relating to the general lack of strategies and policies to promote research within HEIs.

Conclusion

All over the world, universities are increasingly asked to enhance their role as engines of economic development in the knowledge and information society. Cornerstones of national innovation systems, they are required to enhance research and technology transfer and serve the local industry and society. In this context, universities are confronted with Intellectual Property issues, and find themselves in a situation where they have to take a position, decide on how far to engage in IP management, and learn how to implement new strategies and process in their institutions. If they do not engage in IP and focus on their traditional activities, a modern university would disregard a number of benefits and opportunities IP management can bring. As discussed in this chapter, these benefits are not simply related to potential commercialization of research through patenting and licensing, which actually requires a significant bit of experience and time. IP management is multi-faceted and can present a powerful tool for universities in developing regions, such as Latin America, to enhance the relevance and applicability of their research. Thus for example, any institution can benefit from using IP databases when deciding on research priorities, and as a resource of ideas and knowledge that can be adapted and exploited for the benefit of society. Furthermore, as technologies are increasingly developed in cooperation among different entities, IP management is crucial to guaranteeing the potential results will belong to the partner who can convert it into a new product or process, while allowing for further research.

In Latin America, the elements of entrepreneurial university models in general, and IPR in particular, have become prominent issues on the agendas of HEIs and policy makers. For universities to integrate IP management in their institutions and generate positive spill-overs for their national economies, it requires first and foremost strong national innovation policies and appropriate legal frameworks. However, it seems, what HEIs need most urgently is practical know-how on all aspects of IP management and potential benefits, advice on implementing IP policies and processes, as well as support in training university staff and students in IP, and in creating an entrepreneurial culture among staff and students. As the term "IP management" frequently is associated to generating patents, and the number of patents registered by a university is increasingly used as indicator of performance, special care should be taken here to convey the right values and information to HEIs in developing countries, keeping expectations on direct financial return realistic. In this sense it must be clear to HEIs, that patents should only be generated if this is the most adequate option for exploiting the research, and that integrated IP management comprises also alternative ways to the patenting-licensing strategy. In this learning process, universities could benefit from working in networks, exchanging experiences and know-how. This could be particularly true for Latin America, due to their common language and history.

The data analysis presented, based on the PILA-Network study on Intellectual Property awareness and use in Latin American higher education institutions, revealed that there is a relatively high level of awareness and active interest in IP among the HEIs middle managers. At the same time, researchers and staff in general are not well informed and trained on the topic. The study demonstrates that IP had been addressed in a more or less regular and structured manner in all 147 HEIs interviewed. This shows that due to international trends, government pressure, and/or practical needs when pursuing R&D and technology transfer, Latin American HEIs find themselves implicated in IP issues. There is, however, still a long way to go for these institutions to integrate IP in their organizations and to develop adequate IP management capacities, as the interviews confirmed. First of all, awareness raising and information on IP needs to be pursued on all levels of the university. Many of the barriers indicated by the interviewed universities, concerning organizational, institutional and strategic factors, may be tackled by informing university leaders about the benefits of an integrated IP strategy and offering success stories and specific advice. Cultural barriers may be reduced by offering specific training and creating an IP culture among staff and students. Basic training should be included in the curricula of engineers and economics. Additionally, more professionals are needed with specific and practical know-how on the multiple components of IP management, from the use of IP databases to IP exploitation. The interviews suggested besides that national intellectual property offices (those institutions responsible for registering IP rights in each country) could take a more active role and cooperate with universities in providing information and training. They could be inspired here for instance by training initiatives offered by many national and regional patent offices (e.g. WIPO, EPO, UK PTO). There are a number of "success stories" and good practice examples, both from developing and developed countries, which can offer guidance to HEIs and policy makers in Latin America. Yet, the extent to which IP management should be pursued by a higher education institution, and the way in which it can enhance its contribution to regional development, depends strongly on the context. Therefore, successful examples from other countries and institutions need to be analyzed carefully and adapted to the specific circumstances.

Recognizing that Latin American higher education systems have to overcome a number of challenges on their way to become engines of knowledge-based economic development, the potential benefits of integrating IP management strategies should not be underestimated.

Questions to Consider

1. Why is IPR relevant for universities?
2. What are the benefits for universities proactively addressing IPR issues?
3. What are the main perceived barriers for integration of IP management in Latin American Universities according to the PILA study?

References

Adams, J. et al. 2002. *Expert Group Report on the Role and Strategic Use of IPR in International Research Collaborations*. European Commission. [Online]. Available at: http://ec.europa.eu/research/era/pdf/ipr-eur-20230_en.pdf [accessed: July 2010].

Alänge, S. 2008. Innovation Processes in a Systems Perspective, in *Competitiveness through Relationships: Innovation Systems in Developing Countries*. Stockholm: Sida/SAREC.

Alänge, S., Lundqvist, M., Scheinberg, S. and Norgren, A. 2009. The Experiences of Entrepreneurial Universities, in *Competitiveness through Relationships: Innovation Systems in Developing Countries*. Stockholm: Sida/SAREC.

Auril. 2002. *Managing Intellectual Property: A Guide to Strategic Decision-Making in Universities*. [Online]. Available at: http://www.ipo.gov.uk/managingipoverview.pdf [accessed: June 2010].

Autum. 2010. *Bayh–Dole Act*. [Online]. Available at: http://www.autm.net/Bayh_Dole_Act.htm [accessed: July 22, 2010].

Arocena, R. and Sutz, J. 2001. Changing knowledge production and Latin American universities. *Research Policy*, 30, 1221–34.

Arocena, R. and Sutz, J. 2005. Latin American universities: From an original revolution to an uncertain transition. *Higher Education*, 50(4), 573–92.

European Commission. 2006. "Delivering on the modernisation agenda for universities – Education, research and innovation." Communication from the Commission to the Council and the European Parliament, Brussels COM/2006/0208 final.

Delanty, G. 2001. *Challenging Knowledge: The University in the Knowledge Society*. Buckingham: Society of Research into Higher Education and Open University Press.

Etzkowitz, H. and Leydesdorff, L. (eds). 1997. A Triple Helix of University–Industry–Government Relations, in *Universities and the Global Knowledge Economy*. London: Pinter Publishers, 155–63.

Etzkowitz, H., Webster, A., Gebhardt, C. and Cantisano Terra, B.R. 2000. The future of university and the university of the future: Evolution of ivory tower to entrepreneurial paradigm. *Research Policy*, 29, 313–30.

European Research Advisory Board. 2006. *Final Report on International Research Cooperation*. [Online]. Available at: http://ec.europa.eu/research/eurab/pdf/eurab_05_032_wg9_finalreport_june06_en.pdf [accessed: July 2010].

OECD. 2003. *Turning Science into Business: Patenting and Licensing at Public Research Organisations*. [Online]. Available at: http://www.oecd.org/document/54/0,3343,en_2649_34797_31174966_1_1_1,00.html [accessed: August 2010].

WIPO. 2004. *Intellectual Property Handbook: Policy, Law and Use*. [Online]. Available at: http://www.wipo.int/about-ip/en/iprm/ [accessed: July 10, 2010].

WIPO. (n.d.). *A Brochure on Intellectual Property Rights: For Universities and R&D Institutions in African Countries*. [Online]. Available at: http://www.wipo.int/freepublications/en/intproperty/849/wipo_pub_849.pdf [accessed: August 2010].

5

Fostering Innovation and Technology Transfer in the Renewable Energy Sector at Latin American Higher Education Institutions: Findings from a Labour Market Survey Undertaken as Part of the JELARE Project

JULIA GOTTWALD, WALTER LEAL FILHO and YOUSSEF
AHMAD YOUSSEF

Introduction

Renewable energy is a relatively new, emerging sector, but one which is of major importance for the sustainable socioeconomic development of Latin Americas countries for two main reasons. Firstly, due to the obvious environmental benefits in respect of the use of reduced or no CO_2 emissions. Secondly, because it offers local job opportunities and contributes towards reducing the dependency on imported fuels. Renewable energy is high on the political agenda of Latin American countries, and most countries have explicit goals to increase the share of energy coming from renewable sources. However, the current potential is not being used despite the high availability of natural resources. One of the main problems is the lack of supportive public policies combined with barriers, such as the lack of available local expertise to plan, design, implement and maintain renewable energy technologies. Due to the innovative nature of this field, universities in Latin America, as providers of research and education, are expected play a crucial role in overcoming these problems. By increasing innovation and technology transfer performance, in particular, universities could become a vector of sustainable socioeconomic development for Latin American countries as a whole, and particularly for the renewable energy sector. Despite the value of the topic of renewable energies, it is not yet as prominently featured on the curricula and research activities of Latin American (and EU) universities as should be the case. In order to address this perceived need, the Joint European–Latin American Universities Renewable Energy Project (JELARE) is being undertaken.

The JELARE project is a cooperation scheme involving universities from Germany, Latvia, Bolivia, Brazil, Chile and Guatemala with the aim of fostering innovative labour market-oriented educational and research approaches in the field of renewable energies at Latin American and European institutes of higher education (HEI). The project is funded by ALFA III, an EU programme for cooperation between the European Union and Latin America, in the higher education and training framework.

The JELARE project partners Hamburg University of Applied Sciences (Germany), Rēzeknes Augstskola (Latvia), Universidad Católica Boliviana, Universidade do Sul de Santa Catarina (Brazil), Universidad de Chile (Chile) and Universidad Galileo (Guatemala) have been chosen based on their academic competence and interest in international cooperation in the field of renewable energy as well as in the modernization and improvement of their current research and teaching activities. Germany, Chile and Brazil represent comparatively experienced and advanced organizations and countries in the field of renewable energy, while Latvia, Bolivia and Guatemala are less developed in this area. This combination not only anticipates future knowledge transfers between the EU and LA, but also the intra-continental exchanges that may take place.

The main purpose of the JELARE project is to improve dialogue, mutual understanding and foster cooperation between EU and Latin American universities, and to contribute to the modernization of the curriculum by means of including the key topic of renewable energies in teaching programmes, research and activities, and hence assist with the implementation of sustainable (energy) technologies and policies in both regions. The aim of the project is not only to improve the academic quality of European and Latin American higher education institutions, but also to strengthen their role in contributing to local economic development and social cohesion.

In order to contribute to its overall objectives, the JELARE project focuses on the thematic sector of renewable energy, an area widely acknowledged as being very important. Due to the current global situation of scarce energy resources, rapidly rising prices for fossil fuels and the impact of climate change, the promotion of renewable energy is of vital importance for sustainable socioeconomic development in Latin America as well as in Europe. For developing countries in particular, local energy generation has great potential for local economic development (more local jobs and reduced dependence on imports). Lack of expertise is a major impediment to the broader use of renewable energies in Latin America. In this context, Latin American HEIs play a very important role in training people (education), providing expert advice (research and technology transfer) and thereby having a positive impact on socioeconomic development.

The specific objectives of JELARE are:

- to develop and implement labour market-oriented research and educational approaches in the field of renewable energies;
- to increase the capacity of university staff to modernize their educational and research programmes and activities;
- to strengthen the link between universities and the labour market, business and public sector in the field of renewable energies;
- to establish a long-term partnership and network between European and Latin American universities.

During the ongoing, three-year project (2009–11) the following outputs are expected:

- a renewable energy labour market survey;
- teaching and research concepts for renewable energies;
- teaching and research pilot modules for renewable energies;
- university staff capacity-building programme;
- recommendation report for European and Latin American universities;
- the set-up of an international JELARE network, with local subgroups in the partner countries.

This chapter presents the key findings of two project surveys that were carried out in Bolivia, Brazil, Chile and Guatemala. The objectives of these surveys were to identify the needs of the labour market regarding education and research in the renewable energy sector and to identify training and qualification needs of university staff in the renewable energy sector. The presentation of the results will focus on the aspects that are most relevant to the topic of fostering innovation and technology transfer in the renewable energy sector at Latin American higher education institutions.

Overview of the Literature

The Latin American region is a region characterized by a set of countries, which were colonized by both Portugal and Spain and which have a rich history. From Uruguay and Argentina in the south, to Mexico in the north, this culturally rich region is a significant economic centre.

In Latin America, private industry accounts only for a small percentage of research and development (R&D). Most R&D is financed by the government and carried out by Latin American public research institutes and universities (Holm-Nielsen et al. 2006). However, traditionally, universities in Latin America have weak linkages to industry (Lopez 1994, Thorn and Soo 2006) and academic research agendas have been disassociated from the needs of the economy (Hansen et al. 2002). Therefore, university research is seldom commercialized. The concept of the 'third mission' related to technology transfer has been introduced only gradually in universities (Thorn and Soo 2006). Fostering the technology transfer performance of universities in Latin America could unleash a significant innovative capacity in Latin America (Thorn and Soo 2006).

Latin American universities could play a key role, not only in terms of education, but also in terms of innovation, research and technology transfer. The overall contribution of higher education research in Latin America remains unclear (Hansen et al. 2002), yet the potential of universities in terms of increasing the technological capacity of a country has been acknowledged (Thorn and Soo 2006). Internationalization strategies by Latin American universities – discussed as an opportunity to access the latest technology and knowledge and thereby improve the research performance (de Wit et al. 2006) – as well as a stronger focus on applied and market-oriented research (including adapting international technologies to the specific needs of the local market) combined with more domestic technology transfer activities could contribute to increasing the local technology capacity.

In terms of innovation, information on the relative performance of Latin American countries is at present rather limited. Drucker's (2001) definition of innovation as being the bringing to the marketplace of a new product, process or service to enhance an existing product or to develop a new enterprise (Drucker 2001) is not widely used. In assessing their innovation performance, Latin American countries use a range of measures, but a lack of objective and reliable benchmarking makes comparisons a difficult task. The use of the word 'innovation' in Latin America may also in itself be problematic given that it is associated most often with invention rather than commercialization of a new product or service. The element of commercialization is less readily measurable despite the need to place a due emphasis on this aspect.

Even though the subject matter of innovation is under debate, there have been many developments which illustrate the potential seen in Latin America in this field. For instance, Brazil was the first country in the world to have widely adopted the use of sugar-cane-based bio-ethanol in the automotive industry. Starting in the late 1970s and throughout the 1980s, R&D in bio-fuels in Brazil placed it at the forefront. Even today, there are more cars in Brazil using bio-ethanol (or a combination of bio-ethanol and conventional petrol, the so-called 'flexi-fuel vehicles') than anywhere else in the world. Another country, namely Venezuela, also had a leading innovative edge in respect of technologies related to oil exploration in the late 1970s, although lack of investments have virtually phased this out. Nowadays, some Latin American countries have agencies or organizations which try to support innovation and these work closely with industry and universities alike. The current state of affairs is better developed in the field of technological transfer.

Currently, international technology transfer (transfer of technology from industrialized nations to less developed nations) is predominantly carried out via trade or foreign direct investment. However, the benefit for the receiving country is often marginal if the technology or know-how does not spill over to the country in a broader sense. To increase the positive impact of international technology transfer, it is of vital importance that the technological capacities of the recipient country are increased and that the technology gap is decreased. It is important for developing countries to develop a domestic R&D capacity in order to identify scientific and technological options, to adapt existing technologies to local needs and to create technologies that are unique to the country (Thorn and Soo 2006). According to Brewer (2008), international technology flows occur not only at the level of products, but also of individuals and projects, however, current data does not capture the full scope of these multidimensional flows. Internationally, technology is also transferred through meetings, projects and informal networking. Some of the international technology transfer research is specifically focused on the topics of climate change and energy technologies, including renewable energy (Worrel et al. 2001, Brewer 2008). The renewable energy sector is not only relevant with respect to the sustainable socioeconomic development in Latin America (as outlined above) – renewable energy is also currently playing an important role in the context of international technology transfer for climate change mitigation.

University technology transfer has increasingly become a topic of international research, and literature on this topic has emerged from many disciplines, such as economics, political science, engineering (Vinig and Van Rijsbergen 2009). The importance of universities expanding their mission from education and research to technology transfer has been acknowledged and analysed by many authors (Thorn and Soo 2006, Horowitz Gassol 2007). Previous comparative analyses of universities from different countries have shown that their technology transfer performance depends to a large extent on national regulatory frameworks (Feldmann and Schipper 2007). However, so far most research on technology transfer is related to developed countries. A significant amount of university technology transfer research has focused on the commercialization of university research and, therefore, mechanisms such as patenting, licensing and spin-offs have been the most studied. Literature acknowledges that there are other ways that research is transferred. However, such outcomes are harder to measure (Nilsson et al. 2010). Some studies have demonstrated that these common indicators for technology transfer (patents, licensing, spin-offs) account only for a minor proportion of the technology actually transferred to the local market (Lester 2005, Agrawal and Henderson 2002). Therefore, there is a need to explore informal technology transfer mechanisms such as consulting, co-supervision, recruitment of graduates, conversations, collaborative research and conferences. In Latin America, informal linkages and university contract research have grown substantially in recent years (Thorn and Soo 2006).

In this context, the studies carried out as part of the JELARE project intended to explore the needs of the renewable energy labour market as well as of the staff members of higher education institutions in Latin America regarding qualifications and the transfer of knowledge and technologies in the renewable energy sector. On the one hand, the labour market survey seeks to give insight into the perspective of companies and other private and public organization on which qualifications are required from employers in the renewable energy sector as well as on the expectations market players have on universities. On the other hand, the university staff survey seeks to identify the needs of staff for increasing their teaching, research and technology performance. Within the JELARE project, the results of these surveys will be used for developing concepts for teaching, research and technology at the partner universities

Methodology

The set of surveys within the framework of the JELARE project was conducted in each of the partner countries Germany, Latvia, Bolivia, Brazil, Chile and Guatemala between March and June 2009. This chapter presents the key findings of two surveys carried out in the Latin American countries, namely Bolivia, Brazil, Chile and Guatemala.

One survey addressed local employers in the renewable energy sector such as companies, governmental organizations and non-governmental organizations. The aim of this survey was to identify the needs of the labour market regarding education and research in the renewable energy sector.

The second survey addressed the university staff of the JELARE partner universities Universidad Católica Boliviana (UCB, Bolivia), Fundação Universidade do Sul de Santa Catarina (UNISUL, Brazil), Universidad de Chile (UChile, Chile) and Universidad Galileo (UG, Guatemala) in order to identify the training needs of university staff in the renewable energy sector as well as their perception of the needs for strengthening renewable energy topics at their university.

For both surveys, a common questionnaire was developed by the Brazilian JELARE partner UNISUL in close cooperation with all other partners The survey design intended to take into account the different local realities and features in the countries involved as well as allowing comparability among the JELARE countries. As the working language of the JELARE project is English, the common questionnaire has been designed and agreed upon in English. Afterwards the questionnaire was translated into the respective local languages and adapted to the local conditions for certain questions. For example, for the staff survey, the departments of the local university or available staff positions were adjusted to the local context. The surveys were carried out by the local JELARE teams in the respective countries. Each partner analysed and evaluated the local survey results and prepared a local report. In addition, UNISUL prepared a transnational comparison of the survey results.

The questionnaire used for the labour market survey addressing private and public companies and organizations participating in the renewable energy market asked for the following information:

- general information about the organization, company or entity;
- employee training and qualifications;
- qualification requirements and market needs;
- the role of higher education institutions;
- general suggestions.

The questionnaire used for the university staff survey addressing staff members of the JELARE partner universities working or intending to work in the renewable energy sector asked for the following information:

- profile of the respondent;
- training interests;
- requirements in terms of renewable energy training and qualifications;
- perception of the need to strengthen renewable energy at own HEI;
- general suggestions.

The survey was meant to be representative, but one has to bear in mind the restrictions and difficulties which are inherent in this category of empirical research. Nonetheless, the use of a survey instrument was deemed appropriate, bearing in mind the fact that data needed to be collected from different countries. More detailed information on the questionnaire can be found in Annex 1.

To bear references to the varying local differences and conditions, each project partner developed its own methodology concerning how to select the survey sample and to receive responses to the questionnaire, for example by telephone or personal interview or written or email questionnaires. Additionally, some partners organized focus groups to gather more qualitative data. The description of the methodology used by each partner draws from the publication 'Renewable energy market needs: a perspective from Europe and Latin America', produced as part of the JELARE project (Guerra and Youssef 2010).

In Bolivia, for the renewable energy market survey, an initial list of companies was obtained from the Vice Ministry of Electricity and Alternative Energies (VMEAE). Companies in other sectors that operate or could be interested in working in the field of renewable energy such as communications, mining and industry were also identified and contacted; 80 per cent of the companies expressed interest in participating in the survey. A total of 30 companies, non-governmental organizations (NGO) and public institutions were interviewed. For the staff survey, first, the university programmes that could include renewable energy topics were identified. Next, the director of each relevant degree programme was asked to provide a list of professors who work in or could be interested in working in the topic. Finally, these people were contacted and the questionnaire was given to nine people who expressed interest in participating. Surveys of people or entities located in La Paz were realized personally by previously trained interviewers. The rest of the surveys were done by fax or email. All of the surveys were entered in the SPSS programme for evaluation. In addition to the surveys, two focus groups were created. The main purpose was to obtain qualitative information from some of the actors previously interviewed to complement the quantitative data of the survey. One focus group comprised three professors working in the field of renewable energies and three representatives from the market. The second focus group comprised four professors, experts on the topic, and two representatives of government entities and international cooperation working with renewable energy. The discussion was guided through a compendium of key questions. The participants' contributions were later transcribed to add key quotations to the survey results (Villegas et al. 2010).

In Brazil, the sample for the market survey comprised 15 companies, of which 13 are in Florianopolis and two in Rio de Janeiro. There were eight responses to the questionnaire for the university staff survey, four from Universidade do Sul de Santa Catarina (UNISUL), one from Universidade do Estado de Santa Catarina/Escola Superior de Administração e Gerência/(UDESC/ESAG) and two from Universidade Federal de Santa Catarina (UFSC). The questionnaires' results and statistics analysis were analysed using Sphinx software (Leite et al. 2010).

In Chile, for companies located in the Santiago area, initial contact for the market survey was established by means of an email or phone call, and personal appointments were then scheduled. Companies located outside Santiago were supposed to answer the survey without a personal interview, but only one company responded. The final size of the sample was 16 companies. The staff survey was conducted among university professors, project managers, and researchers who were chosen for their research and teaching interests within selected academic units. The academic units were selected based on the Domeyko Energy programme,[1] whose objective is to strengthen university capabilities to face issues of national concern. The two surveys were undertaken based on the following criteria (López Robinovich et al. 2010):

- Members of the survey team were not allowed to provide answers and/or fill in surveys in order to provide statistical validation.
- Interviewed contacts could not answer more than one survey; this criterion maintained the statistical independence of the answers provided.
- Personal interviews were given priority. However, potential contacts located outside Santiago were also considered and were approached electronically by email.

In Guatemala, the sample design for market participants was as follows. The case selection was based on a list belonging to the Ministry of Energy and Mines and enriched by key informants. The total number of cases in the list reached 123 companies and organizations, considered market participants. The relevant decisions were the following: it was agreed that the questionnaire should be sent out to 50 of these companies to make up the cases selected in the sample and obtain information from them. This number is equivalent to 41 per cent of the cases mentioned in the original list. In the end, the technical team

---

1   Available at: http://www.derecho.uchile.cl/cda/cda/programa_domeyko/index.html.

was able to obtain data from 51 cases. An examination of key variables – such as number of employees and annual turnover – of the completed questionnaires, confirmed that the sample selected was a cross-section of organizations and companies in Guatemala. Therefore, it can be claimed that this sample was highly representative of the world of renewable energy industries and organizations in Guatemala. Three judges were asked to rate between zero and three which of these 123 companies were the most relevant and most important for evaluation. A selection was made from the list of those 51 companies and organizations that attained the highest scores. In case any of the companies could not be reached, either because of their location or for any other reason, the company in question was replaced by another one with a lower score. The required information was to be given by the highest managerial authority or the one following in rank. For the sample design for the university teaching and administrative staff, it was possible to apply the questionnaire to 20 cases that are equivalent to a census of the renewable energy staff at the Universidad Galileo when the survey was done. Problems concerning whether the results are representative or not are then excluded. For data recording and analysis, all questionnaires were pre-coded on the same sheet where the questions and answers were. Thus, the interviewer recorded this information immediately after finishing the questionnaire. In order to process the questionnaires' contents, the Statistical Package for Social Sciences (SPSS) programme was used, and three databases were created to log the results of each sample (Ruiz et al. 2010).

Findings and Discussion

In the following section, the most relevant survey results for each country, Bolivia, Brazil, Chile and Guatemala, are presented first. The results draw from the publication 'Renewable energy market needs: a perspective from Europe and Latin America', produced as part of the JELARE project (Guerra and Youssef 2010). Finally, a transnational comparison of the responses to the questions most relevant for fostering innovation and technology transfer is conducted.

Renewable Energy Market Survey in Bolivia

The survey results from Bolivia indicate that the renewable energy market in Bolivia is concentrated in the areas of hydroelectric power, photovoltaics and solar thermal energy (Villegas, Aliaga Lordemann and Buch 2010). Most of the private and public organizations operate only in one sector, although a considerable number of them are planning to extend their range of products, especially in the areas of wind power, low-generation hydro power and biomass and/or bio-fuels. Most of the companies currently work in planning and training, whereas only a small number carry out research and development activities or project development (e.g. electrical engineering or plant construction). This is mainly due to the lack of government policies or incentives and the reduced market size. Therefore, except for the hydro power sector, the sector operates with small companies or micro companies, which act almost exclusively as technology suppliers.

The demand for technicians and university graduates in renewable energy is considerably higher than the supply. The lack of specialized technical qualifications is the most common problem for the companies when hiring staff. This situation can worsen in the mid-term, because most of the companies forecast a positive or at least constant trend in their staff requirements. To cover their increasing requirements of renewable energy specialists, the organizations can also train their current staff instead of recruiting new employees. Among the planned capacity-building opportunities, training and learning on the job is the most common. The main motivations for these measures are product and process innovations and, to a lesser extent, market needs as well as government policies and incentives.

According to the companies surveyed, the current state of the higher education institutions regarding renewable energies is far behind the market needs. Cooperation between universities and the market is minimal. However, private and public organizations expect the universities to contribute with more and better *education and training* and to encourage *research and basic development*. In addition, a strengthening of technology transfer activities as well as the joint development of research projects is required.

University Staff Survey at Universidad Católica Boliviana, Bolivia

The most important results of the staff survey at the Universidad Católica Boliviana are:

a)   the insufficient research and development activity in the university;
b)   the huge quantitative and qualitative setback in the field of renewable energy;
c)   the lack of cooperation with the renewable energy market.

The low number of research projects is related to the reduced budget destined for this purpose, whereas the quality responds more to the lack of long-term planning and the deficit of human resources. On the one hand, the university staff does not have the appropriate infrastructure for research activities and their access to information sources is very limited. On the other hand, there is a clear lack of capacities in fundraising and management and in the development of a sustained strategy for research.

The setback regarding renewable energies has similar causes. There is no integral strategy for renewable energy in any particular institute and neither are there formal cooperation mechanisms between different institutes or faculties of the university. The professors do not have financial resources at their disposal to promote a greater inclusion of renewable energy topics, neither do they have easy access to specialized information sources or infrastructure such as laboratories. Furthermore, a lack of mechanisms to detect market developments and to adjust the study programmes to their needs has to be added.

A clear correlation can be highlighted between the staff's training interests and the development plans of the companies. Both actors manifested their intention to operate more intensely in the sectors of wind power, biomass and hydro power. The university staff gives high importance to the need to receive training that allows the improvement of support for the market in the building of capacities and through required services in the field of research. It is consequently very important to design institutional mechanisms that permit a stronger association between the higher education institutions and companies.

The surveys conducted in Bolivia by the JELARE project with higher education institutions and market actors in the field of renewable energies have permitted the analysis of this segment at different levels of interaction. In this sense, three important lessons were learned which reflect the global interaction of the sector as well as its structural aspects: the technological cycle is not linked to the higher education system. This is reflected in very low levels of technology transfer, technological adaptation and innovation and in the lack of technicians and specialized engineers in the country. Education and research are not suited to the market needs because there are no linking or feedback mechanisms with the renewable energy market. Therefore the universities offer insufficient study programmes and develop technological prototypes that do not get exploited by the market and the companies do not have clear incentives to make use of their education, training and research services. Education and research are not sustainable because the higher education institutions lack an integral strategy and financing mechanisms for planned and structured activities in long-term programmes (Villegas, Aliaga Lordemann and Buch 2010).

The results of the JELARE study in Bolivia strongly indicate that the innovation capacity in the renewable energy sector in Bolivia is still very low. Domestic R&D capacity in the renewable energy sector is still in its infancy. Neither private enterprises nor universities are engaged to a large extent in R&D activities. Before universities can play a key role in reducing the technology gap in the renewable energy sector in Bolivia, the capacity of university staff and their research infrastructure, including access to up-to-date knowledge, needs to be increased.

Renewable Energy Market Survey in Brazil

The sample of the renewable energy market survey in Brazil comprised 15 responding companies, of which 13 are in Florianopolis and two are in Rio de Janeiro. In relation to corporate membership, 73 per cent were private enterprises, and the remaining 27 per cent were divided between government and NGOs. According to Leite et al. (2010), the following characteristics drawn from the collected data should be highlighted:

a) The Brazilian market is mainly oriented toward hydroelectric energy generation; 93 per cent of the firms interviewed have some kind of interest in the development of projects related to renewable energy. The research also demonstrates that the majority of the companies surveyed (60 per cent) develop projects in renewable energy through some form of partnership or strategic alliance. On the other hand, 20 per cent stated that they develop autonomous projects, while another 10 per cent outsource the development of such projects. It is very clear that there is an opportunity to enter the universities and their research groups, development and innovation activities through a partnership or outsourcing to the productive sector.

b) There is a lack of skilled workers in the Brazilian renewable energy market 87 per cent of the firms have difficulties in finding skilled professionals to work in the renewable energy area. Thus, there is a significant gap between supply and availability of vacancies for professionals in this area. It is possible to observe from the data presented above that the demand for skilled workers goes beyond the technical area to cover virtually all areas of knowledge, especially the area of management.

c) Results show a scarcity of skilled professionals Regarding the determinants of new skills, several items were identified, with emphasis on:

- innovation in processes (18 per cent);
- innovation in products (16 per cent);
- basic innovations (10 per cent);
- regulation of industry and relevant laws (37 per cent);
- management and market studies (18 per cent).

From these results it can be concluded that there is a great distance between the universities and the market in all the elements of the renewable energy production chain. Thus, there is an urgent need for an objective approach by higher education institutions in response to the demands for future qualified labour. Another aspect underscored by the results is the need for major integration between higher education institutions and public and private companies in the renewable energy field. This means the promotion of a comprehensive reform in current courses offered by higher education institutions, characteristic of the mission of most institutions of higher education. It is also evident that, from the standpoint of the companies surveyed, higher education institutions are outdated when it comes to renewable energy.

Regarding the subjective answers, respondents were asked about the biggest challenge for a wide range of applications and the use of renewable energy in Brazil. Two issues were made clear from the replies: first, that for greater investment in renewable energy, a greater governmental incentive is needed. That is to say, this issue could be resolved by means of an energy policy focused on increasing renewable energy participation in the Brazilian energy matrix. Secondly, with regards to the former question, many companies state that the cost of production and market price of electricity from renewable sources is not very competitive.

University Staff Survey at Universities in Santa Catarina, Brazil

In Brazil, the university staff questionnaire was sent out to staff from three local universities. Eight respondents participated: four from UNISUL, one from UDESC/ESAG and two from UFSC. All the respondents are professors or researchers: 88 per cent of them work in engineering departments while the others work in administration. Regarding the professional development of the professors, it is clear that the universities and their research departments still require massive training/qualification in the renewable energy area. According to the respondents, this need is both technical and managerial. In the latter area, the respondents emphasized both resource and research management in renewable energy. Thus, according to all interviewees, higher education institutions must offer more academic programmes directed towards the renewable energy sector. In this sense, the majority also see the possibility of expanding research and education programmes with both public and private funding.

According to Leite et al. (2010), the main findings of the two surveys conducted in Brazil suggest that there is a significant gap between the renewable energy market requirements and needs and what indeed universities are offering in terms of research and teaching. With regard to the capacity-building, the surveys indicated that, according to the stakeholders, universities are not prepared to supply the market needs. The surveys also indicated that there is a big demand for investments in the universities' infrastructure in order to better respond to the growing market needs for research and training in the field of renewable energy.

Even though Brazil has a long history of innovation in the renewable energy sector, especially in terms of bio-ethanol, the results of the JELARE study indicate that there is a great deficit in domestic technology transfer and cooperation between universities and private enterprises. To foster innovation in the Brazilian renewable energy sector, it seems vital that universities are able to provide the market with appropriately educated graduates and also increase the capacity of their staff – not only in technological aspects but also in research management.

Renewable Energy Market Survey in Chile

The survey conducted amongst Chilean enterprises and institutions in the renewable energy market revealed that renewable energy technologies with the highest development potential in Chile are hydraulic, wind and geothermal (López Robinovich et al. 2010). The companies surveyed showed significant interest in developing projects on their own or jointly. The Chilean labour market currently has a scarcity of potential employees with renewable energy backgrounds, and they still prefer to recruit university graduates; 92 per cent of the companies in the survey state they require new skills from their employees in the renewable energy field. For both short-term and mid-term hiring, the recruiting tendency shows a clear positive increase; 75 per cent of the companies indicate that universities need to develop new courses and skills relating to the renewable energy field. The labour market detects a need for better training of its employees, focusing on in-house training with external support where the main concern is on changes related to the legal framework.

The companies expect universities to contribute, in particular, to the areas of technological transfer, consulting and advising, and research and development; 92 per cent of the companies surveyed indicate that there is a gap between what higher education institutions are currently offering and the needs of the market.

University Staff Survey at Universidad de Chile

The university staff survey at the Universidad de Chile showed that the majority of people interviewed have five or more years of experience in the university (López Robinovich et al. 2010). Their main interests are thermal solar, geothermal, wind and PV. They also demonstrate some experience in curricula design, but not very much. The university respondents showed interest in receiving training in renewable energy, especially in geothermal, wind, hydraulic, PV and solar thermal energy. However, they do not consider training in curricula design to be as relevant as completing pilot modules. The most important issue mentioned regarding the direction for research training is towards finding appropriate funding sources. The respondents considered it most important to improve technical/professional knowledge, keep up to date with the technology changes, access a renewable energy database, attend conferences/workshops and establish internships with the renewable energy industry. The respondents considered it very important to improve the research infrastructure and cooperation between industry and university. They also noted the need to develop research at the university funded by industry or government.

The survey results from Chile show that universities should play a more active role in enhancing the innovation capacity of the country in the renewable energy sector. The scarcity of appropriately educated people is one key impediment to innovation in the market. Universities could overcome this barrier to innovation by introducing long-term measures, such as adapting their academic curricula to the market needs, but also by providing short-term training courses to employees working in renewable energy companies. Moreover, this could also possibly be achieved as a learning-by-doing part of joint R&D projects of consultancy services offered by the universities. After all, companies indicated that they develop projects on their own as well as in cooperation with other organizations, and at the same time university staff has shown keen interest to work more closely with the market actor.

Renewable Energy Market Survey in Guatemala

The survey of the renewable energy market in Guatemala was focused towards private and public companies and organizations directly related to renewable energy (out of the 51 cases, one was a cooperative, three were NGOs and 36 belonged to the private sector). According to Ruiz et al. (2010), the following characteristics drawn from the data gathered should be highlighted:

a) Guatemalan renewable energy industries and organizations are mainly oriented toward hydroelectric energy generation, although wind power is a rising star. The industries and organizations working with renewable energy mainly work with hydro power, biomass and solar thermal energy; however, wind and photovoltaic energy are also being generated in Guatemala, though on a smaller scale. When the renewable energy sector in which companies plan to work is studied, hydro power and biomass strongly feature again, but wind power has a bigger projection of expansion.

b) There is a bias favouring education and training plans but a more practical emphasis is advanced when companies and organizations are confronted with energy generation activities. Regarding the area in the value chain in which companies plan to work, projections towards education and training have priority. However, with regard to those companies that already participate in this market, 'planning, project management and marketing' is the top preference, and 'energy industry' and 'research and development' are second, followed by 'mechanical engineering/plant construction', leaving 'education and training' behind. With regard to the way industries approach their activities, their own development and joint development are preferred.

c) Links to higher education institutions emerged from recruitment needs and direct hiring from a labour force that showed scarce availability of qualifications together with unequal and unsatisfactory performances in the job according to employers. Recruitment is clearly addressed to technicians and university graduates in the renewable energy area of the market. Few organizations hire through external agencies. Almost all of the organizations use direct recruitment and few of them use both. Most employers in the renewable energy sector revealed that they have difficulties when searching and selecting appropriate employees. The main problems faced when hiring are the lack of applicants and the lack of specialized technical capabilities. Currently, multidisciplinary capabilities do not seem to appear among their problems. This view contrasts with the need perceived at the higher education institutions, where a greater emphasis in multidisciplinary subjects is highlighted. Perceptions of employment in the renewable energy sector are critical in the short term and promising in the medium term.

d) The perceived need of better higher education qualifications for the renewable energy workforce is not a 'blank cheque' but specifies certain conditions alongside practical and 'down to earth' low-cost or externally financed training, which means less formal education around titles and less production-oriented education with a less multidisciplinary perspective. In theory, there is an openness of the interviewees towards training and education. Nevertheless, the condition for the above is mainly the possibility of having access to external support, although there would be favourable attitudes towards 'education and training at work' and 'external training', leaving behind 'e-learning and blended learning' and 'long-term external continuous education courses'. Training is planned to be carried out at the companies and organizations. In contrast to the openness towards innovation inferred from other information, the preference is towards the 'strengthening of basic existent capabilities', followed, with a lower score, by 'new specialized technical skills' and with almost no preference is 'multidisciplinary efforts'. There is almost a consensus in the main motivations for new requirements in renewable energy capabilities which include product and process innovations followed by market needs. Finally, there is less emphasis on the legal framework, government incentives and basic innovations, as well as in the areas of information technology and communications.

e) The profile required by companies and market organization forces higher education institutions to rethink their practices and search for greater synergies. There is almost unanimous awareness of the fact that universities need to develop new courses and capabilities in renewable energy. Nevertheless, the tendency is towards additional capabilities in order to complement initial professional education and is not aimed at new professions. An area emphasized by participants in the Focus Group was better coordination within the universities and externally with the private and public sector. What is most expected from universities is 'processes innovation', 'training and education', and 'basic research and development'. With regard to services that could be expected by the market from higher education institutions, technology transfer has a priority, besides the access to the latest knowledge. In any event, respondents perceive that the universities' programmes should be redesigned. The perception of higher education institutions by employers is that they are behind the market needs. The major challenges that the renewable energy market faces, according to the respondents, include: limited financing, inadequate education and public policies, limited support from the government, environmental and social restrictions, lack of information about renewable energy in the population, inadequate technology and the high costs associated with renewable energy.

University Staff Survey at Galileo Universidad

The findings below correspond to the sample drawn from all professors and administrators related to renewable energy at the Galileo Universidad (Ruiz et al. 2010):

a) Staff profile shows a small number of teachers/administrators at the top, leading a much greater number of temporary professors heavily loaded with teaching activities and other full-time jobs. The profile of the GU teachers' teaching structure is no different in its basic characteristics from those of other higher education institutions in Guatemala, namely a very small segment of teachers with administrative duties at the top and a large group of temporary teachers overwhelmingly in charge of teaching at the bottom. Most of the time, the latter work in other universities and/or dedicate limited time away from their primary job to these activities. Research activities show its absence in this context, as opposed to the teaching approach, which has almost a full-time dedication, with no room for other activities. On the other hand, the recent creation of programmes related to renewable energy determines the fact that few teachers show a long-term connection with the GU and therefore the number of courses taught in the last cycle is lower than the number taught in the most recent cycle. Hence their insertion as teachers is very recent.

b) Hydroelectric energy generation is the preferred field of work as well as the respondents' top area of interest, followed by biomass, especially in this last instance, while both expressed preferences towards attaining these goals with formal education higher degrees. Regarding teachers' professional development, a shift towards training and education can be seen when it is contrasted to other areas in the value chain. This shift in behaviour can be attributed either to their academic background or their interest in these innovations, even when they come from professional areas or sectors different from renewable energy. Among the sectors where teachers said they worked, there is hydraulics, which is highly correlated to the potential in Guatemala in this field. This preference is also present in the disclosed interest to work, although the biomass sector here is also selected. In the same way, the interest in receiving training is more concentrated in hydro power and biomass, although wind, geothermal and solar thermal energy also receive special attention. With respect to the forms of curricula development, more formal degrees, such as Bachelor's, Master's or PhDs, are preferred; the technical degree follows these degrees as an option. It is important to observe that this preference is in opposition to the one expressed by participants in the market.

c) Laboratories, research skills and access to scientific databases are urgent requirements, according to the respondents, including greater links with the renewable energy industry and government, not only for learning but also for funding these activities. In research, respondents markedly prefer taking courses about funding opportunities and research management capabilities, compared to fund management as such, which seems reasonable given that lack of funding is perceived as a main concern regarding renewable energy. There is no need for fund management if there isn't any in the first place. Among training requirements, the concern over infrastructure again emerges as the most perceived need, as well as the right research infrastructure, principally relating to laboratories and equipment. Expanding on the above, access to a scientific database also came up very frequently. Although to a lesser extent, significant percentages were also evident relating to the need for more collaboration with the renewable energy industry and the ability to be updated in this field. There is also, in the survey on GU teachers, a concern about research, either funded by the renewable energy market or by government agencies, apart from the need to bind students' practice in the renewable energy industry through exchanges or internships.

Transnational Comparison of Labour Market Survey

An important precondition for innovation and technological development is the availability of qualified staff on the labour market. Figure 5.1 describes the opinion of the respondents in respect of the availability of qualified staff in the field of renewable energy, whereas Figure 5.2 illustrates the problems companies face when finding and selecting suitable employees. The survey results of all countries show that most employers think that qualified professionals are not available to a sufficient extent. In every country, at least a third of companies state that applicants lack technical expertise (Bolivia 54 per cent, Brazil 32 per cent, Chile 33 per cent, Guatemala 41 per cent). In Chile and Guatemala, even more companies stated that in general not enough candidates are available for recruitment (Chile 50 per cent, Guatemala 42 per cent). In all countries

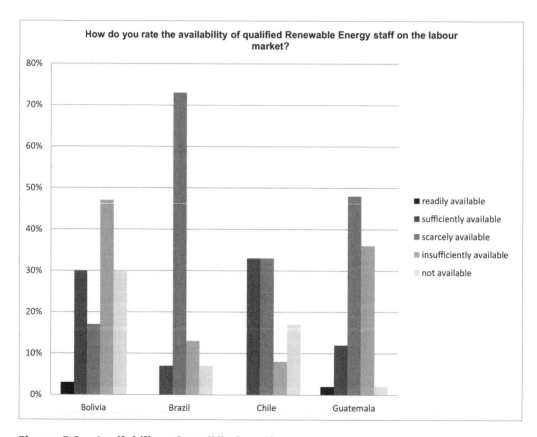

Figure 5.1 Availability of qualified staff

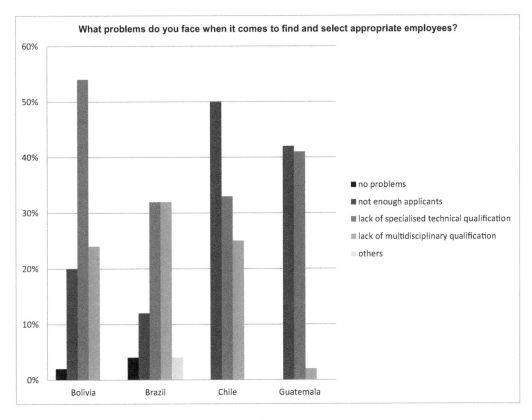

Figure 5.2   Problems encountered finding employees

except Guatemala, the lack of any multidisciplinary qualification was also considered a main difficulty by more than a quarter of the organizations (Bolivia 24 per cent, Brazil 32 per cent, Chile 25 per cent, Guatemala 2 per cent).

As seen in Figure 5.3 on the following page, more than three quarters of organizations questioned in each country stated that universities need to develop new qualifications in the renewable energy sector (Bolivia 97 per cent, Brazil 87 per cent, Chile 75 per cent, Guatemala 94 per cent). Figure 5.4 shows that organizations in Bolivia, Chile and Guatemala believe universities should offer additional qualifications rather than developing new professional profiles (Figure 5.4), whereas the distribution in Brazil is even.

Market actors expect the traditional tasks of training and education and basic research and development from higher education institutions in the renewable energy sector, whereas activities related to technology transfer, such as product innovation, process innovation and basic innovations are expected to a lesser degree (Figure 5.5). However, when asked what types of services offered by higher education institutions they would be interested in using, the service that most attracts the organizations surveyed is, in general, technology transfer (Figure 5.6). This service showed the highest rate of answers in Brazil, Chile and Guatemala, whereas joint research is the most interesting service for the organizations in Bolivia.

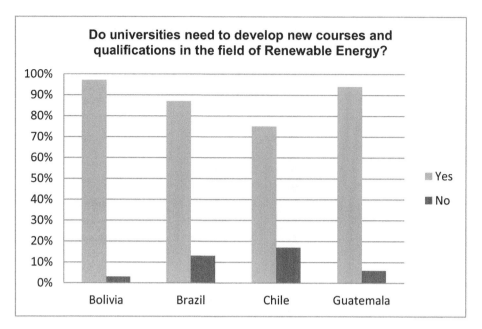

Figure 5.3   Respondents' opinions on the needs for new courses

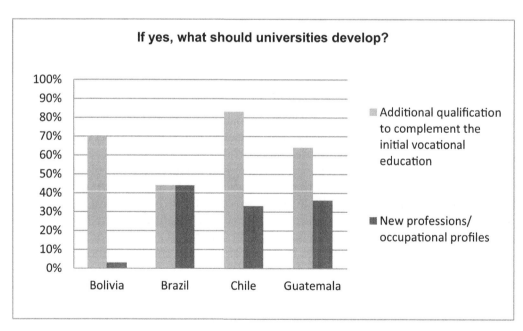

Figure 5.4   Respondents' opinions on which courses universities should develop

The majority of enterprises and organizations surveyed believe that universities are behind the market needs (Bolivia 93 per cent, Brazil 53 per cent, Chile 92 per cent and Guatemala 72 per cent).

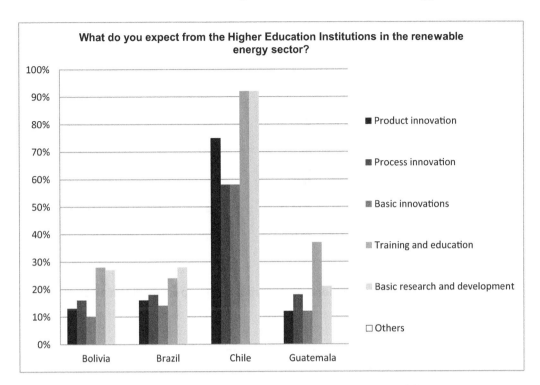

Figure 5.5 Respondents' expectations in the field of renewable energy

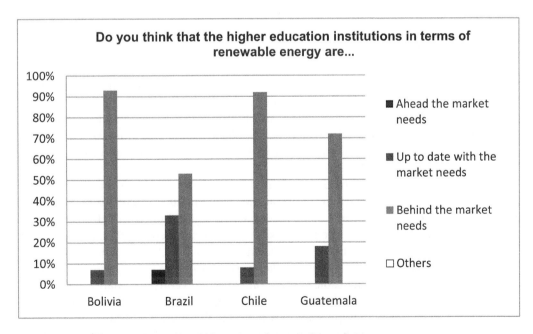

Figure 5.6 Respondents' opinions on the services they may use

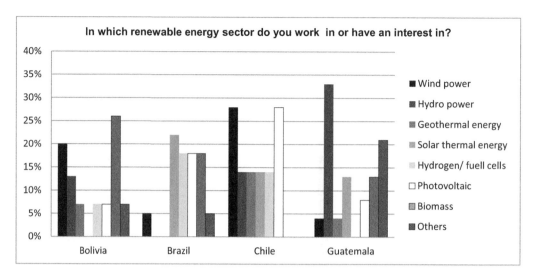

In which renewable energy sector do you work in or have an interest in?

Legend:
- Wind power
- Hydro power
- Geothermal energy
- Solar thermal energy
- Hydrogen/ fuell cells
- Photovoltaic
- Biomass
- Others

Figure 5.7   Respondents' opinions on the market preparedness of HEI

These above results suggest that companies in the renewable energy sector are in principle interested in the 'third mission' of universities. However, currently universities neither fulfil the needs of the renewable energy market for technology transfer and applied research nor the needs of the labour market for educating sufficiently qualified renewable energy graduates.

Transnational Comparison of University Staff Survey

In the four countries surveyed, the university staff showed different interests regarding the kinds of renewable energy in which they act or would like to act (Figure 5.8). In Bolivia, staff members are most interested in biomass and wind power. In Brazil, solar thermal energy followed by hydrogen/fuel cells, photovoltaic and biomass is of highest interest. Wind power and photovoltaics are the key sectors in Chile, and in Guatemala hydro power has the highest priority.

Nearly all university staff who participated in the survey believe that the topic of renewable energy needs to be strengthened at their higher education institute (Bolivia 89 per cent, Brazil 100 per cent, Chile 100 per cent, Guatemala 90 per cent). However, when asked to assess the importance of eight possible measures to achieve this, the responses from staff differ in the four countries. University staff at the UCB in Bolivia advocated partnership with the renewable energy market in order to share knowledge, secure more internships for students in renewable energy companies and constant analysis and design of occupational plans in renewable energy due to technological change and economic behaviour. In Brazil, exchange programmes between the higher education institutions and the renewable energy market, applied technological researches in renewable energy conducted within the higher education institution and funded by the renewable energy market and more academic programmes devoted to the market needs ranked highest. At Universidad de Chile, exchange programmes between higher education institutions

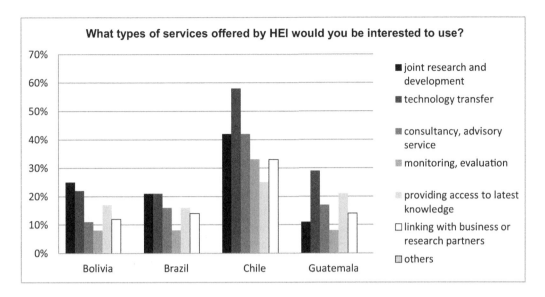

Figure 5.8 Respondents' interest in RE sectors

and the renewable energy market, applied technological research in renewable energy conducted within higher education institutions and funded by the renewable energy market as well as funded by the government agencies are regarded as most important. The staff of Galileo Universidad in Guatemala considered applied technological research in renewable energy conducted within the higher education institutions and funded by the government agencies and by the renewable energy market as most important measures to strengthen renewable energy topics at their higher education institution.

The survey participants were asked to assess their needs regarding a set of seven different training and qualification opportunities. Most university staff felt the strongest need was for better laboratories and equipment infrastructure, participation in networking events in renewable energy (such as attendance at workshops, seminars, conference and/or industry field visits) and more collaboration between their university and the renewable energy industry, but the ranking varies between the countries in the survey. In Bolivia, staff stated that the strongest need was for participation in networking events in renewable energy, more cooperation between the university and the renewable energy industry, as well as access to scientific databases in renewable energy. In Brazil, university staff considered more collaboration between their university and the renewable energy industry, better laboratories and equipment infrastructure and updated technical/ vocational knowledge and skills in their area of teaching/research as their most important needs. In Chile, university staff regarded the need for more collaboration between their university and the renewable energy industry, better laboratories and equipment infrastructure and access to scientific databases in renewable energy as most important. Galileo Universidad stated that its strongest need was for participation in networking events in renewable energy, access to scientific databases in renewable energy and better laboratories and equipment infrastructure.

These results indicate that there is awareness among university staff that universities are not responding appropriately to the needs of the renewable energy market, and that the collaboration between universities and the market, in particular, needs to be improved. Moreover, as regards the perception of the staff questioned, higher academic quality not only requires a better research infrastructure and equipment but also closer contact to the market actors.

The two JELARE surveys have shown that the traditionally weak linkages between universities and industry (Lopez 1994, Thorn and Soo 2006) also apply to the renewable energy sector. However, it became evident that both universities and market players do have a genuine interest in closer cooperation. Even though the traditional fields of university activities (education and basic R&D) are named first by enterprises when ask about their expectation from universities, technology transfer and joint R&D are the services to be offered by universities in which they would be most interested.

Thus the key actors of the renewable energy sector are aware of the potential of universities engaging in the 'third mission' (Thorn and Soo 2006). Nonetheless, it became evident that the universities are not yet in a position to fulfil this role. Not only do most market actors believe that universities are behind market needs, but the university staff, too, has stated considerable deficits in access to knowledge, networks and research funding as well as responding appropriately to the demands of the market.

The responses of the survey participants confirm that for market players as well as universities the classical technology transfer mechanisms, such as patenting, licensing and spin-offs are not necessarily the most relevant mechanisms for increasing the technology capacity of their country. According to Lester (2005), these mechanisms only account for a minor fraction of technology transferred to the local market. The survey results confirmed that there is a crucial demand for informal technology transfer mechanisms, such as conferences, networking events, student internships and other forms of cooperation between universities and industry.

It has become evident that there is a substantial shortage of adequately educated employees in the Latin American renewable energy sector. This not only applies to companies and other market actors, but to university staff too. In order to be in a position to fulfil their obligation to educate future employees according to the requirements of the market, it is essential that the capacity of university staff is also increased. This includes not only dedicated training courses but also, in general, better access to information and knowledge as well as better research infrastructure (e.g. laboratories). In addition, universities are requested to adapt their academic curricula to the demands of the renewable energy market and, at the same time, short-term training offered to employees of local companies might be a short-term solution. These short-term training courses may not only offer an opportunity to respond quickly to the market needs for more renewable energy expertise, but also act as an opportunity to cooperate more closely with enterprises.

In addition, research has shown that in some Latin American countries, e.g. in Bolivia, there is a considerable technology gap which prevents many market agents from acting simply as suppliers of foreign technologies. The survey results also indicate that there is still a long way ahead for decreasing this technology gap in the renewable energy sector and the establishment of a competitive local R&D capacity. However, the awareness and interest of both universities and enterprises suggest that much could be gained if universities could generally better respond to the educational needs of the market, and that universities were to offer more services which can actively support industry in developing renewable energy projects.

Conclusions

These two surveys, simultaneously conducted in four Latin American countries, enabled the investigators involved to experience an atmosphere of transnational cooperation and a favourable attitude towards greater cultural and technical knowledge exchange about renewable energy. Even though the labour market studies cannot claim to be representative except for Guatemala, the surveys enabled researchers to assess the higher education institutions in relation to the renewable energy market from the standpoint of the enterprises. It was observed that, regarding this aspect, there were more similarities than differences between the four countries involved. The survey identified the following facts:

- Most companies in the four countries involved stated that candidates for vacancies in renewable energy positions are not prepared for the market, which means that there is a need for additional qualification programmes. All additional training methods, therefore, are acceptable to the companies, including: company-designed courses, university postgraduate courses, and specialization courses. This allows a broad range of teaching options for universities.
- Most companies see universities currently mainly as providers of education and basic research; however, they signalled an interest in closer cooperation with universities especially in terms of technology transfer.
- With few exceptions, the companies stated that the universities are behind the renewable energy market curve.
- The surveys of university staff resulted in important data indicating that, although there is a gap between market needs and the services offered by the university, there is a growing conscience in the institutions about the procedures needed to steadily close this gap. The investigation also unveils an urgent need for a broader restructuring in academia, following the evolution of the market demands with interdisciplinary professionals who are able to design, operate and manage the new technologies in the renewable energy field. Another important finding from the research is that, although there are different stages of development for renewable energy in the investigated countries, the demands and gaps seem to be very similar.

The analysis showed that there are common internal university demands in terms of enabling a better response to the market, not only in infrastructure but also in faculty and staff training and qualifications. Furthermore, the analysis carried out by partners of the JELARE project also showed the need for better integration with the industry in various fields and activities related to renewable energy, for example in applied research sponsored by industry actors, as well as courses, seminars, and internships for university students. The study also revealed that the staff of the universities involved believe that there must be private industry and government financial support for renewable energy research, together with a constant monitoring of professional trends and market needs. Thus it can be concluded that the staff of the universities involved are conscious of the discrepancy between market reality and academia. This consciousness is manifested in current proposals to close the existing gap through substantial investments in human resources and in teaching and researching infrastructure in the field of renewable energy.

Based on a transnational analysis of the surveys carried out by the universities that participate in the JELARE partnership, the following actions are recommended:

- The promotion of greater integration between university and market through specific actions such as products and services that meet market demands in terms of renewable energy.
- Giving a multidisciplinary and transdisciplinary dimension to the topic of renewable energy in universities so as to offer a holistic approach which integrates the processes of teaching, research and extension and which must be accountable to market needs.
- The allocation of higher investment in university staff qualification for the development of new products and services aimed at meeting renewable energy market needs.
- Investment in the creation of infrastructure for teaching and researching that suits the present renewable energy demands.
- The development of alliances and partnerships with enterprises from private and public renewable energy sectors.
- The development of national and transnational pilot programmes for the expansion of new teaching modalities in renewable energy.
- The creation of a multidisciplinary forum in universities to promote debate about renewable energy in all sectors and departments, whose objective is to develop an integrated institutional vision about the topic.

These actions, along with other institutional initiatives, may help close the gaps that this study unmistakeably disclosed in all four countries investigated. The results also pointed out that, regardless of the varying degrees of renewable energy technological development in the studied countries, the gaps are very similar when the relationship between university and market is discussed. This situation demands immediate action mainly on the university side, so as to follow market trends in the field.

Questions to Consider

1. How can it be ensured that universities respond appropriately to the market needs of the renewable energy sector as well as other innovative sectors?
2. What role could Latin American universities and local enterprises play in reducing the technology gap in the renewable energy sector?
3. What is the relevance of informal technology transfer mechanisms in the context of innovation support in the renewable energy sector in Latin America?

Acknowledgements

We wish to thank the ALFA programme of the EU for supporting the JELARE project. Thanks are also due to the following people who have carried out studies in Bolivia, Brazil, Chile and Guatemala and contributed to this paper: Horacio Villegas, Javier Aliaga Lordemann and Lea Franziska Buch from Bolivia, André Luis Silva Leite João Luiz Alkaim,

José Baltazar Salgueirinho, Osório de Andrade Guerra, Mariana Eliza Ferrari, Mariana Dalla Barba Wendt and Rodrigo Antonio Martins from Brazil, Francisca López Robinovich, Guillermo Jiménez Estévez, Luis Vargas Díaz, Manuel Díaz Romero and Natalia Garrido Echeverría from Chile, Cyrano Ruiz, Ericka Tuquer, Lourdes Socarrás, Nelson Amaro and Robert Guzmán from Guatemala.

References

Agrawal, A. and Henderson, R. 2002. Putting patents in context: Exploring knowledge transfer from MIT. *Management Science*, 48(1), 44–60.

Brewer, Thomas L. 2008. *International Energy Technology Transfers for Climate Change Mitigation: What, Who, How, Why, Where, How Much ...* and the *Implications for International Institutional Architecture*. CESIFO Working Paper Series No. 2408.

Drucker, P. 2001. *Innovation and Entrepreneurship*. New York, NY: HarperCollins Publishers.

Feldmann, M.P. and Schipper, H. 2007. Bringing science to life: An overview of countries outside of North America – Introduction to the special issue. *The Journal of Technology Transfer*, 32(4), 297–302.

Guerra, J.B. and Youssef, Y.A. (eds). 2010. *Renewable Energy Market Needs: A Perspective from Europe and Latin America*. Palhoca: Unisul.

Hansen, T.N., Agapitova, N., Holm-Nielsen, L. and Vukmirovic, O.G. 2002. *The Evolution of Science and Technology: Latin America and the Caribbean in the Comparative Perspective*, LCSHD Paper Series No. 80, Washington, DC: The World Bank,

Holm-Nielsen, L., Thorn, K., Brunner, J.J. and Balán, J. 2006. Regional and International Challenges to Higher Education in Latin America, in *Higher Education in Latin America: The International Dimension*, edited by H. de Wit, I.C. Jaramillo, J. Gacel-Ávila and J. Knight. Washington, DC: The World Bank, 39–69.

Horowitz Gassol, J. 2007. The effect of university culture and stakeholders' perceptions on university–business linking activities. *The Journal of Technology Transfer*, 32(5), 489–507.

Leite, A., Alkaim. J., Guerra, J.B., Ferrari, M., Wendt, M., Martins, R. and Youssef, Y.A. 2010. Brazil, in *Renewable Energy Market Needs: A Perspective from Europe and Latin America*, edited J.B. Guerra and Y.A. Youssef. Palhoca: Unisul, 57–70.

Lester, R.K. 2005. *Universities, Innovation, and the Competitiveness of Local Economies: A Summary Report from the Local Innovation Systems Project – Phase I*. MIT Industrial Performance Center Working Paper 05–010.

López Robinovich, F., Jiménez Estévez, G., Vargas Díaz, L., Díaz Romero, M. and Garrido Echeverría, N. 2010. Chile, in *Renewable Energy Market Needs: A Perspective from Europe and Latin America*, edited by J.B. Guerra and Y.A. Youssef. Palhoca: Unisul, 71–96.

Nilsson, A.S., Rickne, A. and Bengtsson, L. 2010. Transfer of academic research: Uncovering the grey zone. *The Journal of Technology Transfer*, 35(6), 617–36.

Lopez, S. 1994. Technology transfer in the Americas. *The Journal of Technology Transfer*, 19(2), 25–33.

Ruiz, C., Tuquer, E., Socarrás, L., Amaro, N. and Guzmán, R. 2010. Guatemala, in *Renewable Energy Market Needs: A Perspective from Europe and Latin America*, edited by J.B. Guerra and Y.A. Youssef. Palhoca: Unisul, 127–56.

Thorn, K. and Soo, M. 2006. *Latin American Universities and the Third Mission: Trends, Challenges, and Policy Options*. World Bank Policy Research Working Paper No. 4002.

Vinig, G.T. and Van Rijsbergen, P. 2009. *Determinants of University Technology Transfer – Comparative Study of US, Europe and Australian Universities.* [Online]. Available at http://ssrn.com/abstract =1324601.

Worrel, E., van Berkel, R., Fengqi, Z., Menke, C., Schaeffer, R. and Williams, R.O. 2001. Technology transfer of energy efficient technologies in industry: A review of trends and policy issues. *Energy Policy*, 29, 29–43.

Villegas, H., Aliaga Lordemann, J. and Buch, L.F. 2010. Bolivia, in *Renewable Energy Market Needs: A Perspective from Europe and Latin America*, edited by J.B. Guerra and Y.A. Youssef. Palhoca: Unisul, 29–56.

de Wit, H., Jaramillo, I.C., Gacel-Ávila, J. and Knight, J. (eds). 2006. *Higher Education in Latin America: The International Dimension.* Washington, DC: The World Bank.

Annex 1

Structure of Questionnaire Addressed to Private and Public Companies and Organizations Participating in the Renewable Energy Market

1. General information about the organization, company or entity:
   - type of organization (private, NGO, public, etc.);
   - business sector of organization;
   - interest in developing renewable energy projects/applications;
   - sector of renewable energy in which it is active;
   - area in the value chain in which it works or plans to work;
   - ways of developing renewable energy activities or projects;
   - overall turnover of the organization in 2008;
   - turnover of the organization in the field of renewable energy in 2008.

2. Employee training and qualifications:
   - total number of employees;
   - number of employees in the field of renewable energy;
   - assessment of the availability of qualified personnel in renewable energy;
   - field of activity of renewable energy staff;
   - educational and professional background of the personnel employed in renewable energy;
   - recruitment mechanisms applied to renewable energy personnel;
   - problems faced in finding and selecting appropriate renewable energy personnel;
   - predicted renewable energy employment trend of organization (in general; in the short term (next 2 years); in the medium term (next 5 years)).

3. Qualification requirements and market needs:
   - plans for renewable energy training;
   - need for new qualifications for the personnel required for renewable energy;
   - drivers for new qualifications at organization;

- perception of the need for new courses and renewable energy qualifications developed by universities;
- type of new courses or qualifications required.

4. The role of higher education institutions:
   - expectations of higher education institutions for renewable energy;
   - interest in services provided by HEI;
   - perception of how well higher education institutions are updating their understanding with respect to labour needs.

5. General suggestions:
   - perception of the largest challenges facing the increased use of renewable energy in the country;
   - suggestions regarding issues not mentioned in the questionnaire.

Structure of Questionnaire Addressed to Staff Members of the JELARE Partner Universities Working or Intending to Work in the Renewable Energy Sector

1. Profile of the respondent.
   - position at HEI;
   - department of current appointment;
   - area of current academic/professional involvement in renewable energy;
   - sector in renewable energy in which they work or are interested in working;
   - number of years of experience in renewable energy;
   - number of years of experience in curriculum development;
   - number of years of experience in research management.

2. Training interests:
   - interest in receiving training in renewable energy technologies;
   - interest in receiving training in curricula development;
   - interest in receiving training in teaching modules;
   - interest in receiving training in research management.

3. Requirements in terms of renewable energy training and qualifications:
   - need to update technical/vocational knowledge and skills;
   - need to keep up with major technological change;
   - need to learn skills for curriculum development about renewable energy;
   - need for better research infrastructure;
   - need for access to a scientific renewable energy database;
   - need for participation in networking events related to renewable energy;
   - need for more collaboration between university and the renewable energy industry;
   - priority of individual training needs.

4. Strengthening renewable energy at own HEI:
   - perception of the need to strengthen renewable energy at own HEI;

- only for those who answered YES in the previous question: measures regarded as important for strengthening renewable energy at own HEI;
- more academic programmes devoted to the market needs;
- exchange programmes between the HEIs and the renewable energy market;
- HEI's partnership with renewable energy market in order to share knowledge;
- applied technological research in renewable energy conducted within the HEIs and funded by the renewable energy market;
- applied technological researches in renewable energy conducted within the HEIS and funded by the government agencies;
- more internships for students in renewable energy companies;
- constant analysis and design of occupational plans in renewable energy due to technological change and economic behaviour.

6

A Model for Innovation and Global Competitiveness: The Monterrey International City of Knowledge Program (MICK)

MARTHA LEAL-GONZÁLEZ, JAIME PARADA-AVILA, MARCELA GEORGINA GÓMEZ-ZERMEÑO and LORENA ALEMÁN DE LA GARZA

Introduction

In order for a country or regional area to attain sustained growth, the investment in science, technology and innovation must be accompanied by a review of its policies and mechanisms, in order to ensure the proper and effective use of the invested resources. These actions should result in the strengthening of the spatial dimension of innovation, where the region or the state, in Mexico's case, happens to be the core for national production and innovation networks, and it is on this scale where public policies and the interactions between companies, researchers and universities are most important for the promotion of innovation.

Since the creation of the National Council for Science and Technology (CONACYT) in the 1970s, the Mexican government has been actively involved in designing and creating programmes, tools and mechanisms to promote science, technology and innovation (STI) capabilities at the national level. In recent years, state governments have taken an active role in promoting STI at the regional level, and have created agencies and bodies to help with the task. CONACYT is perhaps the better known institution created by the federal government to foster STI, and it may well be considered the core of the National Innovation System (NIS). In a broad sense, NIS represent an innovation ecosystem, which we define as the set of elements (agents, organizations or institutions) whose activities and interactions result in the production, dissemination, assimilation and conversion of technological knowledge into new products or services or advanced manufacturing technologies.

In June 2009, the Technology and Science Law explicitly introduced the concept of innovation, defining it as 'the development of a new product, design, process, service, method, organization or added value to an already existing one'. Although the concept might seem relatively simple, the process driving it is rather complex, since it requires the implementation of actions that must consider sociological and educational factors at the local, regional and global level.

In the new knowledge economy, innovation plays a central role in socioeconomic processes. At the macro level, it manifests itself as the dominant factor of international competitiveness and of national economic growth. It also determines the international patterns of world trade. At the micro level, technological research and innovation is considered as a growth promoting agent for business and society at large (Alemán 2010).

In the last nine years, the NIS has undergone a series of transformations, promoted mainly by structural reforms in several government agencies and legislations at the federal level, which have made possible to start decentralizing several key federal programmes to promote entrepreneurship within the academic researchers, and to reinforce the industrial sector's awareness of the long-term benefits that a close relationship with the universities and research centres may bring, in terms of global competitiveness.

It is important to note that CONACYT's role is virtually the same across the country. However, at a regional level, it depends on the local actors (academia, enterprises and state and local governments), and on how well the policies, tools and instruments are used and complemented to achieve an effective regional innovation ecosystem (RIE).

Accordingly, the creation of new public policies and strategies for the attraction and retention of technology-based companies in the state of Nuevo Leon, has been carried out under an appropriate framework for innovation, that goes by the name of Monterrey International City of Knowledge (MICK), that provides a Triple Helix structure and access to funds for research and innovation, as well as the establishment of a technological research and innovation park, PIIT (Parque de Investigación e Innovación Tecnológica), as a core of the RIE.

The PIIT research park, is the main instrument in which the tools, policies and strategies to incentivize cooperation between universities, research centres and companies, designed by the state government, come together to achieve the transformation of research into new products and services, and to lead the conversion of the local industry into a eco-friendly one, through more efficient operational processes and a focus on new business models and technologies, nesting the most promising in its incubator facilities.

In this chapter, we will review the actions taken at regional level in the state of Nuevo Leon for the establishment of new policies designed to accelerate the development of a knowledge society, and their effect in the productive and technological capabilities of the regional industry and the innovation ecosystem.

The Role of CONACYT as an STI Policy Maker and its Programmes

Since antiquity, knowledge has been the driving force of economic growth and social well-being. The ability to innovate and create new ideas that eventually turn into products, processes and organizations has always driven economic development. For David and Foray (2002) this tendency is not only limited to information and high-technology sectors, since it has gradually expanded to all the other relevant fields. Because of this, society in general is leaning towards activities that require a high degree of knowledge.

When we research the available literature on innovation, several definitions stand out that showcase its different dimensions (Edgar and Grant 2009). For instance, innovation can be incremental or radical in its nature and it can manifest itself through products, positions, users, social networks, environments or even in paradigms, since it is based in concepts of discontinuity, such as new markets, new technologies, new rules, new business models, unimaginable events, among others. According to Edgar and Grant (2009), the commonly held concepts of innovation refer only to a level of 'novelty', or new products or processes, usually adding an advance dimension of speed. Trying to categorize innovation has resulted in considerable debate, therefore affirming that we need to distinguish between product innovation and process innovation, concluding that in essence, the architecture of innovation is knowledge, the awareness of the components that form the environment and how these join together.

According to Malian and Nevin (2005), innovation comes from the Latin word *innovare* which means renewal or doing something new; in a metaphorical way, innovation reflects the metamorphosis of a current way of doing things into something new, preferably better. In this way, innovation is achieved by challenging creativity, because a product or idea can be utilized or applied. Innovation can be taken to environments where it can become something tangible (Sternberg, Pretz and Kaufman, 2001).

Conceição and Heitor, cited by Alemán (2010), conceive innovation as an association between creativity, idea generation, initiatives and risks. In similar fashion, Filis and McAuley, cited by Alemán (2010), point out that group or individual creativity is the beginning of innovation; nevertheless, it does not mean that it is the only sufficient condition to achieve it.

Finally, innovation and creativity are intimately linked in order to propitiate change, generate new ideas and applying them. According to Martins and Terblanche, cited by Alemán (2010) creativity and innovation can be considered as overlapping terms or coinciding stages of the creative process, idea generation and implementation.

In Mexico, over time, the innovation concept has been internalized and is no longer recognized as an isolated fact that emerges out of entrepreneurial people, that are able to successfully take advantage of technological and scientific developments, but that it is instead a complex process included in the NIS, where the micro and macro components of the economy make possible the birth and application of the technological innovations and their impact on the country's social and economic growth.

The role of the federal government in the NIS is mainly carried out by CONACYT, which regulates the framework to that supports and promotes STI. Accordingly, the Council establishes policies, legal framework, programmes, instruments and evaluation mechanisms to modify the performance of the other key actors in STI activities.

CONACYT is the entity responsible for dictating STI policies for the federal government, and disposes of an important portion of the total federal budget reserved for science and technology. Programmes such as the Scholarships Program, the National Researchers System (NRS), the System of Public Research Centres and the funded programmes for fostering science and technology are directly under its administration.

In 2006, the total budget administrated by CONACYT amounted US$508 million, which represented 17 per cent of the total federal expenditures in science and technology. The resources were distributed in the main programmes as follows: scientific and technological research (26.6 per cent); scholarship programme (37.6 per cent); and National Researchers System (26.6 per cent). These resources allowed CONACYT to support around 20,111 postgraduate students (44.8 per cent PhDs and 55.2 per cent Masters), 900 scientific and technological projects, and 13,485 researchers with a membership in the NRS programme (Dutrénit et al. 2008).

Mexico must emphasize the STI policy to direct the NIS towards more experimental research, in order to understand the need to produce more relevant products to be transferred to the industry and generate a healthy innovation practice; CONACYT has designated a bigger budget to encourage project proposals in this subject. Since 2001, it has implemented new sub-programmes for technology development and for the creation of new technology businesses under the shelter of the Special Program of Science and Technology (PECyT). The programmes define sectors and regional programmes, based on the strategic knowledge fields, and consist of a proactive policy mix for the promotion of:

- public/private R&D;
- consortia and research networks of excellence;
- private investment in S&T activities;
- university-enterprise linkages;
- innovation and competitiveness;
- intellectual property.

More than 60 funds or programmes have come to life following the objectives of the PECYT. They are designed to promote and fund basic and problem-oriented research, the regionalization of the innovation system, R&D in private companies, support of innovative projects from entrepreneurs, and the formation of highly specialized human resources. The most important programmes and sub-programmes of the current Mexican STI policy mix are shown in Figure 6.1 opposite, and we will discuss briefly the ones that promote innovation and entrepreneurship.

a) Sector funds: With coincident resources provided 50:50 by CONACYT and state ministries or government agencies, the funds aim to promote the development and consolidation of STI capabilities according to the strategic goals of the Ministry. To date, there are 18 sector funds that receive proposals at least once a year. The two main funds are:

- Public Education Ministry–CONACYT fund: promotes the development of scientific and technological research of the highest quality in the strategic areas demanded to strengthen the NIS and the National Researchers System (NRS).
- Economic development based on science and technology fund: The Ministry of Economy and CONACYT's resources combine in this fund to encourage innovation and technological development projects in the industry. Technology transfer is given a boost, as the project selection and evaluation gives better scores to proposals presenting evidence of a company's linkage with universities or public research centres. Companies must present the proposals, and up to 50 per cent of the project expenses are covered by the fund.

b) State (mixed) funds: CONACYT created these funds in partnerships with state or municipal governments, providing 50:50 concomitant resources for a trust, intending to use the PECyT to motivate regional STI capabilities and develop scientific and technological projects according to local demands. In 2008, there were 32 mixed funds.

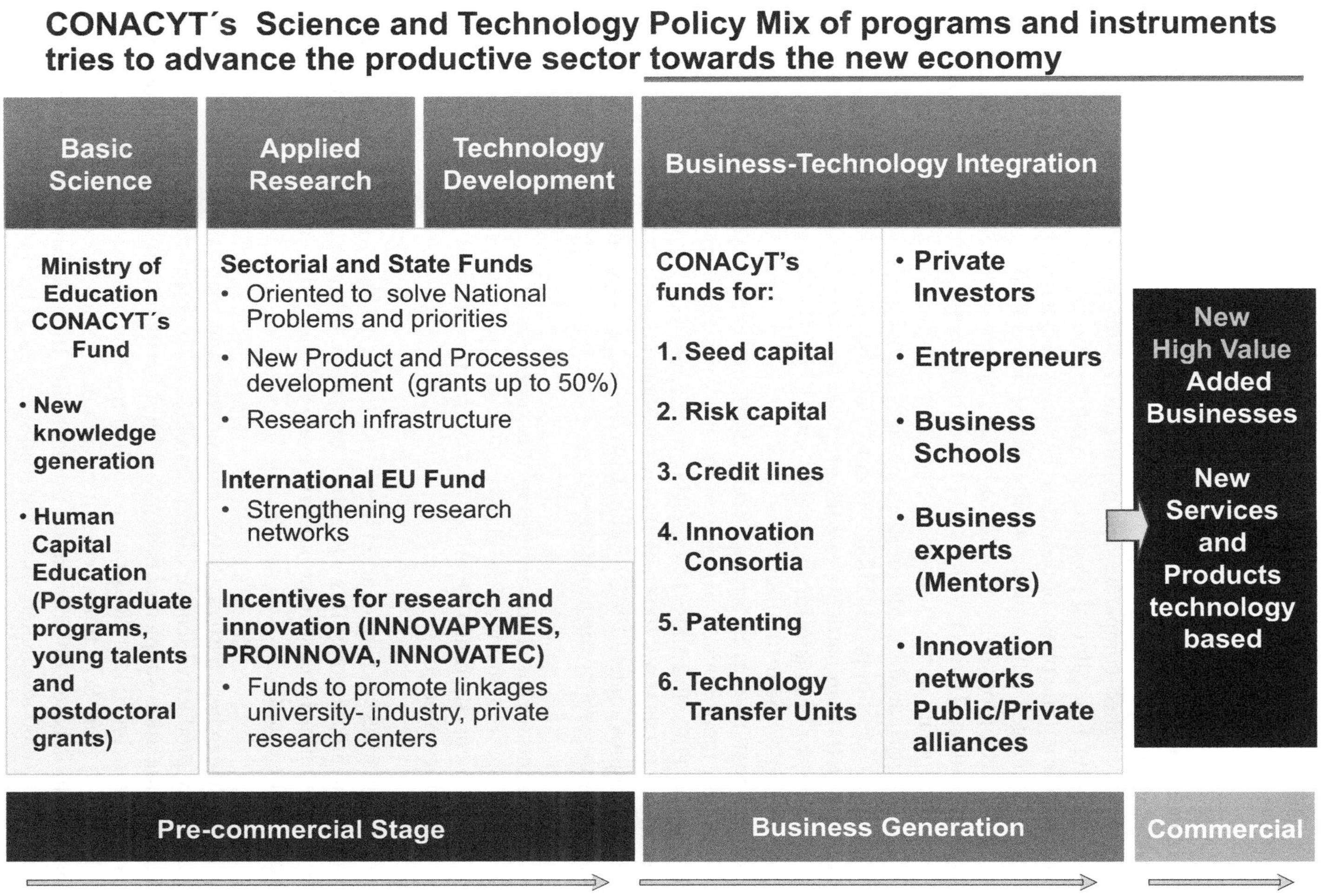

CONACYT's Science and Technology Policy Mix of programs and instruments tries to advance the productive sector towards the new economy

Basic Science	Applied Research	Technology Development	Business-Technology Integration	
Ministry of Education CONACyT's Fund • New knowledge generation • Human Capital Education (Postgraduate programs, young talents and postdoctoral grants)	**Sectorial and State Funds** • Oriented to solve National Problems and priorities • New Product and Processes development (grants up to 50%) • Research infrastructure **International EU Fund** • Strengthening research networks **Incentives for research and innovation (INNOVAPYMES, PROINNOVA, INNOVATEC)** • Funds to promote linkages university- industry, private research centers		**CONACyT's funds for:** 1. Seed capital 2. Risk capital 3. Credit lines 4. Innovation Consortia 5. Patenting 6. Technology Transfer Units	• Private Investors • Entrepreneurs • Business Schools • Business experts (Mentors) • Innovation networks Public/Private alliances

New High Value Added Businesses

New Services and Products technology based

Pre-commercial Stage	Business Generation	Commercial

Figure 6.1   CONACYT's main programs and instruments 2001–2010

c) Institutional funds: CONACYT reserves a large portion of its budget for programmes that are deemed strategic and where the institution is solely responsible for its good performance (AVANCE, scientists' repatriation, researchers' incentives, and formation of human resources in science and technology).

d) AVANCE: (high value added in businesses with knowledge and entrepreneurship): The objective of this sub-programme is to foster new companies that produce or use innovative products and processes resulting from technology and scientific research projects. Established companies can participate in the programme as long as they are developing a new line of products or services. The fund provides resources to be employed during the phase of transition between research and prototype (last mile), as well as leverage in the capitalization phase of the company.

AVANCE is a programme that includes Last mile, Entrepreneurship Fund, Credit Lines Technology Transfer Units and School of Business Fund. AVANCE explicitly calls for proposals in the strategic subjects of information and communications, biotechnology, materials, advanced manufacturing processes, and urban and rural infrastructure development. Public Research Centres (PRC) and Higher Education Institutions (HEI) can participate, if the proposal involves the transfer of technology to a company or has plans for the establishment of a spin-off company belonging to the researcher or the institution.

In the first two calls for proposals, 2003 and 2005, AVANCE received 580 applications, more than 65 per cent of them coming from companies, and the rest largely from PRCs and HEIs: 140 projects were approved. According to CONACYT's Work Report (CONACYT 2008), by the end of 2008, the sub-programme had awarded funds for approximately US$59 million to 215 proposals in the five years since its inception, in the following modalities:

- new businesses based on innovation: 140 proposals;
- technology and business feasibility studies: 44 proposals;
- entrepreneurship fund CONACYT-NAFIN: 25 projects;
- credit lines: 6 projects.

e) Strategic alliances and innovation networks (AERIs): This is a new instrument to promote the links among HEIs, PRCs and companies, to construct networks that will work in the competence scheme, and to elevate the competitiveness of the productive sectors of the country.

f) National Researchers System (NRS): This programme maintains a network of the most highly productive scholars and researchers from across the disciplines that are given remuneration supplements in recognition for their work. Although most of its members work for HEIs or PRCs, only a small proportion of Mexican academics are part of the NRS system. Selection occurs through a peer review system, and maintaining membership is based on continuing productivity. In 2008, the NRS accounted for more than 14,000 researchers in widespread science and technology activities.

g) The Graduate Scholarship Program: This programme constitutes the most important source of funding for Mexican students to pursue graduate education in Mexico or abroad. In 2008, there were around 27,000 active scholarships funded by the programme.

h) IDEA (incorporation of Mexican scientists and technologists to the social and productive sectors of the country): This instrument works under the proposal of a research project that incorporates masters or doctorate degree professionals to a company. CONACYT pays full salary for one year and supports with funds the second year of the project, with the understanding that the company will hire the professional after that time. In 2007, there were 39 masters and doctors carrying out research activities in industry supported by this instrument.

i) R&D Fiscal Incentives and other instruments to promote companies' innovation activities: these incentives worked as a fiscal credit until 2008. It was successful in promoting R&D investment in companies as hundreds of research projects were approved where the criteria applied was innovative products and services, existing linkages among universities and industries, and evidence of the effect in the competitiveness of the company. It returned as a fiscal credit consisting of 30 per cent of the R&D expenditure. In 2006, the programme awarded more than $390 million dollars to 3155 approved projects, benefiting 561 companies from the range micro, small and medium size, and 326 large or corporate enterprises, according to CONACYT.

j) For 2009, the Fiscal Incentives programme has been transformed into three new sub-programmes that provide a better accountability of the resources and financing given for R&D in companies:

- Technology-based innovation for the competitiveness of the enterprise (INNOVATEC): Its objective is to incentivize big companies or corporations to invest in STI, fund private research centres, help with intellectual capital portfolio management, and fund technology projects involving new processes, products and services.
- Technology-based innovation for high value added businesses (INNOVAPYMES): Its main goal is to promote STI in SMEs and fund research projects of innovative products or processes.
- Innovation and Research Development in Precursor Technologies (PROINNOVA): This fund is exclusively to promote linkage between industry, HEIs, and research centres.

Lastly, there is another instrument created in 2009 by CONACYT, the Institutional Fund for the Regional Development of Capabilities in Innovation, Scientific and Technology Research (FORDECyT). This fund seeks to promote the development of technology poles at the regional level, helping with the creation of infrastructure and formation of specialized human resources. It is noteworthy that Nuevo Leon's participation in this programme, alongside the north-eastern states of Tamaulipas and Coahuila, has won funds for the design and building of a biotechnology incubator to be installed at the Research and Technology Innovation Park (PIIT) in Monterrey.

Methodology

This study was carried out with a qualitative focus, since it provides a frame of reference for the subject matter. It is also a study case, whose primary information source is the natural environment of a situation, and the subject cannot be understood outside its space-time.

Stake (2007: 114) points out that 'a case has a unique life, it is something we cannot fully understand, yet we strive to comprehend it', and that its purpose is not to help make a change, but to help realize what is happening, so we can facilitate change. When preparing this report the following remarks by Stake were used:

> We must find the history that bests describes the situation of this concrete investigation, for the benefit of the reader, the case, and the forests. An efficient author is the one who writes only the necessary and leaves the rest to the reader. (2007: 105)

Thus, the study case focused in the MICK programme: an analysis of the structure of MICK's model was carried out, its key components were described in a detailed manner, as well as its key players, their roles and how they relate to the Triple Helix model. For the purpose of this chapter, we will focus on some of the results and programmes that contribute directly to the establishment of new businesses based on innovation and foster technology transfer in the RIS, such as the research park PIIT, its infrastructure and its contribution to the sustainable development of the north-east Mexican states.

Monterrey International City of Knowledge (MICK)

Notwithstanding the efforts of the federal government, there are areas of opportunity that must be resolved at the regional, state, and municipal levels in order to achieve greater amounts of technology transfer among companies and research centres or universities. One of them is the creation of intermediary institutions or organizations with very specific roles and resources, to be used in the promotion of financing funds and mechanisms that accelerate the formation of a critical mass of innovative companies that will catapult the economy of a region.

In 2004, the state of Nuevo Leon initiated a concerted effort to create a systematic approach to attract and create new, high-technology-based companies into its productive sector. The tradition of Monterrey and its metropolitan area as a pioneer in the rational management of resources and industrialization processes in Mexico made it the logical choice for the creation of an efficient innovation ecosystem.

National policies and programmes developed under the PECyT by CONACYT were used to tailor the local government's instruments, and to obtain funds for the promotion of a culture of innovation in the region. The model successfully applied in MICK is based on the following premises:

- a culture of knowledge;
- the establishment of state wide policy and the sufficient allocation of resources;
- the clear and defined roles of its participants and their interaction;
- the definition of strategic areas of knowledge in which the programme focuses;

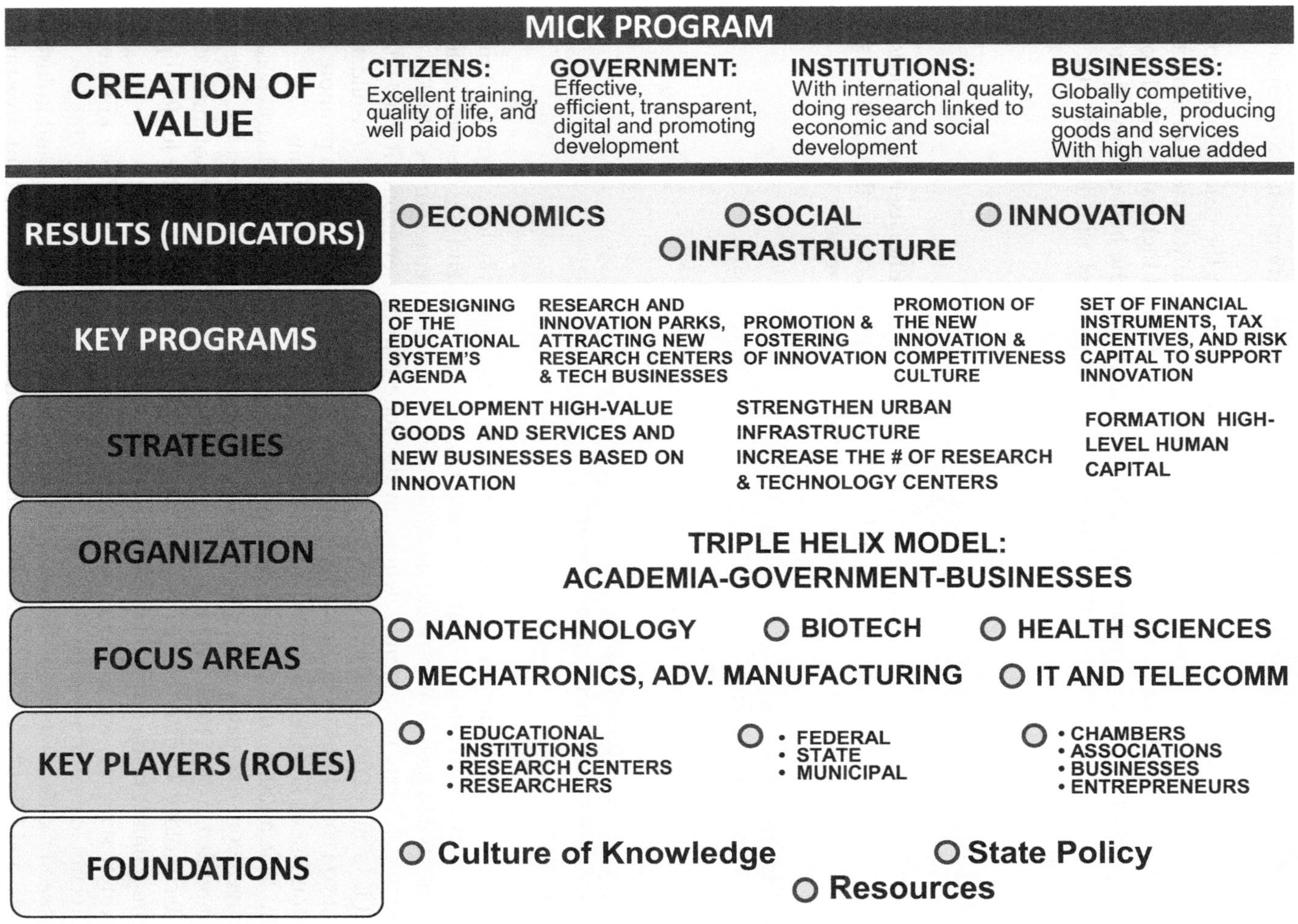

MICK PROGRAM

CREATION OF VALUE

CITIZENS: Excellent training, quality of life, and well paid jobs

GOVERNMENT: Effective, efficient, transparent, digital and promoting development

INSTITUTIONS: With international quality, doing research linked to economic and social development

BUSINESSES: Globally competitive, sustainable, producing goods and services With high value added

RESULTS (INDICATORS)
- ECONOMICS
- SOCIAL
- INFRASTRUCTURE
- INNOVATION

KEY PROGRAMS

REDESIGNING OF THE EDUCATIONAL SYSTEM'S AGENDA	RESEARCH AND INNOVATION PARKS, ATTRACTING NEW RESEARCH CENTERS & TECH BUSINESSES	PROMOTION & FOSTERING OF INNOVATION	PROMOTION OF THE NEW INNOVATION & COMPETITIVENESS CULTURE	SET OF FINANCIAL INSTRUMENTS, TAX INCENTIVES, AND RISK CAPITAL TO SUPPORT INNOVATION
DEVELOPMENT HIGH-VALUE GOODS AND SERVICES AND NEW BUSINESSES BASED ON INNOVATION		STRENGTHEN URBAN INFRASTRUCTURE INCREASE THE # OF RESEARCH & TECHNOLOGY CENTERS		FORMATION HIGH-LEVEL HUMAN CAPITAL

STRATEGIES

ORGANIZATION

TRIPLE HELIX MODEL:
ACADEMIA-GOVERNMENT-BUSINESSES

FOCUS AREAS
- NANOTECHNOLOGY
- BIOTECH
- HEALTH SCIENCES
- MECHATRONICS, ADV. MANUFACTURING
- IT AND TELECOMM

KEY PLAYERS (ROLES)
- EDUCATIONAL INSTITUTIONS
- RESEARCH CENTERS
- RESEARCHERS
- FEDERAL
- STATE
- MUNICIPAL
- CHAMBERS
- ASSOCIATIONS
- BUSINESSES
- ENTREPRENEURS

FOUNDATIONS
- Culture of Knowledge
- State Policy
- Resources

Figure 6.2   Model for the Monterrey International City of Knowledge Program

- the creation of the organizations and structures needed to boost and implement the key initiatives;
- continuous progress and result evaluation;
- its impact on the creation of value for the citizens, the institutions and the companies.

The Monterrey International City of Knowledge programme has the vision of converting Monterrey into one of the most competitive cities internationally, capable of attracting and retaining capital and human talent, for the production of high value added goods and services based on knowledge and innovation, and offer the best quality of life to its inhabitants. An analysis of the structure of MICK's model will illustrate the key components.

Foundations

Culture of knowledge: Some characteristics of the society that identifies itself as *regiomontana* (belonging to Monterrey), are chosen to be cultivated carefully, due to their relationship with the culture of knowledge that the programme is trying to achieve:

- long-term vision;
- participative leadership;
- entrepreneurship and creativity;
- science, technology and innovation;
- digital culture;
- appreciation of knowledge;
- sustainability and social responsibility;
- teamwork.

State policy: A legal framework has been put in place to ensure the long-term continuity of the programme. It includes laws, regulations, mechanisms, and the creation of legal instruments designed to oversee the accountability of the allocated resources. MICK is one of the five strategic programmes defined in the State Plan of Development 2004–2009, and it is included inside the axis of 'Wealth Generation', under the name 'Consolidation of Nuevo Leon's Knowledge Economy and Society'. Its main function is to promote and position Nuevo Leon as a noteworthy global competitor in the new economy.

In March 2004, the law for promoting development-based knowledge became effective. From that date on, MICK's programme began to take institutional life. The law was modified in 2005 to allow the creation of a new organism, the Institute of Innovation and Technology Transfer of Nuevo Leon (I2T2), which would assume the leadership of the programme, being responsible for its execution.

A new state law was approved in November 2009, the Act to Promote Knowledge and Technological Innovation Development of the State of Nuevo Leon. This law was proposed by citizens involved in public and private universities, business and industrial clusters, and it is the first one in Mexico which mandates at least 1 per cent investment of state-level fiscal budget in science, technology and innovation, and the establishment of a long-term plan reviewable every three years.

I2T2 was designed as the official government agency for the promotion of public policies related to science, technology and innovation. As a result, the I2T2 manages and allocates funds for this purpose, designing and operating financial instruments, funds and infrastructure that allow the creation of innovation businesses, formation of the Regional System of Innovation (RIS), formation of intellectual capital, and the management of strategic alliances regarding science, technology and innovation.

Resources: To fulfil the purpose and obtain benefits, the state government has implemented viable financial instruments to sustain the innovation ecosystem, and has agreed to allocate economic resources, concurring with funds from the federal, state and municipal governments, and the academic and the private sectors (Figure 6.3).

The generation and the granting of capital seed and risk funds for projects and companies with a technological profile are essential for the development of a knowledge-based economy. Therefore, the establishment of the Nuevo Leon's fund for Innovation (FONLIN) was fundamental, since it ensures local access to seed and risk capital, for technology-based businesses and science discoveries. The FONLIN is generated from the resources contributed by the Inter-American Development Bank (IADB), I2T2, CONACYT, and other investors.

Nuevo Leon's FONLIN fund provides financing to the strategic areas defined in the MICK programme, such as nanotechnology, biotechnology, biomedical devices, electronics and telecommunications, information technology, mechanical engineering, design and advanced manufacturing, advanced material, and chemical engineering.

The proposals guidelines emphasize that projects that are presented by the industry in collaboration with a university or research centres will be given better rating than those presented by either a university or a company individually. To help companies and private research centres find a suitable research partner within universities and institutes, the I2T2 created the State System of Interaction and Information, Science and Technology (SEIICYT), which began operations in 2008. It is an online system designed to promote technology transfer, networks of collaboration among scientists, technologists, representatives of private industry, and graduates from science and technology careers. Since the start of operations, the system has catalogued more than 600 experts in science and technology in Nuevo Leon.

Other federal financial resources that have been used to fund the MICK programme are:

Technological Innovation Fund: Created in July 2007, with a MXN$500 million budget, for the purpose of strengthening the quality of the production processes of Mexican SMEs. Additionally, this fund will be used to strengthen the development of basic sectors of the economy of knowledge, like nanotechnology, biotechnology, biomedical devices, electronics and telecommunications, information technologies, mechanical engineering, advanced design and manufacturing, chemical engineering, and advanced materials, which are the areas that the MICK programme promotes.

Fund for the Support of Technological SMEs: Created by the Ministry of Economy in September 2007, with a total of MXN$100 million. Its first goal was to provide support for the formation of the Monterrey IT Cluster, which brought together 42 software developing SME's.

State Budget

- Prioritization in the budget for science and technology, allocating fiscal resources to this area for more than 2,000 million pesos from 2004 to April 2008

State (Mix) Funds (Consejo Nacional de Ciencia y Tecnologia (CONACYT) y Nuevo Leon State Government)

- 50:50 State Government: Federal Government contributions. More than 840 million pesos in technological and scientific infrastructure from 2003 to 2008 (includes concurring academia and private sector investments)

Impetus to the investment of more than 1% GDP in science and technology over the next five years

- Encourage private sector participation by creating tools to support innovation and maximizing the portfolio of supporting tools by diverse federal, state and municipal government entities

Programs to support investment in innovation, research and technological development

- Tech Innovation for High Value Added Businesses (INNOVAPYME) $ 700 M
- Tech Innovation for the Competitiveness of Enterprises (INNOVATEC) $ 700 M
- Development and Innovation Technology Precursors (ProInnova) $ 1,200 M
- Companies in Nuevo Leon were awarded the biggest amount of resources in 2009-2010 ($ 350 M pesos in 2010)

Seed Capital Funds and Venture Capital

- Fund to support the creation and startup businesses based on innovation of Nuevo Leon
- Nuevo Leon Fund for Innovation (FONLIN) (2009) with an initial contribution of $95 M ($ 20 M the I2T2, CONACYT $ 30 M, $ 15 M FUNTEC)

Figure 6.3 Resources for innovation activities available in Nuevo Leon

PROSOFT Fund: This fund is used to support the development of the software industry and other services associated with ITC businesses, using resources provided by the state and federal governments. The resources assigned by PROSOFT to IT and software businesses operating in the state in 2004–2008, amount to more than MXN$835 million, combining contributions from the ministry of economy, the state government (through I2T2 and SEDEC), and the businesses themselves.

Seed and Risk Capital Funds: In Mexico, the Ministry of Economy has a seed capital fund to support businesses that are registered with the incubators that are enrolled in, and certified by the Ministry. This fund provides loans to new businesses, at low interest rates and with no collateral, facilitating the access to financial resources for launching their operations. Usually, this type of loans are granted to newly created businesses and, preferably, to those with innovative projects.

Key Players, Roles and the Triple Helix Model

The process of innovation is accelerated by the interaction of different interested parties, such as researchers at universities or research centres, and those in the private sector, focused in bringing new products or services to the market. In this regard, it is important to create structures that act as intermediaries, translating the language of the university to the language of the company and vice versa.

The Triple Helix model has been selected by the state programme MICK because it fits the innovation ecosystem model, allowing for nonlinear interactions and feedback among industry, academia, and government while working together and integrating other actors as required. The Triple Helix model facilitates the identification of policy instruments for industrial development to attain the benefits of the innovation.

At national level, Mexican companies in the productive sector have kept a low profile in the innovation system until recently. CONACYT's instruments for promotion of business R&D, Technology Transfer and technological innovation were reformed in 2002, and since then there has been a growing involvement of Mexican and multinational companies based in Mexico in STI activities.

According to the results gathered in the two National Research and Technology Development Surveys ESIDET conducted by CONACYT in 2001 and 2005, between 2004 and 2005, 23 per cent of a total of 16,398 firms surveyed made some innovation either in product or in process. The survey gives also evidence on the investment in R&D carried out by innovative firms. In 2001 their expenditures in R&D as percentage of their total expenditures in innovation were only 8.6 per cent, while acquisition of machinery and equipment absorbed 66.5 per cent. However, in 2006, the composition of the expenditures changed dramatically: R&D grew fivefold (up to 42.5 per cent) since 2001 and the resources allocated for acquisition of machinery were reduced (down to 39.7 per cent) (ESIDET 2001, 2006, Dutrénit et al. 2008).

Under the Triple Helix model, the auspice of the state and incentives to promote innovation in the strategic industrial sectors, the industry in Nuevo Leon has taken the challenge to improve its competitiveness and enter the economy of knowledge very seriously. Up to date, eight industrial clusters have been formed in the state, working under the concept of *coopetency*, understood as collaboration in the competition.

In agreement with the *coopetency* concept, local, national, and global companies within the same productive sector work jointly and in collaboration with the universities, research centres, and the government to develop greater synergies, economies of scale, and networks of suppliers. This joint effort propels the productivity and competitiveness of its sector, transforming scientific research into new products and services.

The second actor in the Triple Helix model, academia, has been a player on the national scene for quite some time. Mexico's higher education system consists of universities, technological institutes, state educational institutions, and *normal* schools (training of primary and secondary teachers). In 2009, in Nuevo Leon there were 93 colleges and universities with over 150,000 students. Monterrey Tech and the University of Monterrey are two of the most prestigious universities in Latin America. The State University of Nuevo Leon (UANL) is ranked as one of the best state universities in Mexico and it is the third largest university in the country, with 356 researchers registered in the NRS. It has modified its bachelor and graduate programmes to include topics on entrepreneurship and technology management, and has designed continuing education programmes for its researchers, in subjects such as patents, copyrights and entrepreneurship.

The role of the universities of Nuevo Leon in the Triple Helix is twofold: first, they are in charge of producing highly capable human resources in strategic knowledge areas, and second, they create and disseminate new knowledge that in the long or short term might be converted into new technologies that will bring benefits to society at large. In 2008, Monterrey Tech University consolidated its educative system of excellence at the national level with 33 campuses in the Mexican Republic. Since 2005, the institution has grown substantially in the research field: 122 research chairs have been created, 65 of which are at the Monterrey campus. This research chair scheme brings together experienced teachers, young teachers, and students engaged in a specific line of research.

The role of the state government in the Triple Helix, besides the commitment of resources and the design of public policies, construction of educational, telecommunications, urban and scientific-technological infrastructure, has been to organize the structure for public participation in support of the tasks and strategies of the consolidation of the knowledge economy and society, through the creation of Citizens' Councils, and the coordination of citizen participation in Nuevo Leon. These councils increase the interaction among citizens and seek the active participation of civil society. In addition to the creation of I2T2, there are a number of decentralized and citizen-participation organizations that contribute to the development of the programme.

Definition of Strategic Knowledge Areas and Focus on Industrial Sectors

Ten strategic economic sectors, through five technological areas, were defined via a consensus between private companies and universities. The five technological areas are biotechnology, mechatronics and advanced manufacturing, nanotechnology, information technologies and telecommunications, and health sciences.

Organization and Government of the Industry–Academia Innovation Groups

With support from the Ministry of Economic Development of the state of Nuevo Leon and the participation of I2T2, Citizens Advisory Councils were created. Their function is to foster synergies and support the development of strategic industries such as software, aerospace, medical and biotechnology, automotive, electronics and appliances, among others. The Citizens Advisory Councils are defined as groups that include multiple participants from various sectors such as business chambers, professional associations, universities, trade unions and political parties. The members of the Citizens Advisory Councils are organized into strategic clusters, integrated by companies, universities, governmental research centres and institutions. To date, there are eight clusters integrated in the sectors of aerospace, automotive and auto parts, electro-domestic appliances, agro-alimentary, IT and software, health services, biotechnology and nanotechnology.

Strategy of the MICK Programme

The MICK programme centres its strategy on achieving the proposed mission objectives by 2025, as expressed by the state government: 'Monterrey will be placed among the top 25 cities competing internationally, able to attract and retain capital and human talent, to produce goods and services with high value added through knowledge and innovation, and providing the best quality of life for its citizens' (González-Parás 2007). The MICK programme seeks to foster an innovation culture among the inhabitants of the state, increase GDP per capita by attracting knowledge intensive, high technological industries, and engaging in activities that create knowledge for economic benefits.

The core strategic actions identified for achieving these goals are:

- promoting the development of high-value goods;
- promoting innovation in the productive sector;
- increasing the formation of high-level human capital;
- promoting a culture of an innovation society;
- increasing investments in technological research and development;
- promoting new businesses based on innovation;
- strengthening urban infrastructure and cultural options;
- increasing the number of research and technology centres.

MICK's Key Programmes and Progress of Strategic Projects

The deployment of the MICK model resulted in the implementation of strategic projects that were designed to achieve:

- a model of high quality education, that allows its citizens to stay connected to activities that call for a high level of employment and entrepreneurship;

- a higher investment of public and private resources in science, technology and innovation capabilities;
- an urban infrastructure with high human capital formation and investment in the best projects, in order to be competitive and to offer citizens and visitors a high standard of living.

The projects that comprise the strategy are:

1. Redesigning and updating of the educational system's agenda.
   - redesign the content and educational methods for science and technology – Experiential Program of Science in Education;
   - increase connectivity and the use of IT in schools;
   - promote an entrepreneurial culture.

2. Attraction of new research centres and technology businesses.
   - adapt the educational offer of universities based on the needs of industry;
   - accelerated programmes for the formation of scientists and technologists;
   - research and technology innovation parks (PIIT).

3. Promotion and fostering of innovation in businesses, universities and research institutions.
   - formation of key talent in businesses and clusters;
   - integration of specialists and technologists into industries;
   - promote graduate studies and research in the universities;
   - scholarship programme for graduate studies;
   - design innovation instrument using the theory of inventive problem-solving.

4. Create and attract new strategic businesses.
   - regional program on competitiveness and innovation;
   - integration of production chains;
   - expansion of Regional and International Cooperation;
   - INVITE programme;
   - agreement between governors of the north-eastern region;
   - high-tech business incubators.

5. Expanding urban infrastructure and cultural options.
   - 2007 Forum of Cultures;
   - Urban Integration Macro Plaza – Fundidora Park – Santa Lucia Riverwalk;
   - Aerotechnopolis Project;
   - Museums Programme and Science and Technology Interactive Centres Programme;
   - Connectivity 'Nuevo Leon Digital';
   - Sustainability and the environment;
   - Mobility and transportation;
   - Urban and Housing Improvement Programme.

6. Promote the new business culture and the benefits of the MICK programme.
   - stimulate patent activity;

- program for the promotion of scientific-technological knowledge;
- design of the promotion and communication strategy.

7. Improve an entire set of financial instruments, tax incentives and risk capital to support innovation.
    - tax incentives for innovation in businesses;
    - research funds;
    - creation of seed capital funds;
    - Angel Investors in Nuevo Leon;
    - Research and Innovation Technology Park.

Before the construction of PIIT, Monterrey had an excellent network of industrial parks – more than 2,212 hectares – and the existent research centres pertaining to the local universities were isolated within its corresponding campuses.

According to international classification standards, apart from being a fourth-generation park, the PIIT is a semi-specialist park (IASP 2007), oriented towards innovation/incubation (innovation and incubation-oriented [I&IO]), which combines the vocation of research and development (R&D-oriented [R&DO]) (Hu, Lin and Chang 2005).

The PIIT is classified as a semi-specialist park, according to IASP classification, since it favours the high-priority sectors of science and technology for the MICK programme, but it also admits companies or start-ups working in other technology areas, if their strategy and objectives are aligned with those of the programme. The areas of major interest are those established by the MICK programme: Biotechnology, Nanotechnology, Health Sciences, Mechatronics and Advanced Manufacturing and IT and Telecommunications.

A fourth-generation STI park, according to Formica (2009), leverages on:

- brain exchange;
- circular causality in the research domain;
- multiple stakeholders;
- experimental labs.

The international networks that the established and projected centres bring with them, as well as the membership of the park to international associations, such as the Association of Universities Research Parks (AURP), and of the International Association of Science Parks (IASP), the interdisciplinary mix of public and private centres, the spaces and events designed for increased interactions between the tenants and researchers to provoke cross-fertilization and an open innovation atmosphere, the high-technology incubators and state of the art infrastructure in telecommunications, together with the ease of access to funds and seed capital, have already positioned the PIIT as an important player in the research park arena.

The PIIT can be considered a pioneer in the country, and in Latin America, because it is the first park in the region that:

1. Hosts research centres of local, national and international universities. The University of Texas, Texas A&M and the University of Arizona are members of the park.
2. Promotes synergy in the use of infrastructure and equipment, offering joint graduate programmes between the institutions of the park. One example of this collaboration

is the successful Master in Technology Commercialization degree jointly awarded by the Centre of Research in Advanced Materials from Mexico and the University of Texas at Austin, which has already graduated more than 150 students.

3. Strengthens the training of highly qualified human resources and innovation in the strategic clusters of the state.
4. Consists of a joint investment of private capital, public and private higher education institutions and the government at federal, state and municipal levels.
5. Offers high-tech incubators with experimental pilot plants open to the public for product to market development.
6. Promotes a regional innovation ecosystem, offering access not only to scientific and technological infrastructure and promoting linkages between academy and industry, but also facilitating access to grants, funding and seed money for research projects, technology transfer and for the incubation of new businesses.

The conceptualization, design, implementation and deployment of the PIIT project were carried out in record time. Four years after its conception, with all the land allocated to build 30 research centres and three high-tech incubators, eight research centres and the nanotechnology incubator already installed, there is a commitment to long-term investment from society and the state government.

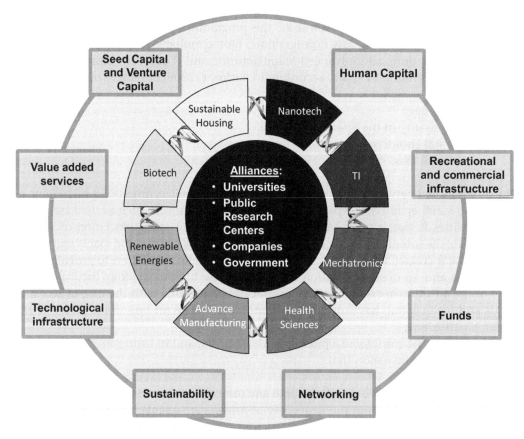

Figure 6.4 International and regional network

The PIIT maximizes the regional innovation ecosystem to promote synergy between universities, research and industry, with support from the state and federal government, newly created instruments for access to venture and angel capital, and a strong international and regional network (see Figure 6.4 opposite).

For the operation of the park, a trust has been created (FOPIIT), which in its guidelines indicates that the park will operate under a condominium regime. The trust is governed by an Advisory Council of Institutions, composed by the tenants that have fulfilled the necessary requirements to settle in the park.

The design of the PIIT facilities meets the expectations outlined in Battelle's study of the characteristics of 'Research Parks of the Future' (Battelle 2007). This study is based on a survey conducted among 134 managers of parks in Canada and the United States, and notes that the research park model which is currently used in North America has evolved from a model used for real-estate development projects, to become a catalyst for regional development.

Some facts about PIIT:

- Total area 70 Ha. (190 acres).
- 7 university research centres.
- 8 public research centres.
- 12 private companies research centres.
- 3 business incubators: nanotech, biotech and renewable energies/housing.
- 3,500 new jobs.
- Recreational and commercial areas.
- 100 per cent of water is re-utilized.
- 40 Ha. expansion planned for 2011.

Location of the Research Park

The PIIT is located in the municipality of Apodaca, Nuevo Leon, on grounds next to the new freeway to the city's main airport. Its proximity to the international airport and the location of a large amount of important industries in numerous industrial parks nearby makes it especially attractive, and promises to be an advantage for facilitating technology transfer and establishing linkages between the research centres, universities and the industry. In choosing this location, taken into account was the experience of other parks reported in studies that relate the park's success to the nature of urban and semi-urban parks, its facilities and its surroundings. The comparative findings of industrial parks in the United States conducted by Money (1970), regarding their location, are still in force, and have been endorsed by different studies conducted thereafter (LaValle 1982, Minshall 1983). The available studies of European parks (Carter 1989, Williams 1982) complement a list of characteristics that identify the importance of the location for establishing a research park:

- The physical space of the park should provide room for expansion of the original facilities for tenants.
- The park should be accessible by road and access systems for community transport.

- The location must have access to quality infrastructure services worldwide.
- The cost of settling in the park must be competitive with other parks available.
- The park must have a nearby airport.
- The park must have nearby residential areas and range of housing prices must be upper-middle class.
- The park must be within 50 miles of an urban centre.
- It must have quality schools in its vicinity.
- It must have easy access to sources of qualified human resources.

Thus, the ideal location for the PIIT was defined as being near the airport, with expansion possibilities, accessible by road, with plans for economic and urban growth, housing development projects in its vicinity, and public transportation facilities. Also, there are several hotels and restaurants within a radius of one kilometre, that serve the airport and nearby business parks. The PIIT is just 20 minutes from Monterrey's downtown.

Regarding the construction of the research facilities, PIIT has a manual of guidelines for architecture and construction which includes elements to protect the environment and also control and generate savings on the consumption of energy, water, etc. All buildings in the PIIT must comply with these guidelines according to the general project. An excellent example of sustainability, environmental care and energy conservation, is the International Baking Centre project from PepsiCo. It will be a milestone in the construction of research centres. The architectural design provides for the use of wind and solar energy, as well as rooftop gardens.

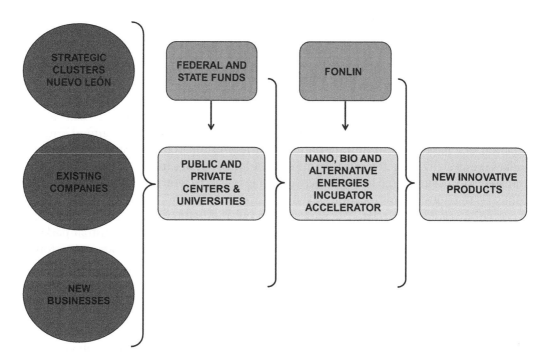

Figure 6.5   Innovation network model for the PIIT

From all the infrastructure built in the park, of note are the three high-technology incubators that will be managed by the I2T2, in the areas of:

- nanotechnology;
- biotechnology;
- renewable energy and sustainable housing.

These incubators will allow companies to scale up their products in order to market tests of their new designs. The network model being followed in order to create innovative nodes within the different universities and public and private research centres located at the PIIT is shown in Figure 6.5. This has helped to create strong linkages between academia and industry researchers in the state of Nuevo Leon.

Findings and Discussion

Notwithstanding the short time span since the formal beginning of operations of the MICK programme, there are already some notable benefits, which are summarized in the following paragraphs. They demonstrate that the approach of the programme, and the sum of efforts, strategies, and actions from the private sector, academia and governmental agencies, are providing the expected results.

Nuevo Leon has managed to fully seize CONACYT's mixed funds, providing resources for the development of science and technology that responds to the needs of the state. Nuevo Leon's mixed fund is the largest in the country: more than MXN$1,000 million from 2003 to 2010, including resources channelled from the federal government, state governments and those contributed by companies and academia to the approved projects.

Regarding Innovation funds, in the two call for proposals (2009, 2010), Monterrey's companies, around 200, have been the leading applicants (387–450 projects) for CONACYT's Incentive Funds for Technology Research and Innovation (MXN$2,500 million). The results of the two calls show that for two consecutive years, Monterrey has taken the uppermost position in awarded funds and projects, exchanging its traditional second place position with Mexico City.

The Triple Helix implemented as a part of the model has contributed to the transformation of the regional culture into one of innovation and one of a flourishing academic–industry partnership. As an example of the success in the implementation of the new culture, the state of Nuevo Leon obtained the first place in research funds from the National Council for Science and Technology (CONACYT), being awarded to projects that present academy–industry linkage, both in economic resources and project number. Moreover, the biotechnology incubator housed in the park PIIT has obtained federal funds for its construction, due to the fact that it is a project carried out by three neighbouring states (Tamaulipas, Coahuila and Nuevo Leon), the academic and the industrial clusters.

As part of building the regional innovation ecosystem, a state fund was created to help launch new innovative businesses (Figure 6.6). FONLIN (Fondo Nuevo Leon para la Innovación), started operations with an initial capital of US$7 million. This fund is composed of federal, state and other international agencies contributions. The call for proposals of new innovative business based on knowledge was opened and 210 projects were received in 2009. There are some companies in the selection process right now, and they involve some

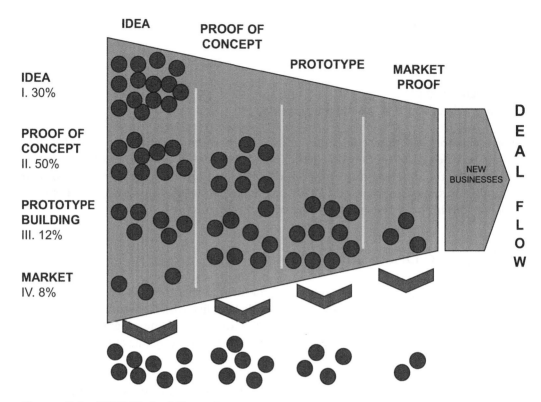

Figure 6.6   FONLIN deal flow stages

new companies that will be nested in the research park incubators. There are 10 companies that are in the prototypes creation stage, being the first ones supported by this fund.

The park is already seen as the core for regional innovation, and its effects and those of the state government's strategies on the regional economy, already look very promising. Besides the biotechnology incubator, the park will house two other incubator facilities, one in nanotechnology and one in renewable energy, 30 research centres, from international, public and private universities, transnational companies and local firms, and public research centres from CONACYT's network, thus positioning Nuevo Leon as a leading region concerning economic development through innovation.

Conclusions

As we have pointed out, the decentralization of the key federal programmes regarding science and technology in the realm of state policies has made the promotion of innovation and entrepreneurship among academia and industry more efficient, as it has increased awareness of the long-term benefits that a close relationship with the universities and research centres may mean in terms of global competitiveness, and to accelerate the introduction of new products to the markets.

The annual average income of the citizens has grown by 8.5 per cent, an increment higher than the inflation rate, which in the past five years has been hovering around

3.3 per cent in average. Nuevo Leon has grown at an annual rate of 5 per cent, while the national average is close to 3.3 per cent, and in the USA is near 3.0 per cent.

This growth rate will continue to scale upwards in the medium and long term, with the consolidation of the programme. The GDP per capita of the state, an annual US$18,465 by inhabitant, is almost twice as great as the national average in 2008.

The leadership of Nuevo Leon in the international markets is corroborated with the dynamics of its exports. In 2004 these represented the 19 per cent of the local GDP. In 2007, the proportion had reached 30.3 per cent, which means that the state exports passed from US$10,400 million in 2004 to US$20,620 million in 2007, with an annual growth average of 26.0 per cent.

A fact that also reflects the real advance of Nuevo Leon in transforming the industry sector towards higher use for innovation and technology is the composition of the exports of the companies located in the state. According to the classification established by the OECD for the sectors and with data from the Ministry of Economic Development of Nuevo Leon, in 2007, the exports of high technology and upper-middle technology represented 72.0 per cent of the total of the state exports and were equivalent to almost US$15,000 million.

The tangible community assets of residents from all regions of Nuevo Leon increased at an unprecedented rate in the last five years, through infrastructure for tourism, community centres, public plazas, roads, pedestrian bridges, rain water collection systems, rural roads and highways, urban public transport systems, sports facilities, recreational public areas, schools, museums, hospitals, and modern spaces devoted to science and technology for the promotion of the knowledge-based economy. Consequently, the size of infrastructure and the state's dynamics to attract capital and create jobs were significantly expanded at a rate well above the national average.

The MICK programme creates favourable conditions for the growth of the innovation ecosystem, because it encourages the development of innovation clusters, formed by the joint efforts of universities, research centres and companies, where the government acts as a promoter of policies and resources for scientific and technological development. Now in its consolidation phase, the programme favours research in the following subjects: aerospace, health sciences, biotechnology, nanotechnology, renewable energy and sustainable housing, information and software technologies, and advanced manufacturing. Because of the proximity of research centres, universities and companies in the same territory, the innovation core formed by PIIT, promotes innovation among the different clusters for their strengthening and 'cross-fertilization' networks.

The state's progress has not stopped; on the contrary, Nuevo Leon is now the *National Leader in Development*, as confirmed by the data that has been presented.

Learning Review Questions

1. What is considered the key for the success of the innovation ecosystem model implemented in Monterrey?
2. What types of interactions are purposefully built according to the model, and which are the innovation strategies and programmes that are implemented based upon these interactions?

3. Do you consider that the model is replicable for any other Latin American region? Explain the key factors of the strategy that you may have to change or take into account when trying to adapt this model to other regions.

References

Alemán, L. 2010. 'Liderazgo para la Innovación en las Cátedras de Investigación del Tecnológico de Monterrey', unpublished Master's thesis, Escuela de Graduados en Educación del Tecnológico de Monterrey, Mexico.

Carter, N. 1989. *Science Park Development and Management*. London: The Estates Gazette.

CONACYT. 2008. *Informe de Labores 2008*. Mexico: CONACYT. [Online]. Available at: www.siicyt.gob.mx/siicyt/docs/contenido/INFLAB08.pdf.

David, P. and Foray, D. 2002. Fundamentos económicos de la sociedad del conocimiento. *Comercio Exterior*, 52(6), 472–90. [Online]. Available at: http://revistas.bancomext.gob.mx/rce/magazines/23/2/davi0602.pdf [accessed: January 26, 2010].

Dutrénit, G., Capdevielle, M., Corona, J.M., Puchet, M., Santiago, F. and Vera-Cruz, A. 2008. *The Mexican National System of Innovation: Structures, Policies, Performance and Challenges: Background*. Report to the OECD Country Review of Mexico's National System of Innovation. Mexico: CONACYT.

Edgar, D. and Grant, K. 2009. Innovación en la práctica y practicando innovación, in *Kick Start: Nuevas formas de enseñar innovación*, edited by A. Mateos, M. Anderson and J.M. Rodríguez. Salamanca: Signum, 13–24.

ESIDET. 2006. *Encuesta sobre Investigación y Desarrollo Tecnológico*. Sistema Integrado de información sobre investigación científica y tecnológica. [Online]. Available at: http://www.siicyt.gob.mx/siicyt/docs/Estadisticas3/Informe2007/Innovacion.pdf.

Formica, P. 2009. *Science and Technology Parks (STP): The Evolution*. [Online]. Available at: www.iked.org/pdf/4TH%20Generation%20STPs.pdf.

González-Paras, N. 2007. Instituto de Innovación y Transferencia de Tecnología. [Online]. Available at: http://www.mtycic.com.mx/?p=articulos&a=20080404.

Hu, T., Lin, C. and Chang, S. 2005. Technology-based regional development strategies and the emergence of technological communities: A case study of HSIP, Taiwan. *Technovation*, 25, 367–80.

IASP. 2007. *Facts and Figures of Science and Technology Parks in the World*. [Online]. Available at: http://www.rtp.org/files/iasp_survey_on_stps.pdf.

LaValle, K.P. 1982. *High Technology Park–A Marriage of Higher Education and Industry*. Report by the Chairman of the New York State Senate Higher Education Committee.

Minshall, C.W. 1983. An overview of trends in science and high technology parks. *Economic and Policy Analysis*, Occasional Paper Number 37. Columbus, OH: Battelle.

Money, M.L. 1970. 'A model for the establishment of a university related research park within a framework of selected management principles', unpublished PhD dissertation, Division of Business Administration, University of Utah, USA.

Stake, R. 2007. *Investigación con estudio de casos*. Madrid: Morata.

Sternberg, R.J., Kaufman, J.C. and Pretz, J.E. 2001. The propulsion model of creative contributions applied to the arts and letters. *Journal of Creative Behavior*, 35(2), 75–101.

Williams, J.F.D. 1982. *A Review of Science Parks and High Technology Developments*. London: Chartered Surveyors and Planning Consultants.

7

The Socioeconomics of Digital Ecosystems Research: Policy Analysis and Methodological Tools from an Argentinian Case Study

LORENA RIVERA LEÓN, RODRIGO KATAISHI and PAOLO DINI

Introduction

In the field of innovation and development studies opinions on the best way to approach the problem of sustainable development vary widely. The perspective (disciplinary, cultural, political, etc., one adopts to define the problem plays an important role in developing innovation strategies. For example, at one extreme the IMF tends to impose expectations which affect the permeability of trade barriers. At the other extreme, various kinds of NGOs adopt different strategies, most of which tend to involve direct intervention or engagement on the ground with respect to development problems. Digital Ecosystems (DE) research starts from the hypothesis that information and communication technologies (ICTs) can play an important role in catalysing (i.e. accelerating) development through processes of innovation. For the innovation potential of ICTs to be maximized DE research maintains that two normative assumptions need to be upheld: the software should be open source, and the underlying architecture should be distributed. DE research, therefore, falls somewhere in the middle of these two extremes. In addition, it places a particularly high emphasis on the importance of the localization, re-interpretation and consequent appropriation of ICTs by the local stakeholders. Where differences of opinion arise, DE researchers see opportunities for asking open-ended research questions, either theoretical or empirical, in support of fostering a constructive debate among the stakeholders. Ultimately, DE research aims to inform and support the processes through which sustainable socioeconomic development (i.e. through innovation) policies are defined and implemented.[1]

These first few words already show that DE research addresses theoretical and applied questions of economic, technological and sociological import at the same time. When

---

1   'Sustainability' is not necessarily a positive concept. For example, some dictatorships or oligopolies have lasted for very long periods, and could therefore be described as 'sustainable'. We mean the term in the narrower sense of what could make economic growth more stable.

introducing processes of innovation in areas such as value generation and technical architectures the role of complex power relationships cannot be overlooked. Further, DE research advocates the exploration of these questions through a combination of action and reflexive research. Therefore, the success of this approach depends on the involvement of local stakeholders in the same social processes, in collaboration with academic researchers. The research discussed in this chapter, in particular, grew out of collaboration between European and Latin American researchers in the context of the Framework Programme 7 EU project EULAKS (Connecting Socioeconomic Research on the Dynamics of the Knowledge Society in the European Union and Latin American and Caribbean Countries). The research was centred on an analysis of the possibilities for the introduction of a DE in the Municipality of Morón, in the province of Buenos Aires (Argentina).

Since the beginning, the DE concept as defined by the European Commission (EC) involved more than technology-led innovation. Other horizontal aspects such as business models, training and knowledge-sharing were an integral part as well (Nachira 2002). Over the subsequent years and during the course of several EC-funded research projects[2] the need to formulate appropriate policy analyses became more apparent. Similarly, governance was originally seen to be relevant to DE open source communities, but the research gradually showed it to be an all-pervasive concept of relevance to every facet of a given socioeconomic-technical context. Innovation in the DE context, therefore, refers to the introduction of a sociological perspective in both the technical and economic dimensions. As will be discussed during the course of this chapter, this leads to several important consequences, e.g. Web 2.0 dynamics, distributed architectures, and ultimately to new forms of governance. In the DE perspective, sustainable socioeconomic development then becomes a natural outcome of this innovation landscape.

Figure 7.1 provides a simplified 'economics map'. The three layers shown can be seen as a historical progression of how the definition of 'economics' has become broader over the past 100 years. In other words, it can be seen as a coarse-grained historical map of innovating the economics discipline itself. Figure 7.2 shows how DE research can be situated on this map. The simplistic two-step progression shown – first introduce ICTs and services, then the social dimension – should not be taken literally, as these two steps usually blend into each other and take place in parallel. They are shown in this linear fashion to highlight their role as the 'backbone' of the claim made by DE research. It is perhaps easier to accept the linear character of this progression as partly reflecting how the concept of development has evolved in the past 100 years, and how it is likely to evolve in the next decades. Thus, DE research is ultimately concerned with testing this high-level framework through a combination of theoretical and empirical studies in a number of different disciplines (Dini et al. 2009, Van Egeraat et al. 2008, Dini et al. 2011).

Figure 7.3 shows the logical structure of the chapter. The next section presents the six hypotheses of DE research together with an abstract rationalization and a brief discussion of the concepts introduced. The abstract perspective grew out of several years of DE research in various contexts (Dini et al., 2008a; Dini et al., 2008b; Botto and Passani, 2008; Dini et al., 2009; Botto et al., 2008; Shaikh et al., 2008; Rivera León et al., 2009; Nicolai, 2009). This chapter's concern is to develop an analytical methodology or 'tool' that is optimized specifically for the Latin American context and that can help in the

---

2   Available at: http://www.digital-ecosystems.org.

drafting of socioeconomic innovation and development policies. Section 3 then offers an alternative characterization of the problem of regional socioeconomic development that is particularly relevant to the Argentinian context, followed by a discussion of empirical

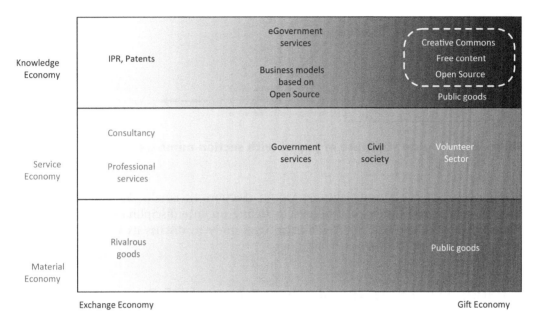

Figure 7.1 Simplified 'historical' map of the main economic fields relevant to DEs

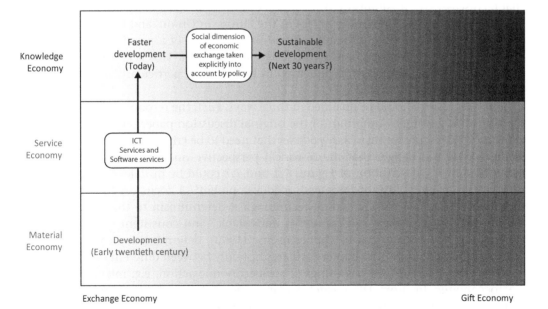

Figure 7.2 The backbone of the DE research argument, from a historical perspective

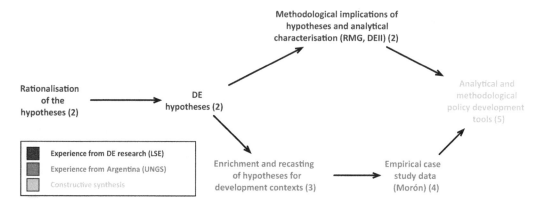

Figure 7.3   Logical structure of paper, with section numbers

data gathered in the Municipality of Morón (Section 4). Finally, Section 5 combines the theoretical and empirical findings to define an interdisciplinary policy analysis visualization tool and use the Argentinian case study to discuss its validity. Section 6 summarizes the conclusions of the findings.

A Rationalization of the Six Hypotheses of DE Research

International cooperation and knowledge transfer among countries has become increasingly important in recent decades, giving opportunity to a set of multiple interaction programmes particularly amongst developed and developing regions. This chapter discusses the feasibility of the adoption of DEs in the Latin American context, based on the experience of deployment of DEs in the European Union, and to a smaller extent in India. At the same time, it paints a broad-brush picture of a possible rationalization of the DE approach from an objectivist, systemic viewpoint. This is consistent with the economic flavour of the research presented in this chapter, particularly in the region of Morón in Argentina.

This discussion should be qualified in three ways. First, the response of DE research to the *normative* starting assumptions of the original discussion paper published by the EC (Nachira 2002) is to treat them as *hypotheses* that need to be critically analysed and tested. Second, there is a danger that the historical perspective on innovation in economics mentioned in the description of Figures 7.1 and 7.2 could be mistaken for a historicist view of the invevitability of 'progress' or 'development'. A focus on ICTs could then make matters even worse by adding technological determinism to the mix. Although the importance of history and context is undeniable (and consistent with evolution), DE research is not historicist in Popper's sense (1993), deterministic or technocentric. Third, the discussion in this chapter oscillates not only between different disciplines, but also between different understandings of socioeconomic action, e.g. microeconomic vs macroeconomic. In short, DE research makes a *bona fide* attempt at piecing together in a rational way the very complex puzzle of innovation and development by adopting a strongly interdisciplinary, scientific and critical approach.

The Six Hypotheses

ONE – ICT LEAD TO EFFICIENCY IMPROVEMENTS

A focus on the technological aspects of ICTs leads to expectations in efficiency improvements in those processes that can most easily be automated; for example, information storage and retrieval or any of the other processes that support the business and economic life of the users of digital online environments. Development and innovation in this case tend to be traditionally interpreted in terms of quantifiable economic measures. If, on the other hand, the focus is on the communication processes enabled by the technology, understanding the nature of the link between the social processes supported by ICTs and the different kinds of possible economic interactions and exchanges becomes more urgent. These two perspectives reflect a dichotomy at the heart of research on ICTs that has been highlighted by Winograd and Flores (1987). This dichotomy corresponds to the two main epistemological viewpoints adopted in the OPAALS project,[3] the European Network of Excellence developing a theoretical framework for Digital Ecosystems (Dini et al. 2008b, Botto et al. 2008, Dini et al. 2009, Dini et al. 2011).

TWO – IMPORTANCE OF THE SOCIAL DIMENSION

The latter interpretation is at the core of a second hypothesis of DE research: *sustainable development is best achieved when the social dimension of economic interactions is explicitly taken into account in the drafting and implementation of development policies.* Even though this hypothesis is not necessarily easy to confirm, there are opportunities for thoughtful reflection and for drawing useful insights from many different theories within the social sciences. The growing economic weight of online social networks, furthermore, also supports this view. The theoretical activities of DE research, therefore, aim to develop new models and understandings (e.g. of innovation) that can explain and support socioeconomic and socio-technical processes of relevance to development. The interplay of the social and technical dimensions are further elaborated through four additional hypotheses.

THREE – COLLABORATION FOR GREATER COMPETITIVENESS

Another consequence of adopting a socioeconomic perspective is that it induces a certain dependence on scale: on average social interactions tend to favour and depend on proximity and a finite number of actors. For an average-sized country, this makes the regional[4] perspective a more amenable scale of study and engagement than the national level.

Three trends, singly or in different combinations, appear to characterize regional economies in many developed and developing countries over the past few decades. First, the amplification of the size and importance of the service and knowledge economies

---

3   Available at: http://www.opaals.eu.

4   When we say 'regional' we are referring to the geographical-political meaning of the term, i.e. a relatively small area such as a province or county, or perhaps a state, depending on the population density. A similar argument makes DE research relevant also to virtual online communities that may not have a recognizable geographical identity.

effected by ICTs suggests a decrease in transaction costs associated with immaterial goods and the impact of a growing dependence on services and labour markets. Second, the emergence and growth of large firms (Multinational Corporation, MNC) in any given region is not necessarily an indication of stability and greater job security. The case of FIAT in Piedmont in the 1960s–1980s is an example of a large company – called a 'keystone' in this case (Iansiti and Levien 2004) – creating an ecosystem of small suppliers. If the keystone loses competitiveness, as indeed Piedmont experienced in the 1990s, the whole region can become vulnerable. In such cases the keystone creates dependence and effectively slows down innovation.[5] Third, the volatility of the operations of many multinational companies, especially those focused on the service sector, renders job security much weaker than it was during most of the twentieth century. As a consequence, for many regions a looser, more dynamic, and more competitive environment appears to reflect better the character of regional economies, the needs of regional development, and the opportunities available to regional actors. In such an emergent market context, it seems plausible to expect that the introduction of ICTs would then facilitate the growth of the local economy. As shown in the next sections, however, ICTs by themselves are not enough.

By any reckoning, in most parts of the world the firm size distribution shows a predominance of micro-enterprises (less than 10 employees) over medium or large-sized firms. The USA has relatively more micro, medium-sized and large firms, while Europe has comparatively more small firms (European Commission, 2010).[6] Small and medium-sized enterprises (SMEs)[7] tend to lag behind larger firms in the adoption of ICT and innovation capabilities. Combining these observations with the trends mentioned above and the first two hypotheses of DE research suggests that investing in ICT adoption policies for SMEs is likely to be associated with higher returns in the form of economic growth, through productivity increases, leading to competitiveness.

The greater role of social interactions in economic life can be leveraged to support and amplify an element of learning in the socioeconomic life of regional actors. This potential is particularly visible in the service economy and for knowledge services. When coupled with the adoption and use of ICTs, this potential can provide an economically sustainable (because it is built into the exchange economy) and self-reinforcing dynamic of growth. This dynamic is not dissimilar to the emergence of complex societies afforded by division of labour and synergy arguments. For example, SMEs whose business models are based on providing software, legal, or training services to other SMEs effect a significant transfer of know-how, in addition to the service itself, that is supported by an economic exchange. This could be argued to strengthen connectivity and absorption capacity in a given regional or online context.

The picture that emerges from these considerations is that of a dynamic and interdependent collection of firms of varying size, but with a predominance of SMEs,

---

5   One should not overlook cases where keystones (i.e. MNCs) had effectively helped the developing process of countries. The United Nations Conference on Trade and Development (UNCTAD) had deeply studied the role of Foreign Direct Investment (FDI) and MNCs in developing countries through its 'World Investment Report' annual series. Available at: http://www.unctad.org/Templates/Page.asp?intItemID=1465.

6   Within the non-financial business economy enterprise population, around 92 per cent of EU firms are micro enterprises. In the US, the share of micro firms in the total number of enterprises is 94.5 per cent while the shares of small, medium-sized and large firms are 3.7 per cent, 1.5 per cent and 0.3 per cent respectively (US Bureau of Census and US Small Business Administration).

7   SMEs are defined by the EC to have less than 250 employees and/or €5m annual turnover.

which has been dubbed a 'business ecosystem' by Moore (1996). In this picture, the socioeconomic 'health' of a region is likely to be characterized by the absence of monopolies or oligopolies and by the presence of a vibrant and innovating ecosystem of small firms that may collaborate as well as compete with one another.[8] From this, a third hypothesis emerges, that greater collaboration *within* a particular geographical region or virtual community leads to greater sustainability of economic growth and greater competitiveness of that region or online community *in the wider market*.

FOUR – OPEN SOURCE

Another question DE research investigates is relevant at all scales and is concerned with the inherent limitations of market signals when they are applied to software. Competition for market share in the sale of commodities and services is unconcerned with the characterization of these objects of economic exchange beyond what the market itself is able to 'sense', i.e. price and production/sales volume. Although the efficiency of the market in finding the right price point has lured many of us into taking for granted that the market is something close to 'intelligent', in fact it is not. At best it exhibits a very rudimentary form of intelligence such as can be observed in connectionist systems. In other words, it is true that the dynamics of markets can improve the efficiency of economic exchange. But the fallacy in relying on the market exclusively lies in the fact that a focus only on price and production/sales volume overlooks the semantic meaning of economic transactions whose significance depends on context. The 'cognitive abilities' of the market cannot cope with such subtleties or abstractions. One of its most glaring omissions is a lack of consideration for the full implications of the commodification of the means of production in the knowledge economy, i.e. knowledge and meta-knowledge, or software.

DE research, therefore, investigates the possible distinction between those aspects of the knowledge economy that can be commodified and those aspects that should not be because they are the means of production of the knowledge economy itself. Depending on one's point of view this argument seems either strange and unwarranted or plausible and legitimate. For example, from the point of view of the material economy, this argument could be criticized for being analogous to saying that it's OK to sell cars but it's not OK to sell car factories, which is clearly nonsense. On the other hand, if some aspects of knowledge are regarded as a public good, then this argument could be supported for embodying some aspects of the extreme opposite interpretation; namely, for example, that it is counter-productive to commodify the air a person breathes because doing so would undercut the lives of those who can't afford to pay for it. The nonsensical proposition in this case is to charge for this particular public good (air). The DE argument, still under development, attempts to find a middle ground for an object of economic exchange that has something in common with the former (e.g. software services in support of business services can and should be charged for) as well as with the latter (e.g. language as a means

---

8   A prime example of this increasingly common phenomenon is provided by the Plone community of OSS companies (http://plone.org/). There are approximately 300 of them distributed around the world. They collaborate in the development and maintenance of a common content management system (CMS) platform and compete when responding to public tenders or seeking private customers. (From a conversation with Roberto Allende, of Menttes S.R.L. Available at: http://www.menttes.com, in Cordoba, Argentina, November 2009.)

of expression and by extension much of the content found on the Web should be freely available to all).

The reason for upholding market mechanisms such as competition is ultimately to maximize the generation of macroeconomic value through efficiency improvements (lower prices and more than proportionally greater production/sales volume). For traditional commodities there is a minimum price that corresponds to maximum macroeconomic output and below which the macroeconomic output shrinks again. One objective of DE research is thus to understand in which areas of economic life competitive market mechanisms lead to the maximization of macroeconomic output at a non-zero price, and in which areas, instead, macroeconomic output keeps growing as the price shrinks to zero. It is known that information markets differ substantially to those for the production and consumption of material goods. As a result it is to be expected that competitive markets for service and knowledge production and consumption will also differ from the standard arguments about the efficiency of markets (see for instance Drahos 2002). This means that questions need to be asked about the optimal organization of markets for the supply of the infrastructure of the knowledge economy and increasingly the means of knowledge production, i.e. the world of software, the Web, etc.

The analysis of this question aims to validate the fourth hypotheses, that digital ecosystems are best built on an open source infrastructure. Because tradable goods are 'fair game' when it comes to competition for market share, if software is tradable it becomes a target to the same competitive 'turf wars'. However, software is not an inert commodity but is actually a 'channel' for other things (economic and social processes). Therefore, DE research is investigating whether and to what extent this specific property means that its commodification is likely to lead to far-reaching and in most cases deleterious knock-on effects.

Assuming that there is some validity to this view, open source software (OSS), therefore, has an interesting effect. By changing the status of software from 'fair game' to 'non-tradable', it causes it to disappear from the radar of the market, here meant as the dumb 'machine' mentioned above. Once this decoupling has been achieved, software becomes unfettered by the constraints posed by market dynamics. Then, since software is carrier of social and economic interactions, it becomes better able to interact constructively with the very same social and economic interactions, leading to a 'virtuous circle' of interaction. This appears to be the case in spite of the fact that OSS is never actually and wholly 'free': there are many costs associated with its production, and it can also be packaged and sold, such as some of the Linux distributions. And yet, when open source software is developed through non-market relationships, its role in the economy shifts in an important way: from software or knowledge as a commodity acting as a trigger for market-share 'wars', towards the same software and knowledge supporting collaborative and social interactions largely revolving around its development.

By decoupling the software or knowledge object from an arbitrary attribution of its monetary value and by linking it, instead, to a different kind of value system which is often characterized as the 'gift economy', its role switches drastically. Since it is a medium of communications, it is not just a *result* of collaborative interactions, but it is implicitly also an *amplifier* of the same interactions. OSS development therefore becomes a self-reinforcing process that culminates in global phenomena like the development of Linux. Even if one adopts a sceptical view on the above interpretation of OSS, the predominance of Linux servers in Web environments leads to wonder how it could have become such an important global phenomenon given that OSS is in good part outside the market. Thus, at the very least OSS simply reinforces the perception that the way in which one thinks about the market, should change and be expanded, as research in the gift economy attempts to do.

The integration of a business ecosystem with an open source technical infrastructure leads to a Digital Business Ecosystem (DBE), which was the initial instantiation of the broader concept of a digital ecosystem (Nachira 2002). By contrast, a different example of a digital ecosystem is the knowledge ecosystem being developed by the Indian Institute of Technology, Kanpur researchers as they investigate the transition from an agricultural economy to a service or knowledge economy in their region (Chatterjee et al. 2008).

FIVE – DISTRIBUTED ARCHITECTURE

Following this line of argument, shows how the initial concept of sustainable socioeconomic development has been mapped to a particular kind of ICT to be grafted onto different kinds of social, economic, cultural, and geographical contexts. However, another important hypothesis is still missing in the definition of a dynamic and 'horizontal' DE that can catalyse sustainable socioeconomic development: the fifth hypothesis is that the open source infrastructure must be distributed.

An understanding of technology as embodying cultural values (Feenberg 1991, 2002) calls for the assumption of responsibility on the part of technologists. In other words, a choice of centralized vs. distributed architecture should look beyond purely functionalist properties (efficiency, resilience, reliability). It should also look at the implications of any given architectural choice on the economic and socio-political control of the infrastructure. For these reasons, the computer scientists of the DE community elected to accept, and largely embrace, this normative requirement. A distributed architecture avoids single points of failure, which is a functionalist value, but also single points of control, and therefore is more consistent with a goal of encouraging competitive, rather than monopoly supply of services. In other words, this hypothesis can be rationalized and justified theoretically *ex ante* by making recourse to Feenberg's critical theory of technology coupled with a hermeneutic epistemology. Whether it also leads to technical and economic advantages has been discussed extensively (Razavi et al. 2009, Malone and McLaughlin 2009) and a partial implementation has been completed (Lacueva et al. 2010), so the next step will be to test this hypothesis also *ex post*, through a real DE deployment.

SIX – ECOSYSTEM AS MODEL

Finally, DE research is also about making the software better able to track user needs, autonomously. The sixth hypothesis of DE research is that it should be possible to transform the self-organizing and evolutionary properties of biological ecosystems into the architecture and algorithms of digital ecosystems, i.e. that the concept of ecosystem can be treated as a *model* and not just as a *metaphor*. A very active area of DE research, therefore, is focused on building a mathematical framework that can usefully bridge cell and evolutionary biology with computer science, formal and specification languages, and logic.

A CRITICAL DISCUSSION OF AN ABSTRACT LOGICAL-SEMANTIC PROCESS MODEL FOR DEs

The argument pieced together so far can be summarized graphically as shown in Figure 7.4. This is a very complex diagram, which was created mainly by following the logical connections explained in the previous section. The main concerns of the DE approach are shown in a reasonably complete form, grouped by a mixture of disciplinary domains and theoretical/applied categories: economics, socio-technical systems, and regional development policy. As discussed more fully in Dini et al. (2011), the concern was to develop a theoretical framework that would ultimately inform policy interventions in different socioeconomic contexts. The simultaneous search for general principles and context-dependent processes led on the one hand to the need to take into account different epistemological positions whilst, on the other hand, made the involvement of the 'local' stakeholders in the customization and localization of the approach paramount.

From the point of view of theory construction, Figure 7.4 can be read also as a mixture of theoretical development and empirical verification. In fact, each hypothesis (blue bubble) can be seen to be supported by a combination of theoretical arguments and verifiable claims, involving in some cases other hypotheses. The theoretical arguments ultimately rely upon a collection of ontological and episte-mological choices which serve a function similar to fundamental axioms. The intention is to show that regardless of one's preferred starting perspective an argument can be made for adopting the DE approach, subject to some hypotheses being proven valid by empirical evidence (not all hypotheses are shown as blue bubbles, only those that appear to be more distinctly related to DEs are).

The figure therefore should be seen as a *collection* of possible arguments that together support the claim that the DE approach is fundamentally innovative and useful in the process of achieving sustainable socioeconomic development. In spite of its complexity, not every relationship can be clearly shown. For example, the 'social dimension of ICTs' bubble is not linked, directly or indirectly, to the open sources nodes in the diagram. This omission is clearly a drawback of this particular diagram, and there are likely to be several others, so Figure 7.4 should be considered only as a partial and 'living' depiction of relevant ideas that will continue to evolve in the coming years, as different theoretical perspectives and/or different arguments are prioritized.

The previous section has traced out a few of the possible paths through this diagram, but others are possible. For example, if one starts with the ontological choice of the exchange economy and economic individualism, the market follows as a logical consequence. A 'healthy' market is free of monopolies, a property that is beneficial to the material, service and knowledge economy alike. Although the theory of public goods is general, its applicability to the knowledge economy is quite relevant to the role of software as a means of production, as argued above. In particular it is relevant to its role as an *infrastructure* supporting online socioeconomic action. This is also dependent on the gift economy and on collectivist ontological and epistemological choices about how to understand socioeconomic action, positions which underpin the open source phenomenon. At the same time, the knowledge economy also implies lower transaction costs, which also depend on the introduction of ICTs. The knowledge and service economies, together with the open source approach, lead to OSS-based business models. The open source approach, in turn, requires and strengthens collaborative practices, which render a geographical or virtual community more competitive (e.g. the Plone case). Open source, collaboration, and lower transaction costs reinforce one another, a claim that appears more plausible if one is inclined to consider social constructivist processes as an important determinant of socioeconomic action. Open source also reinforces the appropriation of technology by its users, an effect that is justified in terms of a non-economic version of individualism. Appropriation of technology, open source, collaboration, market activities in the service sector, and their self-reinforcing interdependencies are all elements of how DEs are defined, and in particular DBEs.

In this manner, a number of interconnected assumptions, theories, and observations can be shown to support *some* of the DE hypotheses. It is interesting to note that the 'storyline' above did not touch at all on the distributed architecture hypothesis. To justify it more elements have to be brought in, as the figure shows. Thus, the scenario as described in the preceding paragraph could correspond to an open source, collaboratively built, *centralized* infrastructure for the support of Web services in the knowledge economy, with many of the characteristics that the DE approach considers desirable and beneficial to sustainable development.

A point that would be difficult to prove, however, is that the absence of a distributed architecture, or of any one of the assumptions, would not be 'innovative' enough and somehow would not be sufficient to 'guarantee' sustainable socioeconomic development. Much more research, over time and in different regional contexts, will be needed to bring the theory anywhere close to demonstrating such a strong claim. More importantly, no such proof may be achievable – or even desirable. In the meantime, a useful course of action has been to attempt to group the hypotheses and the arguments in ways that are empirically measurable and ultimately verifiable. In so doing, the intent has been to 'recruit' policy-making as an additional *applied* research dimension, to support the parallel *theoretical* and *empirical* efforts. Having presented the theoretical perspective, the rest of the chapter is concerned with balancing the empirical research results from the region of Morón, near Buenos Aires, with a policy analysis methodology in support of applied regional development policy design and deployment.

The arguments presented so far are not new to development discussions. In fact, if the node 'Digital Business Ecosystem' is deleted from Figure 7.4, and if all the arrows that point to it point instead to the desired objective of sustainable socioeconomic development (light grey box), nothing in the arguments presented would change. In other words, the concept of a DE, or a DBE, is nothing more than a particular way to organize and rationalize a set of assumptions, theories, observations, and hypotheses whose relevance, individually or in other combinations, to innovation and development themes is already well-established. Let us therefore use the term 'digital ecosystem' or 'digital business ecosystem' as a convenient shorthand for a particular way to organize a socio-technical-economic system combined with the context-dependent and multi-stakeholder process to create it. Such a shorthand might acquire greater weight if the DE approach is attempted over many years and in many locations, so as to double-check and verify – or falsify – the many claims and choices made in its theoretical rationalization and in its practical implementation. This would demonstrate that indeed this particular set of hypotheses is needed – and also what happens when some of the hypotheses are not applied.

The rest of this chapter discusses how the problem of integrating ICTs into socioeconomic development policies can be operationalized in practical terms. The

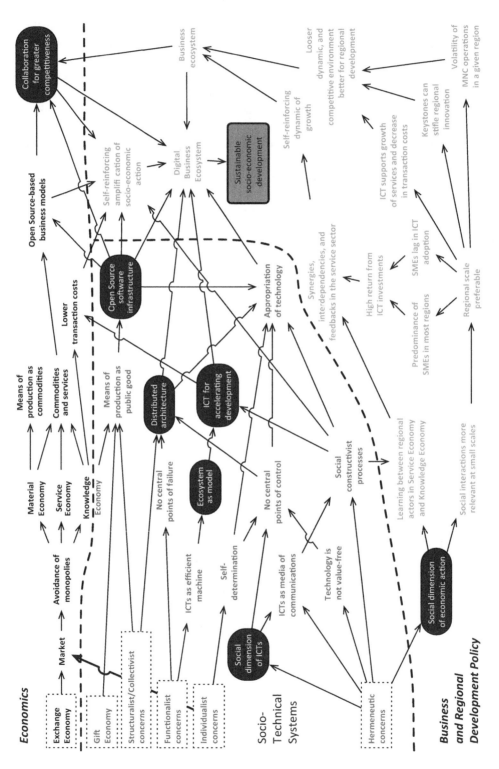

Figure 7.4 Exploring the implications of the DE backbone with a logical-semantic process model

perspective is mainly analytical and leads to a policy analysis visualization tool that can be utilized in the context of policy-making and implementation. The empirical case study discussed necessarily carries some methodological implications. Even more importantly, it brought into greater focus important determinants not only for the characterization of a region's readiness for DE adoption in development contexts, but also for the operationalization of policy interventions, which are discussed in the last main section of the chapter.

REGIONAL MATURITY GRADE AND DE IMPACT INDEX

Different deployment experiences of DEs in the European context revealed the need for a methodology for planning and implementing DEs that resulted in a set of metrics for estimating the 'maturity grade' of localities seeking to deploy a DE, and the need for an impact index for understanding the long-term implications of the dynamics of its implementation

The Regional Maturity Grade (RMG) or Territorial Maturity Grade (TMG) served as a tool for regional analysis. The tool was used to describe a given territory from a socioeconomic point of view by measuring the dynamics and modifications resulting from a development intervention. The RMG is useful for understanding the regional background and it has usually been applied within feasibility studies for the deployment of a DE (Passani and Giorgetti, 2009). The RMG function is composed of three key elements: Social Capital (SC), Innovation Capacity (IC) and the relation between SMEs and ICTs (ICT). Its weaknesses are related to its descriptive nature and to the fact that it does not allow for the analysis of feedbacks emerging from the implementation of a given set of policies.

Figure 7.5, on the next page, shows how the DE hypotheses map to the elements of the RMG function. The two-headed arrows mean that the hypotheses and the regional policy indicators reinforce each other. The 6th hypothesis 'Ecosystem as model', which underpins DE research in bio-computing, is connected with an arrow that points towards the regional indicators only since, if it is successfully demonstrated, it was always only expected to increase the functional properties of the software. In other words, it is equivalent to a new release of the technology towards something that is more efficient, more reliable, etc. However, whereas the other hypotheses have been substantiated to varying degrees by DE research as well as by many other development and innovation studies, the sixth hypothesis has not been proven yet, so the arrow is shown with a dotted line.

As DE research evolved there was an increasing interest from policy-makers and researchers in understanding the socioeconomic impact of DEs. An impact index of DE deployments was therefore defined (Van Egeraat et al. 2008) as an aggregate composite indicator. A multiple-account Cost-Benefit Analysis (CBA) global methodological approach was used. Four evaluation accounts were defined in order to provide an overall assessment related to DE deployment: Financial, User/Consumer, Economic Development and Social. The framework did not consider any *ex ante* impact assessments, *ex ante* evaluation, or progress evaluation. This turned out to be a limitation when trying its implementation, especially since no real and complete cases of deployment existed for its full validation.

This conceptual framework then raised the question on how could a Latin American region be situated in this framework and theoretically and empirically be compared *ex ante* to any European deployment case in terms of readiness and possibility of

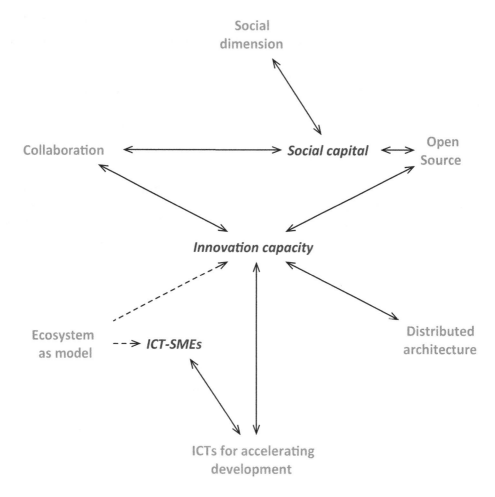

Figure 7.5   Mapping the DE hypotheses to the RMG indicators

successful deployment, given the considerable structural differences in the two regions. This stimulated a debate on the role of collaboration among regional socioeconomic stakeholders in Latin America, on linkages and on their impact on innovation activities, as well as on the role of intermediate institutions in speeding up innovation processes. The problems mentioned regarding different scales and absence or inadequacy of certain issues motivated the introduction of new concepts related to collaboration networks that went further than the triad of innovation capacity, social capital, and ICT-SMEs relationships as initially introduced in the RMG. For instance the connectivity level of the firms and their absorption capacities were introduced (Yoguel et al. 2009, Cohen and Levinthal, 1989, Powell et al. 1996, OECD 2001, and Van Egeraat et al. 2008).

Building on the above rationalization and evolution of methodologies, therefore, this chapter proposes a new methodological framework that integrates concepts related to ICT adoption, connectivity and absorption capacities and recognizes the strong influence of social capital over these, particularly on innovation activities that lead to development. To link the new ideas to the RMG perspective, Figure 7.6 shows a similar comparison to the

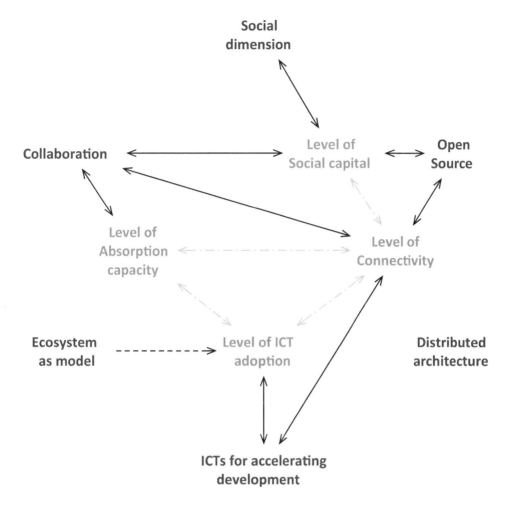

Figure 7.6 Mapping the DE hypotheses to the new indicators

DE hypotheses, where feedbacks between the new indicators are also shown (Yoguel et al. 2009, Antonelli 2008). Whereas most of these feedbacks are fairly self-evident (e.g. social capital reinforces connectivity, and vice versa), the feedbacks between (a) ICT adoption and connectivity and (b) absorption capacity and connectivity are not so straightforward. This can be explained through Figure 7.6, if it is seen as reflecting the characteristics of a specific region or territory.

First, the technocentric assumption that the introduction of ICTs leads to greater connectivity is avoided. ICTs can certainly facilitate and accelerate the circulation of knowledge, but only when some social, communication, or collaboration ties already exist. If there is a very low level of connectivity not only should the ICT adoption-connectivity arrow disappear, but the connectivity dimension should disappear too. Thus, whereas at a theoretical level it can be said that the relation exists, at an empirical level this relation is dependent on the presence of a certain level of development of both dimensions in a given context; if either one is really low, the relationship may disappear. The same argument applies to the relationship between absorption capacities and connectivity; however, in this case empirical evidence shows that a minimum level of absorption capacities is required to both generate linkages and to be considered as an 'attractive' organization to connect with (Erbes, Robert and Yoguel 2010).

The next section describes a methodological tool oriented towards the mapping, evaluation and modification of scenarios related to ICT adoption processes among multiple agents, while preparing the ground for a discussion of how some of the hypotheses of this methodology could be tested in the Argentinian context.

Measuring Collaboration Networks Through DEs in Latin America

A new conceptual framework based on concepts more suitable to international cooperation projects common to the Latin American context has been developed. This framework takes into account the methodological basis for the implementation of development projects such as the '*Marco Lógico*' approach (Camacho et al. 2001). It also situates both previous methods and tools developed in previous research projects (i.e. the RMG and the Digital Ecosystems Impact Index).

The pre-feasibility analysis of a DE implementation in a region relies on the idea that the technology involved in a network is not a mechanism that by itself *generates* innovation and connectivity in firms. The main vision, instead, is that ICTs strengthen and accelerate (catalyse) pre-existing relationships and innovative behaviours, allowing the users of these technologies to enrich their productive activities. This is very important when evaluating the role of ICTs in the implementation of a collaboration network. How does a policy-maker know if a region is prepared to transform technology into a catalyst of a local innovation system? What are the priorities for each region to enforce this process?

The reason for referring to the framework here presented as 'methodological' is that it is concerned with the analysis of policy options and implementations, which necessarily take place over time. Thus, the policy analysis tool to be described below is meant to be used as part of a continuous 'analysis-intervention-analysis' feedback loop. The effect of the policies on a particular region can thus be tracked by seeing how the indicators behave over time, as represented visually by the tool. As a consequence, this approach has strong methodological implications for data gathering and coordination of policies in ways that can be easily monitored. This chapter does not go as far as developing these practical aspects. Rather, it explores the plausibility of such a policy analysis tool by building on the theoretical perspective just described and on the empirical data from the Morón case study. The effectiveness of the tool will need to be tested in future research and applied work.

The methodological framework developed is based on four dimensions that summarize what the authors consider the main aspects of ICTs as a networking and innovation accelerator in a specific context: the levels of absorption capacities, connectivity, ICT adoption and social capital.

ABSORPTION CAPACITIES

Absorption capacities are usually defined (Yoguel et al. 2009) as the ability of given actors to recognize external information, assimilate it, and apply it within their system. These capacities are not just related to the access to knowledge and information, but also to the ability to identify useful knowledge and to generate new knowledge. Absorption capacities are not developed automatically. They require time and the development of previous competencies, and are consequently influenced by the framework conditions.

The absorption capacity dimension concentrates indicators of those aspects of the local environment that allow agents to understand and modify their context, such as innovation capacities, human resources qualifications and characteristics, and quality management of firms and organizations, among others. Absorption capacities are key for firms and organizations in understanding their environment. This understanding makes them able to achieve their objectives more efficiently. This set of indicators could point out 'innovation-based agents', able to develop learning processes under dynamic and adaptive strategies, by analysing their context. On the other hand, very low absorption capacities will show firms with lack of strategy, with no interest in innovation activities and without qualifications.

CONNECTIVITY

This axis is related to the potential of the relevant stakeholders in the region to establish relationships and linkages with other relevant stakeholders (internal or external to the region). As was the case for the absorption capacities axis, 'connectivity' is not just the simple interaction with other agents, but rather selected exchanges and the ability to prioritize relationships according to the *use* and *utility* that these could give to the (network of) stakeholders.

This axis takes into account not only firm-to-firm linkages, but also institutional and organizational relationships. Also, it is interesting to underline that linkages could be analysed beyond the dual indicator based on the existence/absence of the relationship, for example considering the quality or the impact of that interaction.

Vessuri (2003) indicates that there is a strong relationship between absorption capacities and connectivity, since the good development of the former in many cases could enrich and empower the frequency and quality on the latter, and vice versa. Other approaches in the same direction can be found in Erbes et al. (2010) and Antonelli (2008). In the particular case of Morón, however, the analysis of the data collected showed interesting issues that should be taken into account in order to achieve a thorough understanding of the connectivity level in organizations, especially if the intention is to compare them with absorption capacities (Barletta, Kataishi and Yoguel 2010), ICT adoption and social capital indicators.

ICT ADOPTION

ICT adoption takes the form of a prerequisite for establishing collaboration networks among enterprises through DEs. Although it is a prerequisite, this approach to development is not technocentric, since the success relies on the capacities of the region of reference and its actors/agents. Thus, through DEs technology plays a catalysing role of dynamic cooperation processes highly influenced by the interaction of absorption capacities, connectivity and social capital.

This variable is oriented to measure the existence and use of different technologies related to information and communication, such as basic broadband infrastructure diffusion and its characteristics, and more complex ones, such as the properties of ICT use in production processes among enterprises.

It is interesting to note that these three dimensions could be analysed separately but, because of the dynamics of their interaction, it is more useful and informative to analyse them jointly. This is particularly important when evaluating policies related to the adoption of new technologies. For instance, first approaches to supporting ICT use in developing countries only considered the ICT adoption dimension, leaving behind both, connectivity and absorption capacities. The result is an increase in the *stock* of available technology, but without business and networking enablers, due to the lack of pre-existing absorption capacities (i.e. firms that do not understand the benefits of ICT use) and connectivity (very weak relationships and links between firms and between these and support institutions and organizations).

SOCIAL CAPITAL

DE research has increasingly recognized social factors as central to the competitive challenges of the knowledge-based economy (Van Egeraat et al. 2008: 11–12, 36–7, 57–9 and 63–4). The density and structure of social networks is crucial for acquiring democratic organization in a society, and thus also in business interactions. The OECD (2001) defines social capital as '*networks together with shared norms, values and understanding that facilitate cooperation within or among groups*'. Following Steinmueller (2004), 'social capital' considers formal organizations in society and social networks, including 'communities of practice'. The concept of 'social capital' is thus central for a complete analysis of collaboration networks for innovation.

Under this conceptual framework, a region (political-geographical concept) is understood as a localized system of interaction in which networks of stakeholders play a central role. This recognition supports the analysis of the role of social capital and knowledge exchange as relevant elements for local innovation. Generation and accumulation of social capital is mostly based on trust and made possible as actors share norms, values and understanding (Bruno et al. 2008). The effect of higher social capital tends to accelerate the convergence of a successful implementation of ICTs in boosting regional development. A low level of social capital represents an obstacle in achieving this objective.

The above discussion can be represented graphically as shown in Figure 7.7. Each of the axes, or determinants described above, corresponds to one of the circles in the figure. The arrows try to express a quantitative maximization exercise, as will be discussed in Section 5. The graph shows that in the maximization of the three axes (i.e. where the three circles overlap) there is a 'successful' area related to the deployment of DEs for innovation in a given region. As will be discussed below, this framework allows the graphical identification of the stakeholders studied (i.e. enterprises) in the region, as well as their characterization. The equilibrium, or 'success area', is attained when most of the enterprises in the region are located at the intersection of the three axes or, in other words, where the values of the characteristics/axes are at their maximum.

Figure 7.7 would be better represented in a three-dimensional way (this is why social capital is shown geometrically as a cylinder). For this effect, social capital would act as an 'elevator' for the maximization process of the three axes. For example, a strong social capital in the region would 'push up' the other three indicators along the three axes, and

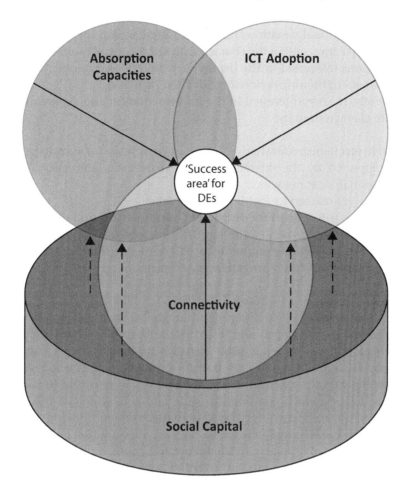

Figure 7.7   Determinants of the 'successful' deployment of collaboration networks through DEs

thus accelerate reaching maximum values in each axis. The opposite would happen with a low level or weak social capital.

The character of the proposed visualization tool also allows comparing relatively different regions and countries, since the framework conditions remain 'internalized' and aggregated in the measurement of the different determinants, thus enabling the formulation of tailored policy options.

DEs for Socioeconomic Development: The Case of Morón, Argentina

CONTEXT AND METHODOLOGY

The findings and results on deployment plans at the European level confirmed that there are important differences in regional needs, requirements and opportunities for

DEs. Typically, the regional variations reflect the differences in innovation capacities, in enterprises' ICT capacities, and in the characteristics of the social capital of a given region. Despite this, regions interested in the deployment of DEs are typically characterized by their support for strengthening regional innovation capacities.

More precisely, regions interested in the implementation and deployment of Digital Ecosystems are characterized by:

- an interest in mechanisms for sharing and for open diffusion of knowledge within local clusters, supported by the interaction and Europe-wide/international cooperation between regional/local networks;
- a need for easy-to-use services with high user value;
- a shared interest and support for distributed infrastructures and Open Source;
- an interest in the promotion of the knowledge 'embedded' within local territories, and the recognition of the importance of knowledge-sharing and best practices through regional innovation programmes and plans.

One of the core objectives of DE research is thus to provide regional stakeholders with new approaches and strategies for fostering sustainable regional development.

After being studied, developed and tested in the European Union, DE research was further extended to Latin America. The activities undertaken were mainly oriented towards partnership building, knowledge transfer and sharing of experiences. The central focus of the activities is the extension of existing European networks to Latin American and Caribbean (LAC) research communities. The aim is to stimulate the collaboration between communities and networks engaged in research on multidisciplinary approaches concerned with the role ICTs and new media have on the evolution and dynamics of the Information and Knowledge Society in the European Union and LAC countries.

One pilot case study was planned in Argentina, province of Buenos Aires, and more specifically in the city of Morón; with applicability to the metalworking sector. When meeting policy-makers and researchers of the region, and presenting the 'European' methods for planning the deployment of DEs and assessing/evaluating their implementation, it was revealed that these ideas were rather ahead of applicability as no real use cases were already taking place, and thus no real benchmark case (or zero case) existed.

Thus, the first step was the compilation and generation of data for the case of Morón. For this, different stages of research were conducted in order to determine the characteristics of the enterprises and institutions in the region, among which three were of particular importance: the search for secondary data for the characterization of the region of analysis; the use of specific data generated in previous projects by the Universidad Nacional de General Sarmiento (UNGS) research team; and the planning and execution of different fieldwork surveys in order to complete the gathering of key data categories. This work was conducted with the objective of achieving comparability of the different regional cases (i.e. when comparing Latin American and European regions).

The process of data collection was based on two main sources. Firstly, the official data generated locally by the Municipality of Morón; secondly, the data published about the region in other research projects (i.e. a project that studied 50 enterprises in the metalworking sector in the region, and a second one that studied 67 enterprises in the region across different sectors that allowed the socioeconomic characterization of the region and the elaboration of a database of 90 enterprises). Additionally, several research projects developed by UNGS research teams were studied, particularly one study focusing on the characterization of different organizations in the region (with 15 in-depth interviews with NGOs' leaders). Finally, two fieldwork studies were developed oriented towards the institutional mapping of the region: one focusing on the institutional networks, and the second focusing on the production networks of the region.

In order to obtain a good understanding of the capacities, linkages and objectives of the different institutions in Morón, 22 in-depth interviews were conducted with leaders and key players of different organizations; notably the Municipality (and those areas of the administration linked to the production sector), business organizations (chambers of commerce and technology centres), knowledge centres (universities and technical schools) and social organizations (NGOs, cultural centres). In addition, further qualitative research was conducted (through in-depth interviews) in five enterprises that were identified as outliers in the engagement of R&D activities, in order to identify their main problems and challenges when developing R&D. Based on the data analysis, a study on the competences of firms and institutions was developed, including an analysis of the networks and the impact of these linkages on the adoption of ICTs.

The following sections present a general description of the region and the findings of the different analyses undertaken.

GENERAL CHARACTERISTICS OF THE MORÓN REGION AND ITS ENTERPRISES

Morón is located on the west side of the Argentinian capital of Buenos Aires. The area is characterized by having experienced significant economic growth in the 1940s, based on a strong development of the manufacturing industry as a consequence of different national policies. The metalworking sector and the textile industry are historically important for the west region of Buenos Aires (Llach and Gerchunoff 1998). Morón concentrates around 900 manufacturing enterprises, of which 60 per cent are in the manufacturing of machines, food and textile industries (INDEC 2010), and 350 institutions, including those related to social care and those supporting the manufacturing sector (Municipio de Morón 2008).

Enterprises in Morón are relatively small (Audrestch et al. 2009). 86 per cent of the enterprises surveyed had less than 150 employees and they have on average 38 employees.[9] In terms of sales, the annual average is of 10.2 million Argentinian pesos, or US$2 million per year. 40 per cent of all enterprises are family businesses, with just one business unit for 98 per cent of the cases. Only 5 per cent of all enterprises receive foreign capital investment. In terms of production practices, only the 35 per cent of all enterprises has a certification on a quality norm (i.e. ISO 9000), which shows a lack of formality of production practices. About 98 per cent of firms have at least a computer, while 95 per cent of these firms have Internet access. The commercial use of these technologies remains limited: only 2 per cent of enterprises engaged in e-commerce between 2007 and 2008.[10]

The enterprises with the best performance indicators are those of the metalworking sector. The sector includes activities related to the production, modification and repair of mechanical components. The food industry and the textile industry remain important to the region but were relatively less present in the sample studied.

---

9   Based on a fieldwork study by UNGS undertaken in 2007–2008 (Kataishi et al. 2008, Borello et al. 2008).

10   Based on a fieldwork study by UNGS undertaken in 2007–2008 (ibid.).

THE METALWORKING SECTOR'S ENTERPRISES IN MORÓN

When analysing enterprises in the metalworking sector, 26 per cent of all enterprises produce auto parts; 29 per cent produce capital goods; while the rest pertain to the classification of 'other metalworking producers', including enterprises offering services.[11] Enterprises also diverge in the degree of differentiation of the products they offer: 51 per cent of enterprises produce differentiated products, 16 per cent offer products that could be considered as 'commodities', and about 30 per cent produce intermediate products.[12] Competences in firms are generally low, with levels of training, R&D, and work organization practices that promote knowledge circulation almost equal to zero. About half of all enterprises have obtained a certification in support of quality assurance policies. With respect to strategies, the analysis shows that 70 per cent of firms are implementing or had implemented strategies supporting the investment in physical equipment (69 per cent) and other strategies related to the increase of the value added of products (67 per cent). There are also improvements related to the layout of products and an increase of specialization of products where firms can acquire competitive advantages (60 per cent of all firms). This latter strategy is more common in smaller firms.

CONNECTIVITY OF ENTERPRISES

The first stage of the empirical analysis was the construction of the commercial networks. Understanding this connectivity is particularly relevant for DE research because of the importance that networks have in DEs deployment, and because commercial networks in the private sector refer to the transaction of products and services between agents in the network. The understanding of commercial networks provides valuable information related to the construction and characterization of knowledge networks.

The survey questionnaires were designed to allow the construction of linkages arising from the commercial networks. This included questions related to innovation strategies, the connectivity of agents, and the acquired capacities for the implementation of innovation practices in firms. Each surveyed enterprise was questioned on their five main clients and suppliers, out of a network of 787 enterprises. This network is shown in Figure 7.8.

Figure 7.6 shows the commercial networks of firms in Morón. Each of the circles (vertex and nodes) represents an enterprise, while each line shows a linkage between the firms. The diameter of each vertex is associated to the number of linkages that a given enterprise has with other agents. Each colour shows the area where the activity takes place (red, for Morón and its area of influence; green, for the federal capital; and yellow, for the rest of Argentina). All the firms that were not linked to any other firm were eliminated from the analysis.

The methodology used for further analysis consisted in cleaning up the network, keeping only those nodes with the highest number of linkages. The criterion used was the 'degree of the linkages', defined as the number of linkages 'owned' by each vertex. So if a given vertex has two linkages with other agents, the referenced agent would be of 'second degree'. From the selection of enterprises/nodes of a degree greater or equal to 2,

---

11   Data produced through fieldwork in Morón.

12   Thanks to José Parra (IDEB Morón) and Javier Terrani (Municipality of Morón) for their support in the classification of firms by degree of product differentiation.

the configuration of the network changed considerably, and notably eliminating the 'tree patterns', and revealing a rather simple network with non-complex commercial linkages (see i.e. Giuliani 2004, and Giuliani and Bell 2004 for similar studies on knowledge-based networks). For further methodological discussions about this survey, an in-depth analysis can be found in Barletta, Kataishi and Yoguel (2010).

Figure 7.8   Commercial network of enterprises in Morón, different sectors

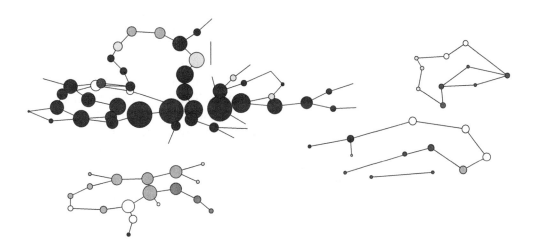

Figure 7.9   Sectoral networks, enterprises with more than one commercial link

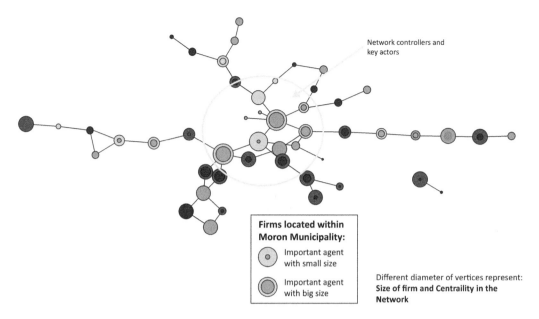

Figure 7.10 The metalworking sector network

Figure 7.9 shows the 'clean' network. Four different networks emerged, represented as four different groups. These groups match the most important sectors of the region in terms of employment. The most complex, in red, represents the metalworking sector. The other networks, not analysed in this study because of their relatively small importance, are those of the food industry (green) and the textile industry (two networks, in violet).

The main difference between Figure 7.8 and Figure 7.9 is that in the latter the diameter of each of the vertices is based on the betweeness index.[13] This index is associated with each vertex, and it takes a greater value when an agent (node) in the network allows other vertices to link with key sections or key players in the network. This allows the identification of gatekeepers in the network.

The metalworking sector network was further shortened following criteria of data availability and relevance,[14] resulting in the network presented in Figure 7.10, which is the object of analysis of this chapter.

The metalworking sector network is composed of 33 enterprises: 26 of them in the Morón area (10 from Morón, 12 from Haedo and 4 from El Palomar), while the other 7 enterprises are from the area of influence of the Morón. The colour of each vertex in the Figure shows the geographical location of each enterprise (yellow for the Morón area and the area of influence, grey for the federal capital and the rest of the country). This shows that the core of the system and its gatekeepers are located in the Morón area.

This shows the great potentialities for public interventions at the local level, particularly those related to the support for greater connectivity among agents. The local government as well as other relevant institutions could identify the main actors and stakeholders in

---

13   See Leydesdorff et al. 2009.

14   Two nodes were eliminated from the network, both supermarkets, clients of two enterprises in the metalworking industry.

the region and involve them in local policies for increasing the connectivity of economic actors.

INSTITUTIONAL NETWORKS

According to official data, there are 350 institutions in the Morón area (Municipio de Morón 2008). Two fieldwork studies were undertaken for the collection of primary data of 37 of these institutions, including those of most relevance for the economic activities of the region, other key areas of priority for the Municipality, and other social activities (i.e. NGOs).

In general, the institutional network of Morón is characterized by having low capacities in terms of the availability of human resources (between three to six persons), and low use of ICTs (used mainly for administrative purposes or basic use, such as Internet and communication through email). The exceptions of this characterization are the Municipality and the universities of the region.

With respect to the qualification of human resources, most of the employees have basic secondary education, while the most qualified personnel take part in the legal and accounting activities of the institutions. The access to positions that involve strategic decision-making responsibilities is limited to people having tacit linkages, or based on personal linkages with other employees of the institution.

CONNECTIVITY OF INSTITUTIONS

In order to analyse the institutions at the local level, two main groups were selected: social organizations, and organizations related to the economic activities of the region. The objective of including social organizations was to understand the way these were structured as well as to understand the characteristics of the social capital in the region.

Following the same methodological process as for the case of the industrial networks, the complete network composed of 147 institutions is first presented in Figure 7.11; Figure 7.12 then shows the network of *second degree*, distinguished by the centrality degree and the type of institution. Two main actors emerged from the bottom part of the figure. These were the IDEB Centre and the Area for Local Development (SDEL) of the Municipality, which could potentially play the role of regional catalysts.

The IDEB Centre of Morón is an NGO, that engages and links all the socioeconomic local actors that work for the development of SMEs in the region. The Centre is in charge of offering services and conducting actions in the support of the creation of new SMEs in industry, trade, services and any other production sector that implement their activities at the local level. In order to carry this mandate, IDEB has a double role. Firstly, it is a place for the integration and sharing of local development projects; and secondly, it serves as a technical support institution for SMEs at the local level. The Undersecretary's office for Local Economic Development (SDEL) of Morón is in charge of the Directorate for Trade, Industry, Promotion of Exports, Employment, and the Social Economy. The office is in charge of achieving growth in the local and regional economy, promoting local trade, promoting the increase of industrial activities, following and facilitating the exporting activities of enterprises in the

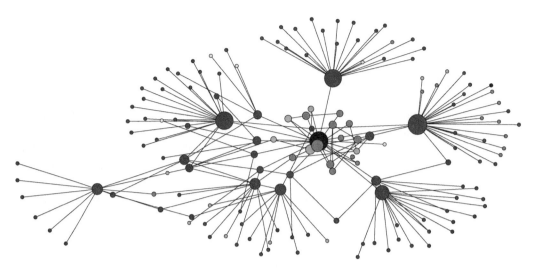

Figure 7.11 Connectivity of institutions in Morón

region, and promoting employment growth. One of the main differences between the IDEB Centre and the SDEL of the Municipality is their structure. The IDEB Centre is a very small organization, composed by a Director and three employees, and supported by a network of 15 consultants that provide the technical support that the Centre offers to enterprises (i.e. training, short courses and technical assistance). In contrast, the SDEL has a more complex structure. It is composed by about 60 people within an organization of 1,800 employees in the local government. The SDEL is structured in three Directorates, which are in charge of the management and coordination of specific projects related to its expertise.

Regarding the competences of the key agents in the network, one important issue is the availability of human resources and the qualifications of these resources in each organization. The IDEB Centre has a resource structure lacking formal specialized qualifications. Despite this, the Director of the Centre has more than 30 years of experience in the implementation of integrated projects that relate the public sector to NGOs and to the business sector. The case of the Municipality of Morón is different, where 90 per cent of all personnel have tertiary education, while the Directors of each of the four Directorates have long experience in the development of government plans in the support of the local industry. The SDEL also studies closely and continuously the characteristics of the local enterprises, including the development of fieldwork studies that help to understand specific demands, weaknesses and strengths of the enterprise sector, with the objective of adapting local policies to a specific group of enterprises (i.e. for providing technical assistance, strengthening the sector or promoting their activities).

In both cases, despite the differences, the institutions have great capacity to diagnose and interpret the business sector. Both institutions have pushed towards interventions based on previous experiences at the local level, by implementing constant monitoring systems and self-evaluation of the activities undertaken.

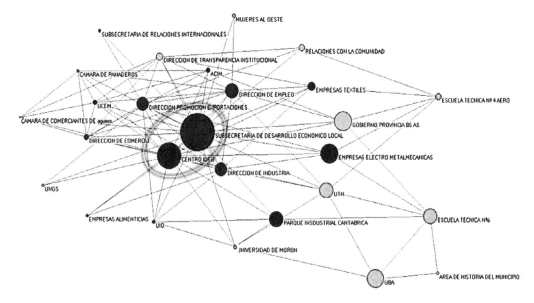

Figure 7.12 Network of second degree of the institutions in Morón

Mapping Complex Socioeconomic Interactions for the Development of Sound Development Policies

The conceptual framework presented in Section 3 is able to map local readiness and the structure of socioeconomic interactions in a given region towards the deployment of DEs. This is possible thanks to a (mathematical) maximization process through the use of several indicators serving as proxy variables for the definition of the main variables of the conceptual framework. The analytical framework is an expressive qualitative tool (3 domains/axes: ICT adoption, connectivity, and absorption capacity, influenced by social capital), as well as a quantitative representation (the triangular coordinates along the same three axes) of data that characterizes well the properties and characteristics of the business and institutional collaboration networks in the region under study. The benefit is the relatively simple way in which these tools can provide a quick graphical overview of the relative positioning of each region studied.

Several secondary and primary sources exist in the EU to approximate quantitatively the axes of the conceptual framework. In Latin America, however, statistical systems are generally less developed, generating comparability problems not only between Latin American countries and the EU, but also amongst Latin American countries. These problems are particularly important when looking at science and technology indicators, use and diffusion of ICTs, and the performance of institutions. Regarding this lack of systemic and periodic official information in many Latin American countries, the main methodological challenges are to generate primary data from specially built case studies and surveys, and to study the availability of secondary sources including those available from other research projects.

MATHEMATICAL CONSIDERATIONS FOR THE POLICY ANALYSIS VISUALIZATION TOOL

Figure 7.13 presents an example of the mapping exercise and characterization of the enterprises in a given region. The original intention was to show the characteristics of a company – or if using aggregate variables of a group of companies, or a region – as a single point in the diagram of the three circles shown in Figure 7.7. This would have provided a clear geometrical visualization of the characteristics of the enterprises in the region relative to DE adoption. However, as Figure 7.13 shows, the information depicted according to the schema of Figure 7.7 is defined in a three-dimensional space (social capital is neglected for a moment). Therefore, the schema shown in Figure 7.7 can only be some kind of projection of the points that appear inside the cube shown in Figure 7.13. In fact, this is precisely the case: the projection is none other than the same system of axes looked at from behind and below the origin, towards the reader and along the long (green) diagonal that joins the origin to the green dot (the vertex of the cube that is closest to the reader in Figure 7.13).

Depicting the state of the object of analysis as a 'geometrical average' in this manner is actually more precisely described as a vector in the three-dimensional space defined by the three characteristic determinants. The dot that is showed in the projected plane of Figure 7.7, therefore, is nothing more than the projection of the tip of such a vector. This fact highlights the drawback of this otherwise very intuitive and expressive representation: all the vectors that fall along the long (green) diagonal mentioned above will be projected to the same point, the origin of the three axes in the projected plane. These vectors correspond to cases where the three characteristic determinants of absorption capacity, connectivity, and ICT adoption have equal numerical values. Thus, plotting single points will not be able to distinguish cases where, for example, all three indicators have maximum (equal) values from cases where the values are near zero (as long as they are still equal).

For the above reason another graphical form was adopted, known as a 'radar chart' (e.g. in Microsoft Excel). This is what is shown on the left side of Figure 7.13. The three points shown inside the cube are mapped to three triangles, obtained simply by joining the three values of the three determinants when drawn on the axes of the three circles. The colours of the triangles correspond to the dots in the cube, to aid the visualization. Each point in the cube, or triangle in the radar chart, represents an enterprise. The green triangle indicates maximum values for all the indicators; the blue triangle indicates a different company, with relatively high values of connectivity and ICT adoption, and low absorption capacity; the red triangle, on the other hand, has relatively high connectivity and absorption capacity, but low ICT adoption.

The average of all the triangles from a given sample of companies for a given region gives an aggregate indicator for the region that is comparable regardless of the differences of the framework conditions (as introduced in Section 3). In other words, it presents macroscopic information from the aggregation of microscopic information. Equally, it shows information from a microeconomics perspective (i.e. by looking at individual enterprises), and helps in deducing corresponding macroeconomic information (i.e. by looking at the relative position of the object of analysis), which can inform policy-makers in relation to innovation and development policies.

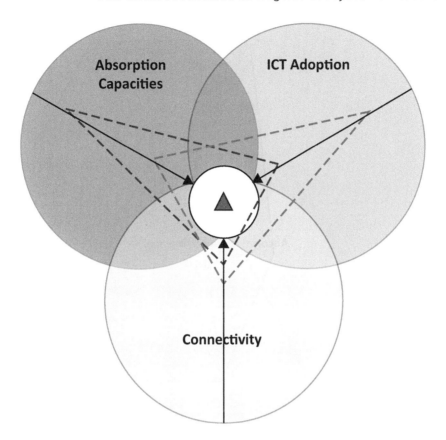

Figure 7.13 Mapping the characteristics of a set of enterprises in a given region

Whereas the above depiction is useful and informative, it has one drawback in that it misses one of the intentions of Figure 7.7 to show maximum readiness for DE adoption at the *centre* of the diagram, i.e. at the intersection of the three axes. Fortunately this can be remedied with a simple variable transformation, as follows. First let us introduce a few definitions:

a = absorption capacity level
c = connectivity level
i = ICT adoption level

A = maximum absorption capacity level for a give sample of companies
C = maximum connectivity level for a given sample of companies
I = maximum ICT adoption level for a given sample of companies

a_j = absorption capacity level of company j
c_j = connectivity level of company j
i_j = ICT adoption level of company j

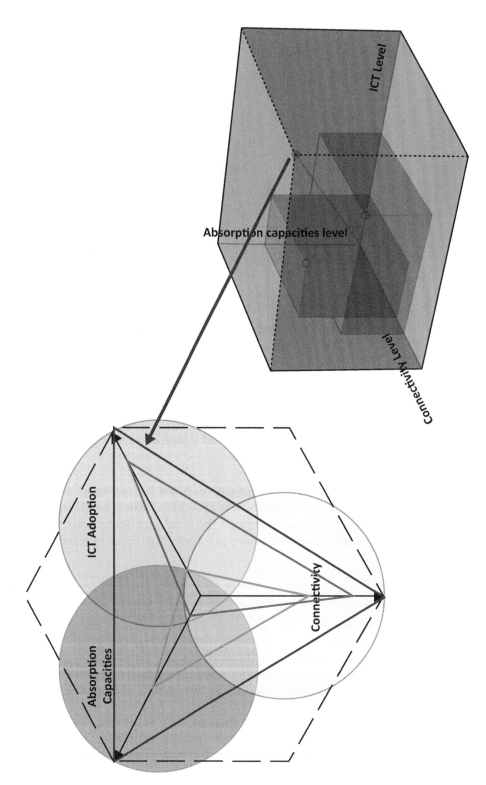

Figure 7.14 Policy analysis visualization tool (using inverted variables)

Now new 'starred' normalized variables are defined, to obtain

$$a_j = (A - a_j) / A = 1 - a_j / A$$
$$c_j = (C - c_j) / C = 1 - c_j / C$$
$$i_j = (I - i_j) / C = 1 - i_j / A$$

In terms of the new variables the representation of the determinants behaves as desired, with smaller triangles approaching the centre indicating *greater* DE adoption readiness, as shown in Figure 7.14. This figure shows the same three cases above, where the triangles are drawn using dotted lines in order to highlight that they correspond to starred variables. The large green triangle of Figure 7.13 has been mapped to a point at the origin in Figure 7.14, shown as a small solid green triangle.

MAPPING THE MORÓN DATA ONTO THE POLICY ANALYSIS VISUALIZATION TOOL

In the previous section it is automatically assumed that normalized variables should be used. This is a consequence of the fact that the quantification and mapping of real data presents some very difficult challenges.[15] It is possible to build quantitative values for absorption capacity, connectivity and ICT adoption for each firm, but the problem is the normalization: how can values for the same indicator be compared for different companies, when the activities of these companies that contribute to the indicator could be different? Even more complex is a more general comparison with other experiences and regions (i.e. in different parts of the world). To propose an answer to these questions first it is needed to define indicators that are both simple and expressive.

The quantification used depends on YES/NO responses to a set of questions that were put to the companies analysed, as follows:

- Absorption capacity
  - Firms that have some level of complexity in their labour organization (i.e. rotation, multitask);
  - more than 10 per cent of their personnel is professional (graduates and postgraduates);
  - formal R&D department;
  - did training activities during the last year;
  - have a quality insurance policy.
- Connectivity
  - Firms that in the last two years were connected with other firms, science and technology institutions, or the local government with one or more than one specific objectives (related to innovation activities).
- ICT Adoption
  ICT adoption is the average result of eight dimensions:
  - availability of equipment (company has at least one computer);
  - has a maintenance area for their information system;

---

15   The discussion in this section draws on Barletta, Cohan and Kataishi (2009).

 – modernity of the equipment (the average computer availability is higher than or equal to a PIV or equivalent with 1GB of RAM);
 – Internet availability;
 – gained access to new clients through ICT use;
 – formation management system based on ICTs (average per cent of tasks digitized and average per cent of information in digital format);
 – mean of employees that have access to ICT use;
 – positive effects of ICT on firm's organization (considering firms that declared that ICT has a positive impact on performance regarding ICT use in information transmission, ICT use to improve the interactions among members of the corporation, ICT use in supervision tasks, production area ICT integration and non-production areas ICT integration);
 – e-commerce (buy and sell in national and international operations).

If the majority of the answers to these individual components were considered to be above a subjectively estimated threshold, the corresponding indicator for that particular company was set to 'high', quantified as 1.0. Otherwise it was set to 'low', quantified as 0.0. The crudeness of this discretization criterion is compensated by the generality of the resulting aggregate indicator, which enables comparisons between different regions. For each indicator, the aggregate is simply the fraction of firms that scored 'high', expressed as a percentage. The results of this analysis for Morón were:

absorption capacity:	51.6 per cent
connectivity:	45.4 per cent
ICT adoption:	41.2 per cent

There was no attempt to quantify social capital. These values are plotted in Figure 7.15 on a reverse radar graph, following the convention of Figure 7.14. The size of the circle of 'DE readiness' in Figure 7.15 is purely speculative.

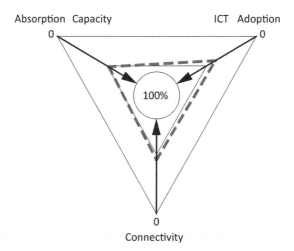

Figure 7.15 Aggregate DE readiness indicators for Morón (using inverted variables)

It is impossible to define or specify the 'correct' absolute values of the components of the indicators. Thus the graphs that can be drawn with this methodology necessarily can only provide relative comparisons. These can still be very useful, however, and can be applied at different scales. If each indicator ranges over a set of possible values, even if these are arbitrary as long as the same quantification criteria for that indicator are applied across the sample the data could still be normalized, which would make the tool an essence a visualization of a benchmark analysis. At a larger scale, the data from different regions, obtained in the same way, could be very fruitfully compared on the same graph.

POLICY MIXES FOR ENTERPRISES AND REGIONS

The policy analysis tool presented above should be complemented with a set of policy actions in relation to the stages of the deployment process of a DE. The objective of this section is to describe the connections between the visualization tool presented and specific policy actions that would be able to modify the characteristics of the business sector in a given region.

Being able to map enterprises in the way described above also has strong implications in terms of policy-making and particularly in terms of the implementation of different policy mixes in the regions of analysis, with the aim of building collaboration networks for innovation and sustainable socioeconomic development through DEs. Figure 7.16 represents graphically the three dimensions that have been described before together with the representation of hypothetical enterprises as dotted triangles. This is shown together with sets of different possible policy mixes applicable to each possible scenario in a given region.

The blue triangle is an example of a case where enterprises are not connected, but show both ICT adoption and absorption capacities of higher-to-medium levels. Secondly, the red triangle shows an example of an enterprise with no absorption capacities, but that is highly connected to the production and institutional systems in the region, together with a significant use of ICTs. Finally, the yellow triangle is an example of an enterprise with no use of ICTs but with good levels of absorption capacities and connectivity. The bright green triangle has intermediate levels of all three variables, similar to the aggregated Morón case, and the dark green triangle at the centre again corresponds to companies that have high levels of all three (where 'high' must necessarily rely on some benchmark, as explained).

For enterprises represented by the blue, red, and yellow triangles different combinations of policies are required, as indicated in the figure. It is important to underline the main steps that lead to the policy-making focus of this section. Figures 7.13 and 7.14 showed the importance of mapping the interactions in 3D (three perpendicular axes) to a 2D representation (three axes within circles). Following this methodology, the feasibility studies would try to map the conditions in which the agents' actions take place for each configuration of a given enterprise, in order to identify behavioural-based clusters. It is expected that relatively homogeneous characteristics among firms will be shown, together with some outlier cases that will have to be analysed in isolation. This will end in a similar representation to the one shown in Figure 7.16, showing firms positioned following the results of the analysis of the characteristics of the determinants shown in Figure 7.7, enabling the diagnosis of the situation of a given region as an aggregate if benchmarked with other regions.

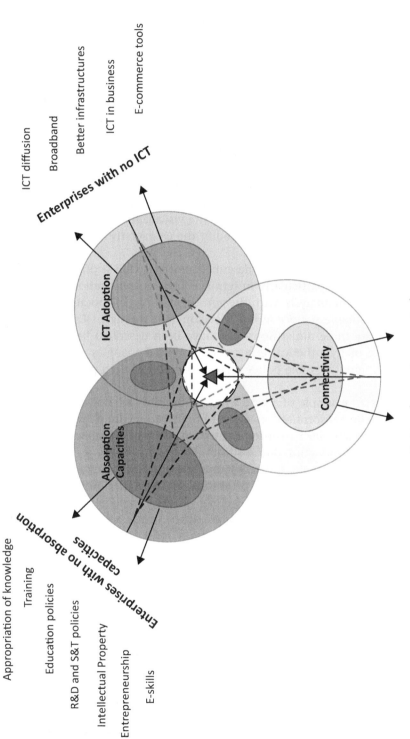

Figure 7.16 Policy mixes for enterprises and regions (dotted triangles are possible representative cases of companies or regions, individual or averages)

As is well known, the elaboration of policy mixes is not an easy task, especially in developing countries (Vessuri 2003), since it implies several sets of issues that affect not only the elaboration of policies per se but also the effectiveness of interventions given the institutional and resource-related limitations as framework conditions triggering innovation. Despite this, this proposal is focused on the development of policies oriented towards specific issues that the methodological process itself is meant to detect.

Policies can be developed by relying on different criteria. Two of them are of interest for this chapter. On the one hand, the mechanisms that may drive policy-making processes can be based on the average position of firms shown in Figure 7.16. On the other hand, policies could be oriented to benefit a given critical group characterized by the lack of one or more attributes (e.g. a group of enterprises with no connectivity). The area where the majority of firms are positioned determines the policy priorities. The lack of some elements implies a relatively precise set of policies aimed at modifying the positioning of firms according to different strategic objectives and priorities (i.e. the shapes of the triangles characterizing the firms) as shown in Figure 7.16.

For example, if the results of a given study were to show that most of the 'agents' are similar to the blue triangle, actions should then be oriented to stimulate connectivity among firms and between firms and institutions. Having acknowledged this, there would be several sets of policy practices available for governments to implement and promote, such as fiscal incentives for collaboration, promotion of linkages among components of the local innovation system, PPP-oriented policies, etc. The same logic can be applied to other possible situations derived from the figure: concentration of firms similar to the red triangle implies that policies should be oriented to enforce firms' capacities. If the firms were similar to the yellow triangle, the need for implementing efforts towards ICT adoption and use would be revealed. The possible policy-making actions are determined by the underdevelopment and under-representation of the dimensions considered. It is also possible to find characterizations where interventions on more than one circle are needed.

One last thing to consider is the relative importance of each dimension and of its practical implications (absorption capacities, connectivity and ICT adoption). Traditional interventions in developing countries are normally focused on the bottom and left-hand side of Figure 7.16, concerning connectivity issues but especially absorption capacities in enterprises.

In comparison, ICT-related deficiencies are usually associated with resource-driven polices, as the main goal is to 'connect' these technologies to users or firms, and the first step usually consists in the acquisition of the technology itself, which can be done for example through financial assistance and support. Connectivity and absorption capacities are more complex issues that would probably require much more than only financial resources, but rather medium- and long-term strategic approaches to policy-making (i.e. education and entrepreneurship policies; technology transfer; collaboration of the triple helix). From this perspective, the key element that emerges from this complex system appears to be the absorption capacities of agents (Yoguel et al. 2009). Nevertheless, the modification of each determinant is very much related to complementary development policies to innovation that involve education, science and technology and socioeconomic transformation, among others.

As mentioned above, the proposed methodological framework has the ability to give a macroeconomic view based on microeconomic data and, most importantly, it makes it possible to reach qualitative conclusions based on quantitative data. It is also an ideal tool for measuring regional performance in the developing world, with the view of comparing this performance with developed countries without the logical bias related to the different stages of development. The implications in terms of policy-making are significant and are to be exploited in parallel when introducing innovation policies.

LESSONS FROM THE ARGENTINIAN CASE STUDY

The methodological framework presented above, together with the analyses conducted in the region of Morón, constitute initial key data for the planning of the deployment of a DE in the region, especially since it sets the basis for understanding the existing framework of institutional networks and their role in supporting innovation processes in the region.

There are two criteria that determine the emergence of key stakeholders in the region. The first, and most important, is related to the quality of the linkages and the positioning of the agents within the institutional network. The second is related to the level of competences and absorption capacities of the key agents and organizations in the network, which would not only allow a better functioning of the network, but would also induce positive effects and spillovers to the rest of the actors in the network. These elements, in the framework of a DE, provide interesting starting points when planning policies oriented towards the construction of effective collaboration networks in support of innovation.

Table 7.1 summarizes the production and institutional networks identified and selected in Morón. The characterization of the networks and the identified competencies of the organizations are directly linked to the deployment of DEs. The findings give interesting insights related to the social capital of the region, the heterogeneity of the

Table 7.1   Production and institutional networks identified and selected in Morón

Identified networks	Sub-networks	Selected network	Qualitative criteria
794 manufacturing enterprises (from the 900 firms mapped in Morón)	3 networks: metalworking sector, textiles and food industry	Metalworking sector	Network complexity, number of agents, importance of the production chain
154 Institutions and organizations (from the 350 institutions registered in Morón)	2 networks: social and production networks	Production network	Network complexity, impact in production related actors
Network chosen	**Identified candidate organizations**	**General competences: qualitative approach**	**General ICT use**
Metalworking enterprises	10 metalworking enterprises	Low	Low
Production-oriented Organizations and Institutions	2 local organizations	Medium	Low, medium

findings, and the existing linkages between the regional actors at the social and cultural levels. Additionally, the data obtained on production networks, far from the traditional statistical analyses, is key for the formalization of a network towards the realization of an ecosystem: the understanding of the linkages and competences of the agents is central for the design of the deployment strategy suitable for the region. Finally, the identification of gatekeepers sets the basis for the nomination of the regional catalysts that would be ideal for leading the effort of the construction of a DE.

As a result of both analyses some organizations were identified, both enterprises and local institutes, whose role is particularly important in the region, and that could act as 'regional catalysts' in a DE (Salminen et al. 2004). In the case of the enterprises, 10 organizations were selected as the best-positioned within the network. Even though the organizations differed significantly in some characteristics (i.e. size of the enterprise), they also share similar competencies and absorption capacities. All of the identified gatekeepers have relatively low competences, mainly because of the absence of practices that promote knowledge-sharing between employees; low quality standards; low use of ICTs (notably in the production networks); and almost no R&D activities.

Regarding the local institutions, the focus was on the two main gatekeepers that mostly control the network: the IDEB centre, and the Undersecretary for Local Economic Development of the Municipality of Morón (SDEL). In terms of the competencies, the SDEL has significant technical capacities, based on strong work teams with specialized professional knowledge. Both institutes also profit from long experience and strong informal linkages. Regarding ICT use, the SDEL uses more specialized ICT tools, whereas IDEB makes basic use of ICTs.

The gatekeepers identified have a strong position in the networks studied. Nevertheless their knowledge flows are limited in both cases. Both networks also have low and limited capacities, which could represent a bottleneck or limitation when these actors try to implement coordinated actions. All gatekeepers have a relatively low use of ICTs, which shows the potential difficulties when trying to implement projects related to the introduction and diffusion of new technologies, such as DEs.

Conclusion

This chapter analysed the implementation process of DEs assuming a dependence on specific regional contexts. The first section summarized the state of the art of DE definitions and goals related to the socioeconomic aspects of DEs theory, and underlined the relevance of DEs as an approach that considers technology adoption as a social process, driven by social networking actions and collaboration and their impact on innovation processes in enterprises. This implies at least three important elements. First, there has to be collaboration among social actors (in other words, connectivity among agents is required for the implementation of DEs). Second, it is required that social actors have something to offer to other actors, otherwise the collaboration may not be possible and/or sustainable (it can be said that learning capacities and absorption capacities have to be heterogeneous and close to the state of the art, and possibly determined by local common practice). Third, it is supposed that ICTs can amplify both connectivity and absorption capacities.

This research was motivated by the desire to strengthen the link between theoretical and policy-oriented DE research. The interaction with an institution new to DE research, Universidad Nacional de General Sarmiento, added a great deal of complementary insight to the DE hypotheses and methodologies relevant to sustainable socioeconomic development through innovation. A new improved understanding through the integration of three distinct research perspectives has been presented: theoretical, based on hypotheses and assumptions to be verified or falsified when applied to the Latin American context; qualitative and quantitative empirical data gathering and analysis, including the visualization and analysis of networks of firms and institutions; and applied, focused on the development of a policy analysis visualization tool. The main contribution of this tool is the possibility of comparing relatively different regions through the aggregation of their regional characteristics and framework conditions (i.e. stage in the development process), and allowing the formulation of tailored policy options.

The tool aimed to visualize the main dimensions of policy-making that are relevant to sustainable development and consistent with the DE hypotheses. Although the tool was successful in this, as Figure 7.6 shows some of the DE hypotheses, for example distributed architecture, are not related to the four determinants: absorption capacity, connectivity, ICT adoption and social capital. In other words, everything that has been described so far in this chapter could be achieved using a centralized architecture for the infrastructure and services of an ICT deployment. As a final consideration to be explored further in future work, therefore, a fifth dimension should be added: 'Level of participatory governance', which may be more compatible with a distributed than with a centralized architecture. By governance is meant for example the manner in which OSS communities of SMEs and developers are organized (as in the Plone case already cited). Communities of firms could organize themselves in a manner similar to how communities of OSS developers organize themselves for those aspects of their work that require coordinated collaboration (standards, business modelling languages, regulatory environment, run-time coordination of complex transactions ...). This is an argument for (1) the benefits of more structure in the market than the atomized[16] model of neoclassical economics and (2) a bottom-up process for arriving at such a structure.

Figure 7.17 shows a new version of Figure 7.6 in which this additional indicator was added to provide a more complete mapping to the DE hypotheses. Additionally, the appropriation conditions (understanding them as micro-meso-macro formal and informal regulations as elements of the framework conditions, able to restrict or promote some production activities and/or behaviours) of each context could affect the connectivity and ICT adoption dimensions and their relationship, and hence ultimately the innovation processes in a given region or territory. This research is therefore indicating that an effective strategy to achieve sustainable socioeconomic development is through the integration of processes of social innovation with the adoption of information and communication technologies in an economic context characterized by a balance of competition and collaboration.

---

16   The metaphor of a collection of rational agents interacting only through market boundaries as a collection of gas atoms probably originates from the fact that in an ideal gas the particles do not interact, i.e. they do not even collide. Granovetter calls such agents, or the description of such an economic system, 'undersocialized' (Granovetter 1985).

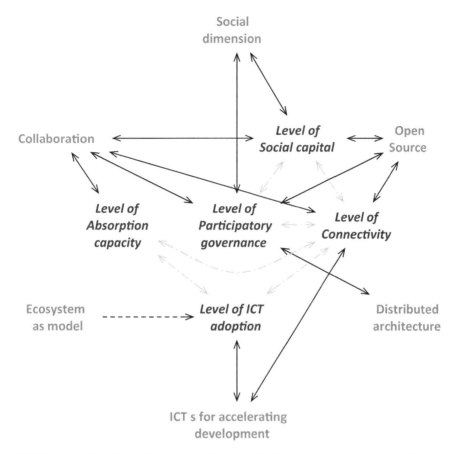

Figure 7.17 Introduction of a new policy indicator, for future research

Questions to Consider

With the aim of stimulating discussion with other researchers and complementary disciplines (innovation studies, development economics, economic sociology), the following questions should serve as a basis for further research:

1. What is the role of governance in enabling different ways of organizing collaboration networks that lead to innovation and the enhancement of the role of knowledge creation and sharing for development (Berdou 2011)?
2. How can all these ideas be reconciled with the LAC tradition and interpretation of innovation and development studies (i.e. Arocena and Sutz 2003, Sorlin and Vessuri 2007)? And how do these compare to European perspectives?
3. How can the innovation perspective of developing countries (i.e. LAC perspective) contribute to a constructive dialogue with a more hermeneutic, post-structuralist, postmodernist, and non-functionalist view of development through collaboration (Latouche 1998)?

Acknowledgements

The authors are grateful to Professor Robin Mansell for reading this chapter and for her very helpful feedback, and to Dr Antonella Passani for her helpful and insightful critique. The research discussed in this chapter was funded by the EU-FP7 EULAKS Project, contract number RTD-217190. Paolo Dini's time was also supported by the EU-FP6 OPAALS Project, contract number IST-034824.

References

Antonelli, C. 2008. *Localised Technological Change: Towards the Economics of Complexity*. London: Routledge.

Arocena, R. and Sutz, J. 2003. *La, innovacíon y el desarrollo en un mundo global: Una propuesta desde el Sur*. Cambridge: Cambridge University Press.

Audretsch, D., van der Horst, R., Kwaak, T. and Thurik, R. 2009. *First Section of the Annual Report on EU Small and Medium-Sized Enterprises*. European Commission: EIM.

Barletta, F., Cohan, L. and Kataishi, R. 2009. *Conectividad comercial y capacidad de absorción. Un, análisis de la red de firmas metalmecánicas del partido de Morón*. Buenos Aires: RedPyMEs.

Barletta, F., Kataishi, R. and Yoguel, G. 2010. *Encuesta a empresas industriales y de servicios sobre conectividad, capacidades e innovación. Enfoques teórico y metodológico*. Buenos Aires: RedPyMEs.

Berdou, E. 2011. *Organization in Open Source Communities: At the Crossroads of the Gift and Market Economies*. London: Routledge.

Borello, J., Kataishi, R., Robert, V., Silva Failde, D. and Suarez, D. 2008. *Difusión de Tics en las empresas manufactureras del partido de Morón*. FLACSO-México, septiembre. [Online]. Available at: http://goo.gl/zXhD4 [accessed: 21 June 2013].

Botto, F. and Passani, A. 2008. 'D7.1: *The Relationship between Community Networks and Digital Ecosystems*. OPAALS Deliverable. [Online]. Available at: http://files.opaals.eu/OPAALS/Year_2_Deliverables/WP07/ D7.1.pdf.

Botto, F., Dini, P., Briscoe, G., Chatterjee, J., Iqani, M., Marinos, A., Pattanaik, D. and Rivera-Leon, L. 2008. *Foundations of the Theory of Associative Autopoietic Digital Ecosystems: Part 2*. OPAALS Deliverable D12.1, European Commission. [Online]. Available at: http://files.opaals.eu/ OPAALS/Year_3_Deliverables/WP12/D12.1.pdf.

Bruno, N., Miedzinski, M., Reid, A. and Ruiz Yaniz, M. 2008. 'Socio-cultural determinants of innovation', Technopolis, Europe Innova Innovation Watch, Systematic Project.

Camacho, H., Cámara, L., Cascante, R. and Sainz, H. 2001. *El, enfoque del marco lógico: 10 casos prácticos. Cuaderno para la identificación y diseño de proyectos de desarrollo*. Madrid: Fundación CIDEAL, Acciones de Desarrollo y Cooperación.

Chatterjee, J., Prabhakar, T.V., Sarkar, R., Pattanaik, D. and Rajagopalan, R. 2008. *D7.3: India's Rural Case Study Folio*. OPAALS Deliverable. [Online]. Available at: http://files.opaals.org/OPAALS.

Cohen, W. and Levinthal, D. 1989. Innovation and learning: The two faces of R&D. *The Economic Journal*, 99(397), 569–96.

Dini, P., Lombardo, G., Mansell, R., Razavi, A., Moschoyiannis, S., Krause, P., Nicolai, A. and Rivera-León, L. 2008a. Beyond interoperability to digital ecosystems: Regional innovation and socioeconomic development led by SMEs. *International Journal of Technological Learning, Innovation, and Development*, 1(3), 410–26.

Dini, P., Munro, A., Iqani, M., Zeller, F., Moschoyiannis, S., Gabaldon, J. and Nykänen, O. 2008b. *Foundations of the Theory of Associative Autopoietic Digital Ecosystems: Part 1.* OPAALS Deliverable D1.2, European Commission. [Online]. Available at: http://files.opaals.eu/OPAALS/Year_2_Deliverables/WP01/D1.2.pdf.

Dini, P., Iqani, M., Rivera-León, L., Passani, A., Moschoyiannis, S., Nykänen, O., Pattanaik, D. and Chatterjee, J. 2009. *Foundations of the Theory of Associative Autopoietic Digital Ecosystems: Part 3.* OPAALS Deliverable D12.10, European Commission. [Online]. Available at: http://files.opaals.eu/OPAALS/Year_3_Deliverables/WP12/D12.10.pdf.

Dini, P., Iqani, M. and Mansell, R.E. 2011. The (Im)Possibility of interdisciplinarity: Lessons from constructing a theoretical framework for digital ecosystems. *Culture, Theory and Critique*, 52(1), 3–27.

Drahos, P. 2002. *Information Feudalism: Who Owns the Knowledge Economy?* New York, NY: New Press.

van Egeraat, C., O'Riain, S., Kerr, A., Sarkar, R., Chatterjee, J., Stanley J., Rivera León, L. and Passani, A. 2008. *A Research Agenda for Bridging Digital Ecosstems to Regional Development and Innovation in the Knowledge Economy – Preliminary Report.* OPAALS Project WP11 D11.1.

Erbes, A., Robert, V. and Yoguel, G. 2010. Capacities, innovation and feedbacks in production Networks in Argentina. *Economics of Innovation and New Technology*, 19(8), 719–41.

European Commission. 2010. *European SMEs, under Pressure.* Annual Report on EU Small and Medium-sized Enterprises 2009, Directorate-General for Enterprise and Industry.

Feenberg, A. 1991. *Critical Theory of Technology.* Oxford: Oxford University Press.

Feenberg, A. 2002. *Transforming Technology: A Critical Theory Revisited.* Oxford: Oxford University Press.

Giuliani, E. 2004. *Laggard Clusters as Slow Learners, Emerging Clusters as Locus of Knowledge Cohesion (and Exclusion): A Comparative Study in the Wine Industry.* LEM Papers Series 2004/09, Laboratory of Economics and Management (LEM), Sant' Anna School of Advanced Studies, Pisa, Italy.

Giuliani, E. and Bell, M. 2004. When Micro Shapes the Meso: Learning Networks in a Chilean Wine Cluster. SPRU Electronic Working Paper Series 115, University of Sussex, SPRU – Science and Technology Policy Research.

Granovetter, M. 1985. Economic action and social structure: The problem of embeddedness. *The American Journal of Sociology*, 91(3), 481–510.

Iansiti, M. and Levien, R. 2004. *The Keystone Advantage: What the New Dynamics of Business Ecosystems Mean for Strategy, Innovation, and Sustainability.* Boston, MA: Harvard Business School Press.

INDEC. 2010. Database derived from 2001 National Census. [Online]. Available at: http://www.indec.gov.ar/cgibin/Rp,WebEngine.exe/PortalAction?andMODE=MAINandBASE=CPV2001ARGandMAIN=WebServerMain.inl.

Kataishi, R., Erbes, A., Delfini, M., Roitter, S. and Yoguel, G. 2008. *El, rol de las instituciones para el fortalecimiento de las cadenas de valor. El, caso del sector metalmecánico en el Municipio de Morón.* Buenos Aires: RedPyMEs.

Lacueva, F.J., Vea-Murguía, J.I., Fernández de Alarcón, P. and Navamuel, J. 2010. *Test Plan. Evaluation Report and Recommendations from Beta-Testing of P2P Infrastructure.* OPAALS Deliverable D5.9, European Commission. [Online]. Available at: http://files.opaals.eu/OPAALS/ Year_4_Deliverables/WP5.

Latouche, S. 1998. *L'Autre Afrique: Entre don et marché.* Paris: Albin Michel.

Llach, L. and Gerchunoff, P. 1998. *El, ciclo de la illusion y el desencanto.* Buenos Aires: Ariel.

Malone, P. and McLaughlin, M. 2009. *Implementation of Identity, Trust and Accountability Models.* OPAALS Deliverable D3.11, European Commission. [Online]. Available at: http://files.opaals.eu/OPAALS/Year_3_Deliverables/WP3.

Moore, J.F. 1996. *The Death of Competition: Leadership and Strategy in the Age of Business Ecosystems.* New York: HarperCollins.

Municipio de Morón. 2008. 'La, guía de Instituciones'. Interactive CD-ROM. [Online]. Available at: http://www.moron.gov.ar/participacion_comunitaria/guiadeinstituciones.php.

Nachira, F. 2002. 'Towards a network of digital business ecosystems fostering the local development'. Discussion paper. [Online]. Available at: http://www.digital-ecosystems.org/ [accessed: 15 February 2005].

Nachira, F., Nicolai, A. and Dini, P. (eds). 2007. Introduction – The Digital Business Ecosystems: Roots, Processes and Perspectives, in *Digital Business Ecosystems Book*. European Commission.

Nicolai, A. 2009. *D11.9: Multi-Stakeholders Policy Framework for Regional Economic Development through Digital Ecosystems.* OPAALS Deliverable. [Online]. Available at: http://files.opaals.eu/OPAALS/Year_3_Deliverables/WP11/D11.9.pdf.

OECD. 2001. *The Well-Being of Nations: The Role of Human and Social Capital.* OECD.

Passani, A. and Giorgetti, M. 2009. Interpreting the Territory for Digital Ecosystems Deployment: A Socioeconomic Analysis of the Extended Area Viterbo-Rieti, in *eGov 2.0: Paving the way for e-participation*. Rome: EuroSpace.

Popper, K. 1993. *The Poverty of Historicism*. London: Routledge.

Powell, W.W., Kopu, K. and Smith-Doerr, L. 1996. Interorganizational collaboration and the locus of innovation: Networks of learning in biotechnology. *Administrative Science Quarterly*, 41, 116–45.

Razavi, A., Moschoyiannis, S. and Krause, P. 2009. An, open digital environment to support business ecosystems. *Peer-to-Peer Networking and Applications Springer Journal*, 2, 367–97.

Rivera León, L., Passani, A. and Pennese, F. 2009. *Preliminary Study on Methodologies for DE Socioeconomic Impact Analysis.* OPAALS Deliverable. [Online]. Available at: http://files.opaals.eu/OPAALS/Year_3_Deliverables/WP11/D11.8.pdf.

Salminen, E., Seppa, M., Rasanen, P. 2004. *Del 31.1: Analysis and specification of current and potential regional catalysts.* DBE Project Deliverables. [Online]. Available at: http://files.opaals.eu/DBE/deliverables/Del_31.1_DBE_Analysis and specification of current and potential regional catalysts.pdf.

Shaikh, M. and Berdou, E. 2008. *D8.3: Review of Open Knowledge Initiatives – Successes and Failures: Evolving Characterisation of the OSS 2.0 Phenomenon*, OPAALS Deliverable. [Online]. Available at: http://files.opaals.eu/OPAALS/Year_2_Deliverables/WP08/D8.3.pdf.

Sorlin, S. and Vessuri, H. 2007. *Knowledge Society vs. Knowledge Economy: Knowledge, Power, and Politics*. New York: Palgrave Macmillan.

Steinmueller, W.E. 2004. 'ICTs, and social capital'. Paper presented at the DRUID Winter Conference, January.

Vessuri, H. 2003. Science, politics, and democratic participation in policy-making: A Latin American view. *Technology in Society*, 25(2), 263–73.

Winograd, T. and Flores, F. 1987. *Understanding Computers and Cognition*. New York: Addison-Wesley.

Yoguel, G., Robert, V., Milesi, D. and Erbes, A. 2009. 'El, desarrollo de las redes de conocimiento en Argentina'. Programa Economía del Conocimiento en América Latina, IDRC-FLACSO, Mexico.

8

Disseminating Innovation by Improving Individual Capabilities: A Brazilian Experience

DAVIDE DIAMANTINI and MARIANGELA TOMMASONE

Introduction

The traditional theories on innovation all agree on what are the instruments and dynamics for *innovation support*: they are developed in a specific territorial system where the forces and creativity of universities and research institutes, along with the enthusiasm and incentives of institutions and the fertile terrain of business converge into the entrepreneurial spirit. This means that the indispensable basic elements of a collective system of creation, diffusion and use of knowledge are identified in the education, in the development and valorization of competent human resources, in a financial system which can sustain innovative projects, in the planning and realization of policies of innovation: elements which are and have a substantial impact on the performance of the "science-technology-industry" system. It is therefore extremely important for all these components to interact with each other aiming for a *broad-based innovation strategy* that is the creation of an integrated system supporting the innovation which is involved with all the fundamental actors (the financial world, academia and institutions). This is even more so when referring to an emerging country such as Brazil.

This chapter will go into depth on one of the fundamental components of the innovation systems, that is the continuous training of skilled human capital which is able to understand and govern uncertainty, risks and opportunities of the innovative process, and to contribute to the economic development of a particular territory.

The first theoretical part will focus on the nature of the two components which are at the base of the knowledge society: on one hand the territory, intended as the physical places in which the development processes take root; on the other hand the knowledge, intended as the patrimony of ability and competences which allow the growth and competition of an economic system.

Afterwards a *literature review* of the principal theories of innovation and development – in particular those based on social capital – focus on the territorial dimension and the development processes of local systems.

A detailed description of the Master's degree program in "Innovation Management for Local Development" organized by the Università degli Studi di Milano-Bicocca together with the Universidade Federal Fluminense di Rio de Janeiro follows and is proposed as a model of *best practice*: this educational experience is designed to give future entrepreneurs not only instruments for the creation of businesses, but above all to help them transform the social and organizational structures of the environments in which public and private actors work. The Master's is concentrated on the different ways local and regional agencies operate together with the private sector in order to fulfill common policies aimed at stimulating the local economies, while also considering the vocational and environmental characteristics of every region.

Afterwards there is an analysis of what this experience brought to the territory and an overall remark on the importance that have the territory and the different actors who interact there for the collective learning process.

The Master's degree program is a significant experience for the Brazilian context: in the past, in fact, very little of the work from research centers has been converted into benefits for the local society, challenging the Brazilian universities to follow a program which could respond to their numerous social issues. The challenge of the research world represents the other side of an even more diffused challenge to Brazilian society: that of entrepreneurship, both in the traditional and innovative sectors. Furthermore, training individuals who are able to govern such dynamics of a global nature and with a strong impact on the territory, introducing and adding economic value to new knowledge, using networks with a heavy local impact involve the role and mission of the universities, and the Master's degree program has principally tried to answer this kind of need.

Therefore, the importance of a policy which aims for life-long training of human capital is emphasized: the fundamental concept of *governance* is introduced to indicate the different processes through which the actors become capable, with a precise definition of the competences, to coordinate each actor's own operational strategies and to define the effective training strategies which can have a significant impact over time only if they make an attentive analysis of the training system.

The conclusions of the chapter focus on the importance of the *links* between the different actors on the territory to start innovative growth processes: in other words, the analysis of the chapter with the concept of network underlines how innovation based on competence networks becomes the key element in processes of socio-environmental transformation, allowing the passage of an instrumental use of technologies and knowledge to a social use.

Literature Review

Over the last few years numerous studies have been carried out on knowledge and its ever growing importance which it is gaining inside the economic area for the dynamics of innovation. The role of knowledge is clearly central in innovation processes. It is considered equal to capital and work, a strategic and productive resource (Winter 1987), at times emerging in respect to traditional "physical" factors with a much more decisive priority (Padula 2002). Knowledge and the processes for its creation, transmission and improvement have become critical factors for achieving competitive advantage in the new socioeconomic context, defined as "informational society" (Castells 1996) or "knowledge society" (Rizzello 1997, Rullani 2004). As a consequence, knowledge and its aspects characterize the modern company which has become a *learning organization* (Senge 1990); moreover, together with other competences and attributes incorporated in subjects (OECD 1998),[1] knowledge assumes great importance for the economy, because it constitutes the human capital first; then, together with the constitution of the formal and informal networks of trust, gives form to social capital.

The economic literature considers these dynamics of innovation in a systemic view (Archibugi, Howells and Michie 1999, Edquist and Johnson 1997, Carlsson, Jacobson, Holmén and Rickne 2002), where innovation is the result of a series of interactions between different actors, who give their contribution with different skills and specializations. Innovation is interpreted, at last, as a "collective" phenomena which requires the contribution of an heterogeneity of different subjects interacting between them (Malerba and Orsenigo 2000). This systemic view gradually led, depending on the perspective chosen, to define concepts such as national innovation system (Freeman 1995, Lundvall 1992, Mowery and Rosenberg 1993, Nelson 1993, Patel and Pavitt 1994), regional innovation system (Amin and Thrift 1994, 1998, Braczyk, Cooke and Heidenreich, 1998) and sectoral system of innovation (Malerba 2002, Breschi and Malerba 1997, Malerba and Orsenigo 1997).

The approach of the learning region and of regional systems of innovation (Florida 1995, Doloreux 2002), for example, emphasizes the structural change of the new knowledge-based economy, which puts the regions at the center of the new territorial competition as collectors and depositors of knowledge and ideas.

Abramovitz (1995) introduced the term *capabilities* to explain the growth factors which do not have traditional productive factors,[2] and recalls Mill (1848) for the concepts of "trust" in the reciprocal relationships between individuals and the ability of individuals to cooperate in the formation of social organizations. The definition of social capabilities is linked to the "technical competencies and political, industrial, commercial institutions of a country": therefore the recall to new institutionalism theories is explicit (North 1995). Abramovitz's approach argues that the social capabilities determine an interactive and cumulative process in which economic growth is supported, and the development favors further reinforcement of the social capabilities.

The approach of the learning region is strictly linked to an important theory that has been increasingly taken into account in the local development strategies: the theory of *endogenous development*, according to which development should take place starting from the resources of each society, defining each society's values and vision of the future, in order to answer the specific and diverse needs of every situation. All of this requires the use of local resources (wealth and raw materials) and the trust in one's own potentials, giving major importance to *education and training* of people who contribute to the overall development (Lundvall 1992). It is an approach which involves local traditions and particularly insists on considering cultural values and on the use of participative and cooperative interaction modalities. This approach considers the rediscovery of the *small dimension* (Schumacher)[3] as a key point, along with the small business and the territorial problematic of development (Bagnasco),[4] of the specificity and regional aspect

---

1   The full definition of human capital given from the OECD contains the following elements: "the knowledge, skills, competences and other attributes embodied in individuals that are relevant to economic activity" OECD (1998: 9).

2   "The requisites of production are Labour, Capital and Land. The increase of production, therefore … is a result of the increase either of these elements themselves or of their productiveness." John Stuart Mill, Principles of Political Economy (1848).

3   Schumacher 1973.

4   Bagnasco 1977.

of the local identities, of the services of proximity of the local actors. In other words, the "base strategy" is seen as one of the few anchors which cross every development policy, from the local experiences of the negotiated planning to the financed interventions of regional development. According to this setting, the local community (urban or rural) is considered protagonist of its own change and therefore taken on as an active subject, capable of producing initiative and experimentation. In this perspective, many experts of this approach say, in one way or another, that local development is a process of *collective learning*, intended as the growth of knowledge inside a technological trajectory, incorporated in a local context:[5] a process of accumulation of knowledge inside a market of local work, made possible by various territorial preconditions, such as geographic and relational proximity. The processes of collective learning in that sense are the basis for greater innovative capacity of business, and therefore greater territorial competitiveness and greater potential for development.

The literature on social capital has investigated various aspects and approaches connected to the different theories of growth and development linked to innovation.

The notion of social capital is extensively traced back to some fundamental authors who laid out the foundations of the concept: Bourdieu (1985) and Coleman (1988, 1990) in sociology, Putnam (1993, 1995, 2000) in political science and Fukuyama in history of economy and sociology (1995). Additionally, the literature on social capital refers to other major contributors such as Granovetter (1973, 1985), Burt (1992, 1997, 2001), Lin (1999), Lin et al. (2001), Portes and Sensenbrenner (1993). As Alguezaui and Filieri (2010) notice, this literature exhibits a general disagreement on the definition of the concept of social capital. The multiplicity of definitions derives from different approaches, levels of analysis and sources. Social researchers perceive differently the sources of social capital as networks (Coleman 2000, Putnam 1995, Burt, 1992, Granovetter 1973), norms (Putnam 1995), social beliefs (Nahapiet and Ghoshal 1998), and rules (Adler and Kwon 2002). Further, there are differences related to the level of analysis undertaken such as an individual (Coleman 2000), a firm (Baker 1990), a geographic region (Putnam 1995), a nation (Fukuyama 1995) or a network (Burt 1992).[6]

Coleman (1990), in particular, uses the concept to indicate a resource which does not exist in individuals and production systems, but in the structures of social relationships. Social capital, therefore, is seen as a collective resource, it is linked systemically to the network structure of relationships, to the stability of the relationships while at the same time to the reciprocal dependence associated to other forms of capital as one of the "production factors." Obviously, these resources vary from subject to subject and can constitute an important advantage for those who consider them at the moment of the development of human capital. Given this concept of social capital and every other extension of it which has contributed to scientific discussion, we can assume that the notion of social capital is like an "investment in social relations with expected returns in the marketplace" (Lin 2001). The definition of social capital, like the set of networks of social relations intended as resources for action, besides being rooted in the tradition of sociology based on theory of the rational choice, refers to the economic sociology researches inspired on the work of Granovetter (1973, 1985). He explained the concepts of "embeddedness" and "informal ties," or all those interpersonal relations which, according to the author, in a specific local

---

5   Cavazzani 2000: 35–72.

6   Alguezaui and Filieri 2010: 891–909.

context have a very broad range in respect to formal ties: their effectiveness is worth more than dense networks of friendship, because they configure broad links of social networks which can considerably influence processes of innovation.

In the Italian literature social capital is defined as the accumulation of what is invested in the relational structures between individuals and organizations: in other words, collective relational goods or networks among the actors, who allow the diffusion of information and knowledge and reduce the costs of diffusion at the territorial level, so that promoting the capacity of coordination and regulation. Some authors underline how through social relationships the cognitive or normative resources (information or trust) become available: they allow the actors to reach objectives that otherwise would not be achievable or that would be at much higher costs (Trigilia 1999); some others underline rather that informal networks and trust stimulate cooperation and reciprocity, producing immaterial and symbolic values (Mutti 1998).

Bagnasco (2001) instead proposed the distinction between a systemic or cultural conception of social capital according to which social capital is the aptitude for cooperation that results from a shared cooperative culture, capable of generating diffused interpersonal trust,[7] and a "relational" or "interactive" conception according to which social capital encompasses the resources for action that result from the fabric of cooperative relations of which a person is part.[8]

Basing on these premises, Rizzi (2003) sees in the social capital the competitive push which can explain the innovation at the territorial level: in other words, the innovative capability of the regional systems is collected to the social capital notion, together with the networking ability, the cultural and social attitudes system, the institutional development. So, the role of government and policy makers in enhancing overall national growth by stimulating the innovative capability of individual regions (Camagni 1992) is recognized.

Some previous studies have suggested that qualified human capital can play an important role in the generation of innovative activities within a sector, if it is characterized by an exchange of high-quality knowledge between the main subjects in this sector (e.g. Bianchi 2001).

Kilkenny et al. (1999) discussed a human capital model that could lead to success and said that the company success is strictly linked to the training level in the firm, besides the overall business experience and the total income. Also, Prais (1995) analyzed how the educational and the training system of a country may promote the overall productivity, and pointed, for instance, to the need to balance educational resources between the general academic issues and the professional life's ones, as well as to encourage vocational training, in order to give employees job-specific technical skills.

It is clear that the human capital idea is based on the fundamental assumption that human beings have abilities and skills that can be improved: this means that they can change their way to act (Becker 1964). As Dakhli and De Clercq (2003) say, the relationship between human capital and innovation at the country level is based in what Bourdieu (1986) denominated "conversions": in other words, different forms of capital can be converted into resources and other forms of economic pay off. At an individual level, this conversion process has been studied and validated by many researchers (e.g. Becker 1964,

---

7   Bagnasco 2003: 359–80.

8   For the reconstruction of the theme of social conditions of development in the areas of industrial districts refer to the works of Becattini (2000a, 2000b) and Bagnasco (1999, 1988).

Gradstein and Justman 2000) and the argument is that "those who are better educated, have more extensive work experience, and invest more time, energy, and resources in honing their skills are better able to secure higher benefits for themselves, and at the same time are better able to contribute to the overall well-being of the society."[9]

At the firms' level, it has been widely taken for granted that continuous innovation and its underlying knowledge play an important role in building firms' sustained competitive advantage (Prahalad and Hamel 1990, Drucker 1993, Nonaka 1994, Grant 1996). In fact, the literature perceives knowledge as the key element of a firm's strategy and emphasizes the importance of strategic activities aimed at managing knowledge (Grant 1996, Huber 1991, Nonaka 1994). Along these, more and more firms chose to follow the *open innovation model*[10] (Chesbrough 2003, 2007) which illustrates the distributed nature of innovation and could prevent the environmental threats through the exploration and exploitation of ideas, technologies, knowledge and capabilities: these derive from the collaboration with players formally or informally linked to the central firm and that are now included in the new product development process (customers, lead-users, suppliers, universities and research centers) (Alguezaui and Filieri 2010).

The importance of external actors – and of the social interactions with these actors as main drivers of firm's higher innovation performance – has been emphasized by several past studies. Powell et al. (1996), for instance, demonstrated that firms embedded in an inter-organizational collaborative network are more likely to realize higher innovative performance, while Landry et al. (2002) stated that increases in participation and relational assets contribute more than any other explanatory variable to increase the likelihood of firms' innovation. In fact, the radicalness of the innovation is primarily determined by the combination of different forms of social capital with the different advanced technologies adopted by firms for production. This effect is especially demonstrated in the social capital taking the form of research network asset.

THE "THIRD MISSION" IN THE BRAZILIAN UNIVERSITIES

This chapter makes us focus on a crucial theme in the dynamics of innovation which explains the importance of the Master's experience from this point of view: the role of university in the local development. In an era when globalization and multinational corporations seem to dominate economic activity, the system of higher education must respond to the increasing complexity and the different needs of society. The transformation into "entrepreneurial universities" is seen by many parties as a solution to the challenges that universities are facing today. According to this alternative conception, the modern university should be understood as "a social system that is inclusive of all universities and their departments, research centers and faculty. The concept implies the idea of "enterprise" or a deliberate effort in institution building, which will require a special activity and energy" (Clark 1998). The circumstances that move to this finding are different (Diamantini 2004). The actors which the university and public research centers have to compete with for the meager public funding are increasingly raising. In addition, the peripheral and central government is obliged to select, finalize and monitor

---

9   De Clercq and Dakhli 2003.

10   Open innovation means that "valuable ideas can come from inside or outside the company and can go to market from inside or outside the company as well" Chesbrough 2003: 43.

closely the very limited resources it has available for research, according to the requests. Even companies, unable to meet demand within their structure of scientific expertise, are forced to rely more and more to outside institutions such as universities or public research in order to find answers to their technology goals. At the same time, public research, because of the relatively scarce resources, has to draw on the business world and finalize, as a result, its research activities towards the objectives of industrial nature. In this way university easily becomes a market player.

It seems evident that, in this context, the dialogue between universities and enterprises is particularly important and represents one of the cornerstones of new innovation policies, as it deals directly with economic and social exploitation of new knowledge, developed in context of scientific and technological research. The concept of "third mission" of the university in fact means "the translation of research into products and new businesses" (Etzkowitz, Webster and Healey 1998) and it used precisely to identify the direct involvement of academic institutions in social welfare, the technological progress and the economic growth of society and territory: the knowledge that they themselves produce becomes socially and economically attainable and usable and goes to be seen as new driver of innovation (Etzkowitz 2004, OECD 1999 and 2002).

The production of scientific knowledge has become undertaking both economic and epistemological, because the economy operates increasingly on knowledge-based resources (Machlup 1962): that is, it has established itself as an alternative engine of economic growth compared to classic triumvirate of land, labor and capital, the traditional sources of wealth. It is less to replace the traditional functions of teaching and research, but to add to these renewed efforts to respond to a new kind of social demand: in this sense, universities are rethinking their traditional organization. Unlike in the past, the interaction between different levels of the innovation system is not limited to a binary relationship, but involves simultaneously all three players in the development of a local system: universities, government, business.

One route for achieving this proactive role for developmental purposes is under way in the Brazilian universities, related to the emergence of a growing concerning with regional development.

The importance of the Brazilian higher education system for the development of the country was officially recognized by a law of 1968, which defined its organization, functions and powers. First of all, these institutions were classified as public or private: the public ones were sub-classified as supported by the federal government, by the state governments, or by the municipal governments; private institutions were sub-classified as profit or non-profit, and, finally, the private non-profit institutions were divided in communitarian, confessional (religious orientation) and philanthropist (Mello and Renault 2006). In the 2007 Brazil counted 183 research universities: 96 public (55 federal, 35 state and six municipal) and 87 private (INEP 2009). The strong public tradition of the Brazilian universities (Velho 2004) is demonstrated by the significant part of the state's R&D investment they absorb and also by the fact that they offer important output like training professionals and researchers, publishing papers and, more recently, applying for patents (Maia de Oliveira and Velho 2010). Universities have developed their activities in a multidisciplinary way, thereby giving a valuable contribution to the development of the country. They are working on three areas: teaching (offering a wide range of courses: graduate or postgraduate Master's and doctoral programs, specialization and MBA), research (contributing to the generation and dissemination of knowledge as part of their educational approach) and what we previously called "third mission", also-called "extending mission" that means participation in community needs: it is seen as a formative process, which articulates the cultural and scientific education and research in a combined way to meet the needs of society.

Although the first academic revolution – when research joined the teaching activity – took place in Brazil under a military regime, universities have benefited from a certain autonomy that allowed them to give space to the articulation of new initiatives aimed at transferring to the companies the knowledge produced in universities. These initiatives were originally developed outside the formal structure of universities, so they were still not the result of the incorporation by the academic world of economic and social development.

Starting from the 1960, the economic development model established in the Brazilian universities a set of activities aimed at emphasizing managerial efficiency and innovation, such as the supply of technological services (as tests, measurements, consultancies, information services), joint research projects with companies, projects carried out by incubated small companies and projects originating with "junior" companies, consulting firms organized by students with faculty staff coaching (Maculan and Mello 2009). It includes also the process by which results of research or a technical idea with potential value developed in the university are converted into one or more commercially successful products through the generation of a spin-off company: but this process is poorly documented and little studied, in Brazil as in many other emerging countries (Botelho and Almeida 2009). This could be due maybe to the fact that the academia showed its interest on the theme of innovation only recently, from the first Brazil's innovation law in 2004, whose regulatory mechanism begun to be implemented only from 2006. Costa and Torkomian (2008) have analyzed many Brazilian academic spin-offs and have noticed that people employed in them are not so young (30–50 years) even if the structures considered in their sample were mainly created after 2001; in addition, they are highly skilled (they obtained at least a bachelor degree), work in high-tech sectors, have a domestic market orientation and, surprisingly, do not have patents developed nor licensed from university.

Although considered as the work less "noble" that the university can play, and even if studies on the entrepreneurial activities of Brazilian higher education institutions are still small (so it is difficult to evaluate how the set of actions and programs promulgated by these institutions have contributed to the country's economic development), Brazilian universities are struggling to give their contribution to the country's socioeconomic development, not only through teaching and research, but also through their "entrepreneurial" activities closely linked to the society.

Methodology

In light of these circumstances, the basic assumption of the Master's degree in "Innovation Management for Local Development" consisted in the exchange of best practices and the application to the Brazilian context of some of the factors above mentioned about the dynamics of local innovation, in order to support start processes of manufacturing and business sector, particularly in the area of Rio de Janeiro. This means that the training program, designed as a standardized one, with an articulated and flexible nature, first of all needed a profound analysis of the innovation needs of the local context, rooted in a broader concept of innovation closely related to science and technology. The promotion of measures to support SMEs and new entrepreneurs in Brazil can play a particularly important role from not only the economic and industrial standpoint, but also from the social one, given the special conditions existing in this country. Traditionally, Brazil benefited from very little public investment, due to a number of structural factors and historical contingencies.

The country is located in Latin America and is a former Portuguese colony that became independent in the 1822; it has been victim of brutal dictatorships, military governments and fragile democratic governments, until the sanctioning of the republic in 1889. Now Brazil is a Federal Republic with 27 states organized into five regions, with a continental area of around 8.5 million km² and a predominantly urban population estimated at about 190 million people in 2009 (IBGE 2009). It is the fifth country in the world for the number of inhabitants, with a very young population and a large variety in the ethnic composition (Amerindians, descendants of white Europeans, Afro-Americans and a small group of Arabs and Japanese in the Middle East). In the past the population has migrated from the northeast to the inland areas (Brasilia and Amazon), but the difficulties of the environment and the scarcity of resources have forced many farmers to abandon their lands and migrate to the slums ("favelas") that surround the city. Nine are the metropolitan areas that exceed 1 million inhabitants where there is the concentration of one-third of the population.

For many years the various governments that have succeeded in power have sought to develop an economy in situations of high protectionism, high foreign debt and high inflation (between 1973 and 1994 there were inflation rates equal to 268 percent). In the short term, inflation has facilitated the growth of some industries but in the long run the protected categories were severely damaged, there was an increase in inequalities of income and a decrease of the savings by the middle classes. These strong economic and social inequalities, besides leading to the formation of the favelas, took out to many families the possibility to give their children an education. As a consequence, Brazil suffers today a great delay in the expenditure for R&D and literacy.

In the overall Brazilian economy great emphasis is given to the promotion of advanced technologies, in particular in the State of Rio de Janeiro, which is a state of excellence since in the field of scientific and technological support services there are six technology parks (Parque Tecnológico from UFRJ, RIO BIO Polo, Parque Tecnológico and cultural Gávea, Technopolis Project, Parque Tecnológico de Xerém and TECNorte, Parque de Alta Tecnologia do Norte Fluminense) and a network of technology incubators (18 in the state, with 80 percent located in the city of Rio de Janeiro). The State of Rio is also the largest software producer in Brazil, with 40 percent of the national production and headquarters of major companies.

For several years the promotion of measures to support small and medium enterprises and to create new initiatives has become a priority which has been shared across the local agencies. Please note in particular, the work done in this area by SEBRAE, the Brazilian SME support agency, which has promoted research and practical initiatives to raise awareness and networking. In its activities, the SEBRAE has always considered very attentively the Italian experience of promotion of clusters of small and medium entrepreneurship for at least two reasons. First, also the Brazilian economy, like the Italian one, sees an absolute prevalence of SMEs in the industrial fabric (according to a research carried out by SEBRAE in 2004, 99 percent of Brazilian companies are in fact SMEs). Secondly, the community of Italians in Brazil has always been characterized as very cohesive and well integrated in the social environment; it has often made significant contributions with regard to risk-taking entrepreneurship and the creation of new business initiatives. Based on the information reported, it seemed evident that a revival of innovation in the Brazilian system could not but pass through a strongly interview to support the launch of new entrepreneurial businesses that were able to introduce a kind of incremental innovation culture: this on the light of what had already partially happened in the Italian context, which was itself characterized by a profile not strictly based on scientific and technological innovative processes and a reluctance of companies to invest in R&D.

So, the proposal for this training project has been formulated with the objectives to contribute promoting entrepreneurship and the creation of small and medium enterprises in Brazil, particularly in the district of Rio de Janeiro, in order to endorse the development and dissemination of specific expertise on innovation.

As seen before, the educational system and professional training, both formal and informal, is a key component of national innovation systems. So, a first point to be taken into strong consideration when designing a training intervention is the need to communicate highly specialized experiences. These are by nature very diverse and heterogeneous, since they are based on knowledge related to specific problems or abstract and theoretical knowledge. But it is clearly not possible to base the training process on a standard high level of abstraction with a strictly academic program, since this model of knowledge transfer is too remote from practical problem-solving skills necessary for promoting innovative entrepreneurship. It is therefore necessary to balance the dominance of the explicit knowledge on the implicit one and the adoption of a deductive type of approach to problem-solving. Precisely for this reason a training course was designed that combined formal and informal education and was largely devoted to practical experience and learning by doing, which tends to emphasize the role and the creation of tacit knowledge.

Indeed, in a competitive environment for innovation, knowledge must be a set of skills acquired through the theoretical study combined with practical skills, experience and know-how accumulated in the professional field. It also creates a more fertile breeding ground for competition and teamwork. Furthermore, the two processes of training also reflect two different aspects of the process: the training of the academic and formal type is typical of the moment of entry into the new professional environment and as such should be implemented with specialized and more theoretical knowledge; while informal training is characterized by moments of enrichment, maintenance and development of already learned skills through experience gained in the field, therefore concrete solutions to problems along with the application of new skills.

The distinction between the development of empirical knowledge (learning directly on the field through a process of trial and error) and the development of abstract knowledge (starting from theoretical one) corresponds to the distinction between learning by doing and learning before doing proposed by Pisano (1994). According to a case study from the pharmaceutical sector, Pisano argues that the importance of the two training types depends on the openness towards scientific and technological knowledge at the starting point: if it is limited, learning by doing prevails, but if you have a rather developed and established wealth of knowledge, then learning before doing prevails.[11]

---

11   For a different interpretation of learning by doing and learning by doing approaches, see Arora and Gambardella 1994.

The significance of the problem of training resources in diffusion processes of innovation requires a clarification about the difference between the terms resources and skills, which often are interchanged in dealing with this topic, creating confusion in the theoretical framework. A generally accepted contribution follows the trail of studies by Nelson and Winter (1982) and Dierickx and Cool (1989), where resources are identified as the productive inputs already present in the company, physical assets and intangible assets accumulated over time: even if they represent a value, they do not lead to the generation of new performances by the company (Collis and Montgomery 1995, Day 1997). The skills or capabilities are just the routines that combine their resources together. This distinction is necessary to further understand the profile of skills required by managers of technology and knowledge transfer.

An innovation manager, in fact, is required to have a series of skills and knowledge that cover many areas, therefore he needs highly specialized and individual training. This path is characterized by a high level of heterogeneity of contents (bureaucratic administrative knowledge, scientific and technical knowledge, managerial and economic skills, management skills for international networks …) and less amount of time dedicated to training, as well as implicit components which are critical between the skills needed for the many activities.

THE CASE STUDY

The Master's degree program aimed at giving students both theoretical tools and analytical capabilities to implement practices so that they could play key roles as promoters of local development (for example, in business or public policy within their communities or where they would like to be involved). This way they were given the opportunity and the challenge to face critical issues and dynamics of local economic development with a systemic vision and a participatory approach. At the end of the Master's students acquired relevant skills to develop a detailed understanding of new trends of corporate organization in local, national and international areas (with strong emphasis on the Italian experience in the field), analyzing in particular the role and importance of SMEs in local economies, as well as providing insights on the different actors in the area along with their interactions. In the training different strategies to finalize the ideas and recent insights in the field were considered, with emphasis on managerial issues of capacity building, knowledge management, entrepreneurship, funding, building networks, infrastructure and human resources. The program also took into account both the motives and impact of regional and local development policies, the role of institutions that promote the study and the testing of more equitable and sustainable development processes.

In general, the educational goals of the Master's degree consisted in the acquisition of scientific and technical expertise to intervene in relations between local society and socioeconomic development planning, with particular attention given to the development of social capital, the growth of social skills and the functioning of institutional systems of local companies, giving strong emphasis on entrepreneurship, both those of the traditional sectors and those based on modern information and communication technologies (ICTs). The training intended to promote the development of guidelines and specific skills for defining and managing project actions within a regional system, increasingly geared to integrated local development. The Master's in Innovation Management for Local Development has proposed to form a new professional figure who can develop strategies for enhancing local production environments as well as coordinate and manage public or private projects, in order to enhance and improve the competitiveness of a geographical area, to support local businesses and individuals in the construction of an image and a cultural identity which is useful for the recognition of the region's potential. The ultimate objective of the Master's degree was to encourage the employment of students and improve their relationship with the local production systems, enhancing the dynamics of local development and local and transnational productive interdependencies.

The University of Milano-Bicocca and the Fondazione Rosselli offered their expertise at the international level in their respective fields of intervention. In Rio de Janeiro Italian experts spoke in relevant seminars planned as part of the teaching of the Master's, to present and discuss new trends in Italy and around the world on topics as local development, entrepreneurship and networking, critical issues for the objectives of the training program. The Universidade Federal Fluminense made its physical infrastructure – Coordenação Central de Extensão/CCE, Universidade Federal Fluminense – available to students through a department for postgraduate courses and other short courses conducted at the university. The CEE had the following responsibilities: to provide classrooms for the first two modules of compulsory attendance; to put all the information about the Master's program on their website; to provide a secretariat for administrative and teaching purposes during the training. In addition, the Brazilian University offered a program academic coordinator belonging to its teaching staff; he was responsible for the following:

- ensuring the quality and relevance of academic courses of the program;
- monitoring the various educational and work experiences in order to ensure that they are in conformity with the educational objectives of the Master's degree program;
- coordinating the tutoring activities of the Project Work.

Contents

The Master's degree was a 10-month program (calculation of the preparation and planning of the program were not included) with a didactic structure of 1,216 hours, divided into 57 classroom lecture hours, 480 training hours, and 160 project work hours from April 2007 to February 2008. The Master's program was divided into four modules with the following characteristics.

MODULE I: BASIC TRAINING

Local development processes

Educational objectives: to provide a general framework on local economic development by giving students the basics for understanding the subsequent areas of territorial development policies.

Industrial policies and development in Italy and Brazil

Educational objectives to analyze and discuss the public policies for local development, the promotion of industrial districts, clusters and organizational networks in both countries. The characteristics, the main aspects and criteria for evaluation of these policies were discussed with Italian and Brazilian experts in the field.

Entrepreneurship and building networks

Educational objectives: to provide a framework on the issue of entrepreneurship, referring to the profiles of classic entrepreneurs and those based on modern ICTs, the importance of social capital and innovative networks, emerging new businesses and growth paths of SMEs.

Strategic planning in SMEs

Educational objectives: to promote the learning of basic skills for proper spatial planning to support SMEs, promoting entrepreneurship and local development, internationalization and innovation of local systems, and management of SMEs in the medium and long term.

MODULE II: SPECIALIST TRAINING

Management of technological change

Educational objectives: to analyze and discuss the key issues on innovation and technology transfer, with particular reference to SMEs and its relationships with other key actors (universities and research centers, agencies for the promotion of development and other companies). Brazilian, Italian and international experiences were emphasized in the promotion of innovation networks of SMEs, incubators and technology parks.

Social development policies

Educational objectives: to provide opportunities to evaluate functional and coherent policies for local development, examining the formulation and implementation of social policies, as well as the promotion of socio-cultural issues, such as the involvement of local governments, human rights, equal opportunities and social inclusion, the formation of networks for social inclusion.

The new ICTs and Information Society

Educational objectives: to provide an integrated, technological and managerial application of ICT in enterprises, to understand ICT as a tool for promoting social development in the Information Society, and the challenges and opportunities for developing countries.

Networks of learning and tacit knowledge

Educational objectives: to provide and disseminate skills and knowledge of collaborative and cooperative development between the companies operating within the same territorial and innovative contexts, and to create an environment where it is possible to share interests and experiences and offer mutual support.

Financial models for SMEs

Educational objectives: to identify the different forms of financing for SMEs, with special reference to emerging technology-based ones. The formal and informal models of funding: venture capital and angel investors.

Seminars and case studies

Brazilian, Italian and international experts in the public and private sectors were invited to present their experiences on the topics of the Master's program, with the objective of giving students the opportunity to participate in discussions on the topics of training, as well as identify topics of particular interests for internships in Italy and the project work.

PART III: INTERNSHIP

Purpose: The internship was held in qualified public agencies, or with actors involved in projects of local development agencies promoting cooperation between enterprises and institutions, or private companies and consortiums in Italy. It aimed to help students apply and test methods and contents of the training in the workplace. During the internship period seminars with Italian entrepreneurs specialized in "Made in Italy" were also conducted, as well as with policy makers of industrial districts and high-tech clusters.

MODULE IV: PROJECT WORK

Each participant was assigned of a "project work" on a specific theme about the analysis and design of local development, entrepreneurship and training of production networks, combined with research in the field. The participants were introduced to local actors in an area chosen for the collection of data and information that were afterwards processed in a real perspective of intervention. Each participant was guided by a scientific tutor. The start-up of the project work took place after the period of core courses and internships in Italy for a first overview of research opportunities, the opening of contacts and the information gathering, and merged into a final report rated by experts chosen by the participants.

Method of Assessment

At the end of each learning module assessments on the lessons were carried out, proposed by the teacher who was responsible. The positive assessment and attendance of each course were a prerequisite for entering the "trimester" of the project work. The outcome of the planning period and internship, combined with a realization of the project work evaluated by the academic tutor and mentor company led to the completion of the Master's degree.

METHODS OF ASSESSING THE SATISFACTION OF PARTICIPANTS

Students were asked to evaluate each course through questionnaires administered after each training module, which reviewed the following aspects of training:

- relationships and communication with teachers;
- relationships and communication with colleagues;
- the program's ability to meet the demands and perspectives of the participants;
- the availability of the Infrastructure for students during class time;
- development of acquired skills for the future prospects of the participants;
- content of the training;
- the formative periods of activity;
- personal enrichment;
- activity involvement;
- the overall internship program in Italy;
- opportunities to apply what they learned in the course.

Findings and Discussion

Considering the innovative character of the project and since there is no other training program with the same characteristics yet, the overall effectiveness of the project has been considered with a longitudinal evaluation of the introduction and role of the students in the international economic sphere in which they will be operating. This will gradually optimize the planning choices along with an evaluation methodology which is easily transferable to the national system of professional training, elaborated with valid and experimented indicators. With regard to the longitudinal analysis on both the entire evaluative procedure and the impact evaluation of the course on students entering the job market, the analysis, on one hand, verified the employment results of the trained with respect to the attended results of the training program. On the other hand, it verified the existence of an empowerment process which involved the trained and which allowed them to have a more knowledgeable approach to the job market.

The attended results of the training of the participants regarded, in fact, the acquisition of competences (strategic, managerial, technological and marketing), knowledge and necessary instruments to start new and innovative businesses where they live; this shifted to the stimulus of employment through the consolidation of the local productive and entrepreneurial fabric in traditional sectors of low/medium technological content and also intensive sectors in ICT, implementing technological innovation, the integration of training policies and research and industrial applications. These attended results have received positive feedback on the condition and job prospective of the students, five of whom, previously unemployed, found a job at the end of the MBA. The activities in the course and in particular the competences which were acquired in the course during the internships and the project work, were shown in these cases to be particularly important for these subjects to enter the job market. Another student, who was unemployed at the beginning of the program, was able to start a new entrepreneurial activity in the design and production of jewelry sector connected to a Brazilian University incubator, which represented the practical aspect of the competences developed during the period of internship in Italy.

The creation of new entrepreneurial realities by the Brazilian students furthermore helped create links between the university environment and the entrepreneurial one, favoring the interaction for those who need expert skills (the company) and those who can provide specialized skills (the university). This helped to create the basis for an entrepreneurial network between Italy and Brazil (in particular the states of Rio, Espírito Santo and Bahia) and contributed to the development of the local production with the creation of companies oriented towards innovation and technological transfer.

Furthermore, it was possible to improve a Master's course in local development which, through the transfer of know-how at the institutional and entrepreneurial level, could make an important contribution over the long term to the implementation of public policies, of the management of the SME and actions for local development. The bases were laid so that over the long term there could be other programs based on this model, contributing to generating change to the society, the economy, in the companies or even in the entrepreneurial capacity of the individuals. For this reason the attended results implied changes in the attitudes and values of entrepreneurship and contributed to a real behavioral change, stimulating the start of new companies in a sustainable and integrated way to the growing needs of the local actors.

When facing the problem of training for the innovation and local development sector – since the training activity is usually specifically designed for the figure the activity is addressed to – first it was necessary to understand who were the professional figures interested in the problem. The starting point was the idea which in many contexts, even characterized with excellent levels of scientific research, the valorization of the research is particularly penalized due to the absence of ad hoc professionals who are able to guide the passage from an idea to its practical application and to act as catalysts of innovation processes (Butera 1995).

These professional figures are what Diamantini (2004) defines as "innovation managers" or "managers of technological transfer": professional figures which the Master's program is focused on, as they are characterized by a vast range of knowledge on transfer processes, the sources of financing, the ability to introduce elements, innovation policies and organizational changes in companies and contexts which follow innovative behaviors aimed at competing in global markets. From this point of view, they can represent a number of limited targets, but they are strategically crucial: the dynamics of innovation, though a circumscribed phenomenon, have in fact many downfalls on the national socioeconomic system. Because of the limited number of interested subjects and the high profile of the involved competences, is possible to speak of elitist or highly specialized training processes, especially if compared to models for mass training. The technological transfer manager is designated as the catalyst of innovative processes which allow innovation systems and district contexts to improve their own competitiveness and productive capacity.

In Brazil, more than in Italy and Europe, the technology transfer manager represents a rather new professional profile, so it's difficult to find his own collocation in training programs, which means it is difficult to define exact guidelines to follow. The issue of the competences which the actors involved in the development processes should have in order to effectively manage the change processes and the required functions is emphasized by the more and more diffused need to have structured forms of relations between the education system, the training one and other political, social and territorial subjects which are necessary for the planning and development of the services. This leads to the need to find forms of collaboration, coordination and integration which have determined the necessity to revise the organizational and governmental forms of the system.

The need for coordination, integration and renegotiation of roles and tasks make clear that it is necessary to reason in terms of *governance*, rather than with rules and procedures of a hierarchical government. The concept of integration, in particular, stands as a prerequisite for change in the forms of regulation of the system and, above all, of the system of education and training.

THE TERRITORIAL DIMENSION OF THE TRAINING ACTIVITY: A MODEL FOR GOVERNANCE

In the last decades, the competences of the actors have become central in the debate on educational and training policies, thanks to the centrality attributed to the actors in the realization of the innovations and changes. No effective change is possible without changing from bottom up and from the outskirts to the center,[12] inside a process based on practices, learning and sharing of objectives.

In this sense, the vision of the development on which the training intervention of the Master's program is based is centered on a different role of the local actors and above all requires new skills, new competences, as much from the single entity (companies or individuals) as from social groups. This is what approaching to the problem of learning and training means, in a polycentric conception of development based on dynamics of territorial-situated social actions: it cannot but be seen as a *collective* problem, and this is demonstrated by the fact that the vocational and environmental characteristics of the region and the territory were taken seriously into consideration. This is because even a rural territory or an urban suburb of a big city can be seen as an open learning space, where the interactions among people, groups and organizations produce and diffuse information, culture and knowledge. But one needs to ask *for what* does this territory actually educate the people who live and work there.

From this point of view, the same dynamics of the local development can generally be considered like a collective learning process, through which the community *learns* how to know and analyze its own situation, to define perspective of improvement of the local conditions of life, to organize and manage social, economic, cultural and environmental changes: in this way the territory becomes *place* and *contents* of the training.[13] This means that, on one hand, the definition of the situations of people's life and work permits an identification of the most shared training needs, therefore more realistic; on the other hand, the reference to the physical and local socioeconomic context make it easier, on a purely cognitive level, to grasp new theoretical contents, therefore the development of new

---

12   Battistelli 2002.

13   Cf. Caldarini and Susi 1999.

systems of mastery (or rather competences) compared to the surrounding environment, generating in this way new and more effective learning processes. In the district, that is in a defined and circumscribed territory, economic, social and cultural processes take place. On the territory the various social subjects are concretely configured in their experience, behaviors, needs and conditions of life and work, and the basic, institutional and social units are found for the planning of the development; the interweaving between work and residential life accomplished; the various behaviors regarding questions of life and civil liberties are expressed.

As claimed in the literature review when speaking of regional system of innovation (see Florida 1995: 3, Doloreux 2002) and the link between the innovative capability of the regional systems, the social capital, the networking ability, the cultural and social attitudes system and the institutional development (see Rizzi 2003: 4), the notion of territory is used for supporting the innovation process, as place and object of the economic, cultural and social relations, which assume different meanings as reference parameter for the interventions and, before that, for the planning of the training interventions.

First of all, territory has to be considered as a *place of action*. An economically, socially and culturally circumscribed territorial unit must be delimited, which presents concrete and specific problems and tries to define the lines of a possible development. It stands to reason that the training action of the Master's has referred to these situations, in order to contribute to their evolution. It has been held in the State of Rio de Janeiro: even if is the second state of Brazil, behind San Paolo, for GDP and tax revenues, Rio has a very low public investment in health, safety, infrastructures, transports, which has effects on the low level of human capital qualification (13 percent of the total of Brazilian students, compared to 26 percent of San Paolo), on the public administration inefficiency, on the scarce infrastructural apparatus, on the safety, which represents a real emergence.

In the second place, the territory is a *place of participation*, considering that no one can better understand the problems and needs of the population, including training and cultural needs, than those people who live there. For this reason, in the selection of the students who would have attended to the Master's a particular attention has been given to their knowledge of the environment, community, issues related to them; so, they would have been residents in the Brazilian states of Rio de Janeiro, Espírito Santo and Bahia, preferably with a high studies degree, but not necessarily if they had an extensive work experience; their aim had to be to improve the skills and specialization for their careers, adaptability and entrepreneurship. In this way the team who planned and managed the Master's process has been able:

- to develop a training action adapted to the economic and socio-cultural characteristics of the environment (as the result of not only an external investigation, but also of the local forces' representation);
- to use the educational resources of the environment and to contribute to the construction of an integrated training system;
- to give the community which the Master's students belonged to, the guarantee of the social control on the objectives, contents and methods of the training project.

In the third place, the territory as *content* of the training program. One assumption that the planners have taken into great account when planning the Master's program, was the fact that adults work hard in a training program only if they have any hope of finding an answer to their problem, to their situation. This has required also starting from problems of life and work of the people involved, using an in depth examination of these problems with all the necessary knowledge. At the end, students have been required to evaluate different aspects of the training action, including the program's ability to align with their questions, perspectives, life experiences and to valorize the acquired skills in relation to their future opportunities; to evaluate the personal enrichment and the possibility to put in practice in their community what they learnt. So, since life and work problems are those which are born and presented in the territory where people live, the territory itself becomes the object, the contents of the training, as a place of productive and residential life.

In the last place, the territory must be considered as *district*[14] (see Bagnasco 1999: 4, 1988). Separateness is one of the elements which characterizes the training system: separateness from work, society; separateness of the adults' training; separateness of the training activities from the cultural ones, and separateness of both from the territory. During the Master's planning, the finding of an understanding with the other training agencies (school and professional training of the territory) has been important in order to build – or, at least, to pose the problem of – an integrated training system which allowed the concentration of resources and that linked the territory to its processes of economic-social transformation. The territorial dimension, therefore, contrasts the ghettoization of groups of the population and configures as a place of reunification and re-composition of training processes.

The experience of the Master's program in Brazil allowed to foresee, in the articulation of the various phases of the training activities, an alternation between moments of critical and collective observation of local territorial processes, discussions and re-elaborations of personal work and life experiences and finally interventions of experts: as seen before when talking of human capital training as lever of promotion of a country's overall productivity (Bianchi 2001: 5), this different steps are fundamental to implement a successful and virtuous innovation process in a country.

For these reasons, it has been fundamental for the Master's success to put the training activities in a more articulated *system* which could favor the analysis of needs, the evaluation of the activities and the creation of an awareness and information device on the territory: only a system articulated in this way, conveniently connected to the job world and contexts of life (giving the competence for the reading of these contexts), can guarantee a long life-learning process that is, in its turn, a crucial point for the innovation dynamics (see Lundvall 1992: 3). There is a real situation of training only when this is inserted into a more general context, when training another person constitutes the object of research, keeping track of the needs of the people to be trained and the territory in which these people live or operate, of their motivations, when even constant actions of information and awareness are foreseen (in the direction of the people, the environment, the institutions …), together with users' welcoming and orientating actions, training of trainers and activities evaluation. There is training, therefore, when the activity (not necessarily *the course*) is part of a *global device* which has training as its *objective*. In other words, there is training when there is *a group of people who learn* according to an articulated, explicit and shared project.

---

14 In the analysis of Becattini (1989), an industrial district is an agglomeration of economic realities that generates and at the same time takes advantage of economies of scale, and which is reproducing itself over the time.

Figure 8.1   The realization of a 'global' training project (adapted from Susi 1989)

The notion of *global training device*[15] (see Figure 8.1) underlines the fact that training cannot reach its objectives without endowing itself with a set of adequate instruments to understand and face the variety and complexity of the situation.

1. *Analysis of needs and demand* (objective training need and situation-problem): Sometimes people live in a situation which objectively determines training needs that are not able to subjectively translate, totally or partially, into training demand. The same life and work situation poses concrete problems for them: training which wants to be an answer, even if partial to these problems, would be able to motivate adults into participating.
2. *Information and awareness*: In general information does not reach the public or it arrives deformed. But if it is not possible to inform well, a fundamental condition for the involvement of adults in training activities is not achieved. Thus, an action of awareness is needed.
3. *Welcoming and orienting*: This is a key passage as, from one side, it can help people enhance their potential and make informed choices and can support the training

---

15   Susi 1986, 1989; Susi and Caldarini 1999.

motivation; from the other side it is important as agent of change, because can help people overcome the disorientation caused by the changes that characterize the emerging economies and exploit in a positive way the opportunities that are created, by assisting individuals in choices and transitions of job mobility and employment. In addition, the orienting action is intended as a factor of local development, because it can promote a better balance between training, professional qualification and potential areas for regional development.

4. *Training*: The fundamental principle is *diversification of the offering*. Adults live in different situations which require different training possibilities. *Differentiation of the users* and *focus of the target* are important notions to be used and *education of choice and contract* and *education for objectives* are the strategies to be followed. The students have the right to choice and to decide the contents and conditions of the training with the trainers; the learning objectives are defined in operational terms ("to be capable of"). The method of work is a *collective and assisted self-training*. Starting from the hypothesis that the participants already have some competences, knowledge and experience of the problem faced, they assume the responsibility of the training project with the support of experts, who have the role of *entertainers-trainers*. The learning process takes place through the mediation of the group: it is centered on the collective aspect of the problems and collaboration among participants is encouraged as an organization of functional work with the objectives of the project. The trainer unites the questions, makes his proposals, identifies the shortcomings and guides the group to acquire new theoretical and practical knowledge. His role is recognized by the group; his function is defined by the contract.

5. *Training of the trainers*: The trainers are not necessarily teachers by profession, but can be recruited for the occasion from the local population, from those, for example, in the production or service area, professionals (expert farmers, public speakers, researchers, entrepreneurs, etc.). The trainers are continuously trained with a modality of work which puts their experience at the center in order to be analyzed with the help of specialists.

6. *Research*: Research on the training group is fundamental: on its characteristics (age, gender, instruction level and professional situation), problems and experiences, culture and motivations. Research and analysis of the training itself is also important, along with the methodologies, organization, methods and contents, costs and infrastructures.

7. *Evaluation*: The analysis of the results of the training is also fundamental; it must focus on the changes which actually took place in the people and in the organizations, in their lives and jobs, more than a formal exam of the learning objectives established a priori. Any unsuccessful cases or abandonment of the training should be analyzed in depth, together with more effective experimentation and successful situations.

Analyzing the sense and contents of the governance in the type of system just described means trying to understand how the definition of governance is accepted, to identify the processes, the environments and the subjects who are most involved in the change of their manner and content of work.

The governance, emphasizing the concept of "network," must be defined as what Fadda calls "interactive governance,"[16] in which the different actors can coordinate their own intervention strategies and share the necessary knowledge for planning actions and development. As Fadda underlines, however, there is no doubt that in the interactive governance all the subjects must be involved, but a lack of distinction of the roles and weights in the participative processes could block the achievement of the consent or produce unbalanced choices turning at the effective representation power disadvantage and at the advantage of contingent and disproportionate conditioning powers, or worse still, blackmail.

It appears evident how the complex architecture of the schools and professional training governance requires a lot of efforts to achieve the ambitious objectives of integration between systems that are already complex in themselves and characterized with specific types of problems. This put the operators of different institutions, and all the stakeholders involved (see Figure 8.2), in the condition to achieve governance modalities of the whole system, following totally new logics respect to the traditional ones.

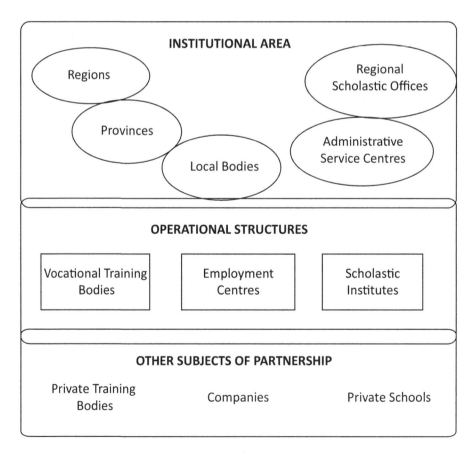

Figure 8.2   Map of the institutional and other actors involved in the governance according to the level

16   Fadda 2003.

DEPENDING ON THE GOVERNANCE ENVIRONMENT, THE SUBJECTS WHO ASSUME A CENTRAL ROLE CHANGE

The students of the Master's can be said to have been introduced into a process of empowerment that allowed them to have a more aware approach to the working world and to the governance processes, to the forms of collaboration and dialogue capable to achieve results which cannot be reached with the traditional approach, in relation both to specific sectors and to the construction of active citizenship. They have been given the tools to reflect and to propose models and hypothesize well-defined pathways. This awareness, in theory, should regard the political, administrative and private system, as everyone must participate in the realization of new policies. But at present, in many cases, the operators of different systems and the different stakeholders don't possess the necessary competences to build new forms of governance through analyses and feasibility studies which identify the various characteristics in relation to the different contexts.

The Master's wanted to provide these potential future operators of the systems not only with motivations and actions seeking to accept "political" responsibility in order to achieve the objectives set, but also, and above all, differentiated skills and a set of transversal competences aimed at realizing complex and desirable processes of governance for innovation.

Conclusions

It should be clear now that the development and competition objectives of a country – all the more so, a country like Brazil which is showing strong growth potential – achieved through training policies dealing with integrated governance of multiple instruments, can be reached only on the condition that networks are installed and developed to be integrated both in the training institutes of excellence and in the production systems, using specialized training models. This implies putting emphasis on participation and co-responsibility, to be done with greater public participation of citizens (active citizenship); but it also demonstrates the need for the system of governance to assume precise "forms," which are "capable of guiding and giving form to existent networks through thoughtful interaction and strategic leadership."[17]

In what was previously defined "knowledge society," these links are configured as real or virtual competency networks, which express modalities through which they exercise territorial governance, promoting agglomerations among the various actors, avoiding redundancy and useless multiplications of structures. The networks of competences (which originate, as seen before, in a regional system of innovation, that is a precise and well-defined territory) derive mostly from the request of public policies finalized on reinforcing the competition of the local territorial systems. They are internally characterized by the presence of different institutions, such as universities, research centers, public institutions, businesses and by the possibility to operate on trans-disciplinary knowledge. They are structures which operate horizontally, according to a synergic and cooperative logic among the various actors, and are oriented towards the market as their mission is to offer research both applied and, above all, applicable to the local businesses.

---

17   Amin and Hausner 1997.

The innovation with the competency networks becomes a key element of the processes of socio-environmental transformation allowing the passage from the instrumental use of technologies and knowledge to their social use. Through the diffusion and sharing of a culture of making innovation, in fact, it is possible to grow in competitiveness, and from the analysis developed before it emerges that, to give continuity to this process and to strengthen choices of innovation, it is important first of all to cultivate talent along with scientific, organizational, managerial and negotiation competences: the Master's has represented a significant example of this attempt, as it aimed at giving both theoretical rudiments of economic and innovation policy, and practical skills of innovation management, analysis of the contests, marketing, research and development, business intelligence, project management and change management.

Secondly, it is necessary to qualify and expand the universities and research centers, to modernize the service infrastructures; to change from an economy based on possession to an economy of access; to protect the most competitive and "futurible" ideas through patent policies which are socially sustainable; integrate the industrial and economic policies with those of knowledge and a good life style. But above all giving importance to young people through ongoing training, guaranteeing them job stability, a worthwhile job in advanced sectors and continuous professional growth. A first step on this way, through *permanent training strategies*, is the transformation of the training system and, in particular, of the universities, which as teaching and research structures must become places of learning and of continuous interaction with businesses, institutions, territory: they are necessary elements to face the challenges of competitiveness and the incorporation of new technologies in order to improve social cohesion, equal opportunities and the quality of life. This is true not only at the European Union level, the Europe of the future based on the "knowledge economy," which for years has been dedicating projects and resources for these objectives;[18] but it can also be applied to Latin American countries, as in our case to Brazil, where the incorporation of the "third mission" of the university[19]can really make the public research universities a fundamental instrument for diffusing knowledge, research and economic development in the country. As shown before, they are currently in a phase of cultural transformation, as the education institutes are playing a significant role in the emerging societies based on knowledge,[20] where in recent years the right environment for the development of a virtuous interaction between university–industry–government has affirmed.[21]

For these reasons, and for the success and positive relapses the Master's obtained, is likely and desirable to aim at replicating such an initiative in other areas which present a minimal potential of development, that is which have such basic components (the level of individual resources, the manner that individuals in the community have developed to interact with and relate to each other, the level of human capital and both generalized and institutional trust) that are able to let a virtuous process of empowerment and innovation

---

18   A fundamental moment was the pathway which was activated in 1999 by the "Bologna Process," where the Ministers of Education of European countries were involved with the construction of a European space of higher education, integrated with research.

19   Etzkowitz 2004: 64–77; Etzkowitz and Klofsten 2005: 243–55.

20   Ferreira et al. 2009.

21   Brazilian universities were created between the 1920s and 1960s with a teaching mission. In the 1960s they started to incorporate research activities in the graduate programs. Since the 1990s, the economic development model has emphasized managerial efficiency and innovation to increase the competitiveness of Brazilian firms.

start. This means that, since there cannot be automatisms nor unique models in the relationships between the training and the scientific structures and productive realities, and since development is defined, depending on the different socioeconomic contexts, as a discontinuous and negotiated process instead of a linear and continuous one, the best practices of learning activities have to be experimented on site, until innovation can be expressed in competitiveness and socioeconomic growth.

This is the reason why the local and regional governments and the citizens are the principal protagonists: no one is able to define from the outside a project of sustainable and feasible change without the help and contribution of those who live in that particular situation. So, as it has been said previously, it is their task to define, sustain and pursue strategies and pathways, to evaluate the potentialities of the productive and scientific system, and to plan the objectives to follow and the instruments to activate with the social forces and entrepreneurs.

Questions to Consider

1. Is the framework of the training system in which the actors operate complete? In other words, do the roles and competences and the instruments of connection between institution, social parts of the territory and other subjects need to be more clearly defined?
2. How can parameters, indicators, instruments, procedures characterizing the evaluation system be defined in the global training device previously defined?
3. If human capital is developed through formal training and education aimed at renewing one's capabilities in order to do well in society, what is the deep nature of the relationship between human capital and the success of a country?
4. Understanding that, within a nation, and even within a region, differences in the levels of human capital and innovative activities do exist, how can the Master's experience, that is an high level and very specialized learning activity, adapt and create value across different cultures and regions characterizing the emerging countries?

References

Abramovitz, M. 1995. The Elements of Social Capability, in *Social Capability and Long-Term Growth*, ed. D.H. Perkins and B.H. Koo. Basingstoke: Macmillan Press.

Adler, P.S. and Kwon, S-W. 2002. Social capital: Prospects for a new concept. *Academy of Management Review*, 27(1), 17–40.

Alessandrini, G. 2001. *Risorse Umane e New Economy*. Rome: Carocci.

Alguezaui, S. and Filieri, R. 2010. Investigating the role of social capital in innovation: Sparse versus dense network. *Journal of Knowledge Management*, 14(6), 891–909.

Amin, S. 1977. *Unequal Development*. New York: Monthly Review Press.

Amin, S. 1990. *Maldevelopment: Anatomy of a Global Failure*. London: United Nations University Press.

Amin, A. and Hausner, J. 1997. *Beyond Market and Hierarchy: Interactive Governance and Social Complexity*. Aldershot: Edward Elgar.

Amin, A. and Thrift, N. 1994. 'Living in the global', in Amin, A. and N. Thrift (eds) *Globalization, Institutions and Regional Development in Europe*. Oxford: Oxford University Press.

Amin, A. and Thrift, N. 1998. 'Globalisation, socioeconomics, territoriality', in Lee, R., Wills, J. (eds) *Society, Place, Economy: States of the Art in Economic Geography*. London: E. Arnold.

Archibugi, D., Howells, J. and Michie, J. 1999. *Innovation Policy in a Global Economy*. Cambridge: Cambridge University Press.

Arora, A. and Gambardella, A. (eds). 2005. *From Underdog to Tigers: The Rise and Growth of the Software Industry in Some Emerging Economies*. Oxford: Oxford University Press.

Bagnasco, A. 1977. *Tre Italie: La problematica territoriale dello sviluppo italiano*. Bologna: Il Mulino.

Bagnasco, A. 1988. *La costruzione sociale del mercato*. Bologna: Il Mulino

Bagnasco, A. 1999. *Tracce di comunità*. Bologna: Il Mulino.

Bagnasco, A. 2003. Social capital in changing capitalism. *Social Epistemology*, 17(4), 359–80.

Bagnasco, A., Piselli, F., Pizzorno, A. and Trigilia, C. 2001. *Capitale sociale: Istruzioni per l'uso*. Bologna: Il Mulino.

Baker, W.E. 1990. Market networks and corporate behavior. *The American Journal of Sociology*, 96(3), 589–625.

Barro, R.J., Mankiw, N.G. and Sala-i-Martin, X. 1995. Capital mobility in neoclassical models of growth. *American Economic Review*, 85, 103–15.

Battistelli, F. (ed.). 2002. *La cultura delle amministrazioni tra retorica e innovazione*. Milan: Franco Angeli.

Becattini, G. 1989. *Modelli locali di sviluppo*. Bologna: Il Mulino.

Becattini, G. 2000a. *Il Distretto Industriale*. Turin: Rosenberg and Sellier.

Becattini, G. 2000b. *Dal distretto industriale allo sviluppo locale. Svolgimento e difesa di una idea*. Turin: Bollati-Boringhieri.

Becattini, G. 2000c. *Dal distretto industriale allo sviluppo locale*. Turin: Bollati Bordigheri.

Becker, G.S. 1964. *Human Capital*. New York: Columbia University Press.

Bianchi, T. 2001. With and without co-operation: Two alternative strategies in the food-processing industry in the Italian south. *Entrepreneurship and Regional Development*, 13, 117–45.

Bostrom, A.K. 2003. *Lifelong Learning, Intergenerational Learning, and Social Capital: From Theory to Practice*. Stockholm: Institute of International Education, Stockholm University.

Botelho, A.J.J. and Almeida, M. 2009. 'Overcoming institutional shortcomings for academic spin-offs: Policies in Brazil', in VII Triple Helix International Conference, Glasgow.

Bourdieu, P. 1985. The Forms of Capital, in *Handbook of Theory and Research for the Sociology of Education*, ed. J.G. Richardson. New York: Greenwood Press, 241–58.

Bourdieu, P. 1986. 'The Forms of Capital', in Richardson, J.G. (ed.), *Handbook of Theory and Research for the Sociology of Education*. New York: Greenwood, 241–58.

Bourdieu, P. 1990. *Le Sens pratique*. Paris: Editions de Minuit [also published as *The Logic of Practice*. Cambridge: Polity Press, 1990].

Breschi, S. and Malerba, F. 1997. 'Sectoral systems of innovation: Technological regimes, Schumpeterian dynamics and spatial boundaries', in Edquist, C. (ed), *Systems of Innovation*. London: F Pinter.

Burt, R. 1992. *Structural Holes*. Cambridge, MA: Harvard University Press.

Burt, R. 1997. The contingent value of social capital. *Administrative Science Quarterly*, 42, 339–65.

Burt, R. 2000. The Network Structure of Social Capital, in *Research in Organizational Behaviour*, vol. 22, ed. B. Staw and R. Sutton. Greenwich, CT: JAI Press, 1–83.

Burt, R. 2001. Bridge decay. *Social Networks*, 23, 333–63.

Butera, F. 1995. *Bachi, crisalidi e farfalle*. Milan: Franco Angeli.

Calderini, M. and Scellato, G. 2003. *Interpretare l'innovazione: Fattori di successo, misure di prestazione*. Turin: Edizioni Fondazione Agnelli.

Caldarini, C. and Susi, F. 1999. Introduzione, in C. Caldarini and F. Giarè (ed.) *Formazione e divulgazione: Sistemi locali e dispositivi globali per lo sviluppo dell'agricoltura*m. Rome: INEA (Collana Studi e Ricerche).

Camagni, R. 1992. Economia urbana: Principi e modelli teorici, La Nuova Italia Scientifica, Roma.

Cardoso, F.H. and Faleto, E. 1970. *Dependência e Desenvolvimento na América Latina*. Rio de Janeiro: Zahar Editores.

Carlsson, B., Holmén, M., Jacobsson, S., Rickne, A. and Stankiewicz, R. 2002. 'The Analytical Approach and Methodology', in B. Carlsson (ed.) *Technological Systems in the Bio Industries: An International Study*. Dordrecht: Kluwer Press, 9–33.

Castells, Manuel. 1996, 2nd edn, 2000. *The Rise of the Network Society*, The Information Age: Economy, Society and Culture, vol. 1. Cambridge, MA: Oxford, UK: Blackwell.

Castells, Manuel. 1997, 2nd edn, 2004. *The Power of Identity*, The Information Age: Economy, Society and Culture, vol. 2. Cambridge, MA: Oxford, UK: Blackwell.

Castells, Manuel. 1998, 2nd edn, 2000. *End of Millennium*, The Information Age: Economy, Society and Culture, vol. 3. Cambridge, MA: Oxford, UK: Blackwell.

Castells, M. (ed.) 2006. *The Network Society: From Knowledge to Policy*. Washington, DC: Center for Transatlantic Relations.

Cavazzani, A. 2000. Problemi di analisi del mutamento in agricoltura, in *Metodologia della divulgazione: Il fattore umano nello sviluppo agricolo*, ed. C. Caldarini and M. Satta. Roma–Cagliari: INEA–CIFDA.

Ciciotti, E. 1998. *Competitività e territorio*. Rome: Carocci.

Chesbrough, H. 2003. *Open Innovation: The New Imperative for Creating and Profiting from Technology*. Boston, MA: Harvard Business School Press.

Chesbrough, H. 2007. Why firms should have open business models. *MIT Sloan Management Review*, 48(2), 21–8.

Clark, B.R. 1998. *Creating Entrepreneurial Universities: Organizational Pathways of Transformation*. Oxford: Pergamon.

Coleman, J. 1988. Social capital in the creation of human capital. *American Journal of Sociology*, 94, 95–120.

Coleman, J. 1990. *Foundation of Social Theory*. Cambridge, MA: The Belknap Press of Harvard University Press.

Coleman, J.S. 2000. 'Social capital in the creation of human capital', in Dasgupta, P. and Serageldin I. (ed.), *Social Capital: A Multifaceted Perspective*. Washington, DC: The World Bank, 13–39.

Collis, D. and Montgomery, C.A. 1995. Competing on resources: Strategy in the 1990s. *Harvard Business Review*, 73 (July–August),118–28.

Costa, L.B. and Torkomian, A.L.V. 2008. Um Estudo Exploratorio sobre um Novo Tipo de Empreendimento: os Spin-offs Acad micos. *RAC*, 12(2), 395–427.

Day, G.S., 1997. 'Aligning the Organization to the Market' in Lehmann, D.R. and Jocz, K.E. (eds), *Reflections on the Futures of Marketing*. Cambridge: Marketing Science Institute, 67–93.

Dave, R. 1976. *Foundations of Lifelong Education*. Oxford: Pergamon.

Desai, M., Fukuda-Parr, S., Johansson, C. and Sagasti, F. 2002. Measuring the technology achievement of nations and the capacity to participate in the network age. *Journal of Human Development*, 3(1) 95–122.

Diamantini, D. 2004. *Il manager dell'innovazione: La formazione nelle professioni del trasferi-mento tecnologico*. Milan: Guerini and Associati.

Dierickx, I. and Cool, K. 1989. Asset stock accumulation and sustainability of competitive advantage. *Managemen Science*, 35(12), 1504–11.

Dakhli, M. and De Clercq, D. 2003. *Human Capital, Social Capital, and Innovation: A Multi-Country Study*. Vlerick Leuven Gent Management School Working Paper Series 2003–18.

Doloreux, D. 2002. What we should know about regional systems of innovation. *Technology in Society*, 24, 243–63.

Drucker, P.F. 1993. *Postcapitalist Society*. New York: HarperCollins Publishers.

Edquist, C. and Johnson, B. 1997. 'Institutions and organisations in systems of innovation', in C. Edquist (ed.) *Systems of Innovation: Technologies, Institutions and Organizations*. London and Washington, DC: Pinter/Cassell Academic.

Etzkowitz, H. 2004. The evolution of the entrepreneurial university. *International Journal of Technology and Globalization*, 1, 64–77.

Etzkowitz, H. and Klofsten, M. 2005. The innovating region: Toward a theory of knowledge-based regional development. *R&D Management*, 35(3), 243–55.

Etzkowitz, H., Webster, A. and Healey, P. 1998. *Capitalizing Knowledge: Intersections of Industry and Academia*. Albany, NY: State University of New York Press.

Fadda, S. 2003. Governance territoriale e Progettazione Integrata, in *Governance e sviluppo territorial*, ed. Deidda D. Formez. Roma.

Ferreira, A., Amaral, M.G., Teodoro, P. and Sousa, G. 2009. The insertion of the public university in the process of innovation and regional development: A case study, in Brazil, VII Triple Helix Conference Annals, Glasgow.

Florida, R. 1995. Toward the learning region. *Futures*, 27(5), 527–36.

Freeman, C. 1995. 'Foreword', in K. Miyazaki, *Building Competencies in the Firm*. New York: St. Martin Press.

Fukuyama, F. 1995. *Trust: The Social Virtues and the Creation of Prosperity*. New York: The Free Press.

Garofoli, G. and Vazquez Barquero, A. (eds). 1991. *Desarollo Economico Local en Europa*. Madrid: Economistas Libros.

Garofoli, G. 1992. *Economia del Territorio*. Milan: Etas.

Gradstein, M. and Justman, M. 2000. Public education, social capital and growth. *European Economic Review (Papers and proceedings)*, 44, 879–90.

Granovetter, M. 1973. The strength of weak ties. *American Journal of Sociology*, 78(6), 1360–80.

Granovetter, M. 1985. Economic action and social structure: The problem of embeddedness. *American Journal of Sociology*, 91, 481–510.

Grant, R.M. 1996. Prospering in dynamically-competitive environments: Organizational capability as knowledge integration. *Organization Science*, 7, 375–87.

von Hayek, F.H. 1937. Economics and knowledge. *Economica*, n.s. 4(13), 96–105.

Huber, G.P. 1991. Organizational learning: The contributing processes and the literatures. *Organization Science*, 2, 81–115.

INEP. 2009. Sinopse de Educacao Superior – 2008. Available at: www.inep.gov.br

Kilkenny, M., Nalbarte, L. and Besser, T. 1999. Reciprocated community support and small town–small business success. *Entrepreneurship & Regional Development*, 11, 231–46.

Krugman, P. 1991. *Geography and Trade*. Cambridge, MA: MIT Press.

Landry, R., Amara, N. and Lamari, M. 2002. Does social capital determine innovation? To what extent? *Technological Forecasting and Social Change*, 69, 681–701.

Lin, N. 1999. Social networks and status attainment. *Annual Review of Sociology*, 23.

Lin, N., Cook, K. and Burt, R. 2001. *Social Capital: Theory and Research*. New York: Aldine de Gruyter.

Lucas, Robert E. Jr. 1988. On the mechanics of economic development. *Journal of Monetary Economics*, 22, 3–42.

Lundvall, B.A. 1992. *National Systems of Innovation: Toward a Theory of Innovation and Interactive Learning*. London: Pinter.

Lundvall, B. 2003. Why the new economy is a learning economy. *Economia e Politica Industriale*, 117, 173–85.

Maculan, A.M. and Mello, J.M.C. 2009. University start-ups for breaking lock-ins of the Brazilian economy. *Science and Public Policy*, 36(2), 109–14.

Machlup, F. 1962. *The Production and Distribution of Knowledge in the United States*. Princeton, NJ: Princeton University Press.

Malerba, F. 2002. Sectoral systems of innovation and production. *Research Policy*, 31, 247–64.

Malerba, F. and Orsenigo, L. 1997. Technological regimes and sectoral patterns of innovative activities. *Industrial and Corporate Change*, vol. 6(1). Oxford: Oxford University Press, 83–117.

Malerba, F. and Orsenigo, L. 2000. Knowledge, innovative activities and industry evolution, Industrial and Corporate Change

Mello, J.M.C. and Renault, T. 2006. 'Integrating entrepreneurial initiatives in Brazilian universities', Ethiopia Triple Helix Conference Annals, Addis Ababa.

Mowery, D.C. and Rosenberg, N. 1993. 'The US national innovation system', in R.R. Nelson (ed.), *National Innovation Systems: A Comparative Analysis*. New York: Oxford University Press.

Mutti, A. 1998. *Capitale Sociale e sviluppo: La fiducia come risorsa*. Bologna: Il Mulino.

Nahapiet, J. and Ghoshal, S. 1998. Social capital, intellectual capital, and the organizational advantage. *Academy of Management Review*, 23(2), 242–66.

Neave, G. 1996. Comparing higher education systems. *Higher Education*, 32(4), 395–402.

Nelson, R. (ed.) 1993. *National Innovation Systems: A Comparative Analysis*. Oxford and New York: Oxford University Press.

Nelson, R.R. and Winter, S.G. 1982. *An Evolutionary Theory of Economic Change*. Cambridge, MA: Harvard University Press.

North, D.C. 1995. *Istituzioni, cambiamento sociale, evoluzione dell'economia*. Bologna: Il Mulino.

Nonaka, I. 1994. A dynamic theory of organizational knowledge creation. *Organization Science*, 5(1), 14–37.

Organisation for Economic Cooperation and Development (OECD) 1999. *Managing National Innovation Systems*. Paris: OECD.

Organisation for Economic Cooperation and Development (OECD) 2000. *Science, Technology and Industry Scoreboard 1999: Benchmarking Knowledge-Based Economies*. Paris: OECD.

Organisation for Economic Cooperation and Development (OECD). 2003. *Main Science and Technology Indicators*. Paris: OECD.

Oliveira, R.M. de and Velho, L. 2010. 'Universities and intellectual property rights in Brazil: A first overview', Triple Helix VII International Conference Annals, Glasgow/Escócia.

Padula, G. 2002. *Reti di imprese e apprendimento*. Milano: Egea.

Patel, P. and Pavitt, K. 1994. National innovation systems: Why they are important, and how they might be measured and compared. *Economics of Innovation and New Technology*, 3, 77–95.

Piccaluga, A. 2001.*La valorizzazione della ricerca scientifica, come cambia la ricerca pubblica e quella industrial*. Milan: Franco Angeli.

Pisano, G.P. 1994. Knowledge, integration and the locus of learning: An empirical analysis of process development. *Strategic Management Journal*, 15, 85–100.

Porter, M. 1986. *Competition in Global Industries*. Boston, MA: Harvard Business School Press.

Portes, A. and Sensenbrenner, J. 1993. Embeddedness and immigration: Notes on the social determinants of economic action. *American Journal of Sociology*, 98(6), 1320–49.

Powell, W.W. and Brantley, P. 1996. 'Magic Bullets and Patent Wars: New Product Development in the Biotechnology Industry' in T. Nishiguchi (ed.), *Managing Product Development*. New York: Oxford University Press, 233–60.

Prais, S. 1995. *Productivity, Education and Training: An International Perspective*. Cambridge: Cambridge University Press.

Prahalad, C.K. and Hamel, G. 1990. The core competence of the corporation. *Harvard Business Review*, 68(3), 79–91.

Putnam, R. 1993. The prosperous community: Social capital and public life. *American Prospect*, 13(4), 35–42.

Putnam, R. 1995. Bowling alone: America's declining social capital. *Journal of Democracy*, 6(1), 65–78.

Putnam, R. 2000. *Bowling Alone: The Collapse and Revival of American Community*. New York: Simon and Schuster.

Rizzi, P. 2003. Capitale sociale e crescita regionale in Italia: una esplorazione, in Scienze Regionali, Franco Angeli, n.3.

Rizzello, S. 1997. *L'economia della mente*. Bari: Laterza.

Romer, Paul M. 1990. Are nonconvexities important for understanding growth? *American Economic Review, American Economic Association*, 80(2), 97–103.

Rullani, E. 1994. Il valore della conoscenza. *Economia e politica industriale*, 21(82), 47–73.

Sachs, W. 1993. Global ecology and the shadow of 'development', in *Global Ecology*, ed. W. Sachs. Halifax: Fernwood Books.

Schumacher, E.F. 1973. *Small is Beautiful: A Study of Economics as if People Mattered*. London: Blond and Briggs. [Italian translation: *Piccolo è bello*. Milan: Mondadori, 1978].

Senge, Peter M. 1990. *The Fifth Discipline: The Art and Practice of the Learning Organization*. New York: Doubleday Currency.

Slaughter, S. and Leslie, L.L. 1997. *Academic Capitalism: Politics, Policies, and the Entrepreneurial University*. Baltimore: Johns Hopkins University Press.

Solow, Robert M. 1956. A Contribution to the Theory of Economic Growth. *Quarterly Journal of Economics*, 70, 65–94.

Subotzky, G. 1999. Alternatives to the entrepreneurial university: New modes of knowledge production in community service programs. *Higher Education*, 38(4), 401–40.

Susi, F. (ed.), 1986. *Regioni, strategie culturali e formazione degli operatori*. Roma: Formez.

Susi, F. 1989. La domanda assente, *La Nuova Italia Scientifica*.

Susi, F. and Caldarini C. 1999. Introduzione, in *Formazione e divulgazione*, ed. C. Giarè and C. Caldarini. Rome: INEA.

Teichler, U. 1993. Research on Higher Education in Europe: Some Aspects of Recent Developments, in *Towards Excellence in European Higher Education in the 90s: Proceedings of the 11th European AIR Forum*, ed. E. Frackmann and P. Maassen. University of Trier, August 1989, EAIR.

Todaro, M.P. 2000. *Economic Development*. Reading, MA: Addison-Wesley.

Trigilia, C. 1999. Capitale sociale e sviluppo locale. *Stato e Mercato*, 57, 419–41.

Velho, L. 2004. *Science and Technology in Latin America and the Caribbean: An Overview*, INTECH/UNU/Discussion paper # 2004.4. Maastricht, February.

Wallerstein, I. 1974. *The Modern World System: Capitalist Agriculture and the Origins of the European World Economy in the Sixteenth Century*. New York: Academic Press.

Winter, S. 1987. Knowledge and Competences as Strategic Assets, in *The Competitive Challenge*, ed. D. Tecce. Cambridge, MA: Ballinger.

World Development Indicators (WDI). Eurostat e MCT – Coordenação-Geral de Indicadores; Institute for Scientific Information (ISI). *National Science Indicators*.

CHAPTER 9

Vertical Integrative Innovation

GUILLERMO SOLANO FUENTES

Introduction

The social benefits of the economic growth that innovation provides are centered on the generation of welfare, employment and the economic activity that makes the market healthy. But for regions with problems of social disintegration, Vertical Integrative Innovation initiatives provide extra advantages, as noted below.

Traditional strategies of innovation assume that those human groups, to which they are applied, have certain social minimums required. These strategies take for granted that individuals have a clear interest in achieving competitiveness of productive projects (businesses or social cooperation initiatives) in an open and dynamic market. However, this is not true for much of the world's population. In Colombia, a country with more than 41 million inhabitants,[1] 17.7 percent of the population lacks basic needs.[2] Some of the groups who are among the poorest segments of the population do not know the concept of competitiveness, or understand the dynamics of open markets.

In economically depressed regions, poverty becomes a major barrier for innovation. The lack of employment or any other source of funding affects the possibilities of development of poorer segments of the population by limiting their access to education or capital to create their own businesses. There are many types of poverty in addition to the economic one; however, many public institutions designed integration strategies as if poor people were "poor overall." As suggested by DABS researchers: "They are not taken into account, for example, their knowledge and skills in the production of wealth, their values, customs, livelihoods and coexistence, not their choice to peacefully build a country." Additionally, unemployment, which in another social environment may lead to the upbringing of enterprises as an alternative for income generation, conducts to an opposite situation where these people have no access to basic means to start their own businesses. In this case, as Amartya Sen puts it, "There is clearly some psychological potential here for a motivational collapse that can be devastating on its own and also conducive to further social exclusion later on."[3]

A research focused on the values' structure of these populations gives us a broader view of the state of scientific phenomenon in Colombia. Many of the youth of the new generations are born in social environments in which science and research are

---

1   According to the latest population census conducted by DANE (National Statistics Department) in 2005. [Online]. Available at: http://www.dane.gov.co.

2   DANE. Multidimensional indicators. 2002–2009. [Online]. Available at: http://www.dnp.gov.co/PortalWeb/Programas/Educaci%C3%B3nyculturasaludempleoypobreza/Pol%C3%ADticasSocialesTransversales/Promoci%C3%B3ndelaequidadyreducci%C3%B3ndelapobreza/tabid/337/Default.aspx.

3   Sen 2000: 21.

not appreciated. Scientific activity is not part of the activities that these young people aspire to devote their working lives. In this case, the cause of the exclusion of innovative entrepreneurship is not the financial limitation but a kind of self-exclusion from a distorted scale of values. As a result of the above, it is possible to find some groups excluded from the innovative activity which, despite living in marginal areas of cities, cannot really be classified as poor. These marginalized people have found ways to earn income through activities outside the law. In this situation, the major barrier to the emergence of productive activities that allow the application of methodologies of innovation is not necessarily the economic constraint, but the lack of alignment between the promise of innovative activity and the expectations and aspirations of these people. In these groups, few people dream of being researchers or inventors. Very often the ideal of successful adult image does not correspond with the innovative entrepreneur, or even with the successful athlete or famous artist, but with the one of a leader of a criminal group. The application of creativity, then, is not related to solving problems in production or launching of amazing products to the market, but with the discovery of novel strategies to evade the law. This situation becomes a downward spiral closing off possibilities for emerging competitive businesses.

This broad view of the situation of communities marginalized from the innovative business activity and the causes for such exclusion makes us rethink many of the assumptions by which research activity has been attempted to be promoted in marginal sectors of the population.

Thus, one of the most important challenges in Latin America is building a social layer that supports the birth of innovative entrepreneurial initiatives and their following development as competitive enterprises. This social layer provides the human resources needed for the flourishing of innovation and small businesses.

In Colombia, some of the people responsible for public innovation policies have been working on increasing the participation of traditionally excluded sectors in innovation activities. For Colciencias (Administrative Department of Science, Technology and Innovation) agency which centralizes in Colombia since 1968 the development efforts for science, technology and innovation, this is one of its biggest challenges: "This is about the knowledge humanistic approach," as called by Maria del Rosario Guerra, former director of Colciencias. She adds: "science and technology themselves are contributing to generate cultural transformations of society."[4]

Some of the most pressing challenges for Latin America and similar countries with weak economies or recent history of internal conflict include the following: building of national social agreements towards the search and benefit of knowledge; increasing coverage of education and its focus on research; and rebuilding confidence in the national scientific capabilities. What for most industrialized societies is clear, which is science is a viable way to build competitive advantages, for societies such as the Colombian, reality is different. Science is perceived as distant, unattainable, and characteristic of other latitudes. The most important question is: is it possible to generate world-class innovation in a society where priorities and values are distant from science? For those who build policies, this situation represents a dilemma. Do you need to follow the examples of more developed countries and allocate as many resources available for traditional R&D (Research and Development)? Or should you prioritize the building of

---

4   Colciencias 2006.

social layers, investing the budget to ensure a human resource that properly values the scientific activity?

Colombia and other developing countries should duplicate their efforts. The institutions that define the strategies to increase the competitiveness of Latin American countries should be doubly effective in their work. While their peers in Europe or the United States strive to ensure the existence of spaces for researchers to provide all the resources they need for the production of knowledge, Latin American leaders must, in addition, create conditions for the existence of such researchers.

This study seeks to discover potential strategies to solve the dilemma. It starts with analyzing local experiences that have been successful in the generation of innovation as well as in the integration of sectors of society that have traditionally been marginalized of research activity. Subsequently an approach is presented that combines three courses of action that would accomplish the objective of achieving social inclusion and innovative efficiency, simultaneously.

Literature Review

Most of the studies published in recent years in Colombia on innovation have benefited from the intervention of Colciencias. These studies are an essential part of the work material used for this research. The public perception survey of science and technology[5] held in Bogotá and published in the 2007 stands out, bearing in mind that one objective of this work is the discovery of mechanisms to motivate some sectors of society about science and technology. This survey is part of the project funded by Colciencias and was conducted by the Colombian Observatory of Science and Technology. The initial purpose of the survey was to participate in the program led by the OEI (Organization of American States) and FECyT (Spanish Foundation for Science and Technology) for the implementation of surveys of public perception of science and technology and the construction of the Ibero-American Manual of Public Perception of Science Indicators. A previous study on this subject with national coverage was the one conducted by Colciencias in 2004 and published the same year with the title *The Perception that Colombians Have on Science and Technology*. This second work broadened the information contained in the Bogota study of perception at the national level. Another Colciencias publication, *75 Ways to Generate Knowledge in Colombia*, provided valuable information about how communities have integrated themselves into the research activity.

About the formation and reconstruction processes of personal values scale, valuable information was extracted from the book *Innovative Experiences*, published by the DABS (Administrative Department of Social Welfare) in 2003 in which experiences of reintegration of individuals in situations of extreme poverty and vulnerability were collected. An interesting insight into the status of the personal values of Colombians can be found in the study *Our Identity* by the CENEC (Cultural Studies Center) and RADDAR which was published in 2006 in three volumes. The article "Intercultural science education and capabilities approach" by Liliana Valladares published in *CTS* magazine (Ibero-American Journal of Science, Technology and Society) addresses the issue of science education in communities whose cultures do not correspond to Western standards. In

---

5   Colombian Observatory of Science and Technology 2008.

particular she reviews the case of indigenous people in Mexico and the commitment to generate a dialogue between traditional knowledge and that provided by modern science.

For the analysis of ParqueSoft, Maloka and Tecnoparque cases, the wealth of material available on the Internet and publications of case studies were used, such as the one conducted by the CESA (Center for Studies in Management) on Maloka or the thesis by Ivan Hernandez, Fernando Alemán and Jennifer Taborda on ParqueSoft.

The abundant international literature about science, technology and innovation provides enough material for the work of contextualization of the Colombian situation in the world. The main reference sources are listed at the end of the chapter.

Methodology

The research behind this work was focused on the analysis of the data available in publications on the subject of science, technology, innovation and society in Colombia. Many studies that have been published so far have lacked the subsequent work of analysis and benefit that allow decision-makers of public policies to increase the effectiveness of their efforts. It seems that many of those responsible for the definition of national innovation strategies are satisfied with the mere publication of studies and they do not consider it necessary to use them to deeply understand the dynamics that drive the generation and use of knowledge in Colombia.

The search for relevant information was conducted in two major fronts. The first includes information available on perception of science, technology and innovation matters in Colombian society. The second front covers successful cases of vertical integrated innovation, mainly those in which an important part of the innovation processes involve sectors of the population traditionally excluded – mostly people from lower socioeconomic strata.

Once the information was gathered, the work was directed towards discovering patterns that allowed identifying common elements in these successful experiences. The aim was to find which innovative practices produce good results in Colombia and integrate the population traditionally excluded from traditional processes of R&D.

Two interviews, one with a psychologist, expert in creativity, with experience in social reintegration projects of young people participating in armed groups and another interview with an entrepreneur, who has been part of Parquesoft and Tecnoparque, complemented the written information with actual first-hand experiences. The interview with the psychologist is included at the end of the chapter.

To have a direction for the approaches of the study and following the guidelines raised by the report of the wise-men mission,[6] the excluding condition to which the raised strategies are focused primarily is the low level of education for much of the population. It was not just thinking about strategies to improve the level of education of the population, but also to find ways to link, within innovation processes, those whose education level is significantly lower than is traditionally required. Several of the examples presented in this chapter show how the successful integration of people with just a couple of years of basic primary education has been accomplished.

---

6   See Aldana et al. 1995.

Finally, a framework was proposed that could serve as a starting point for designing policies that encourage innovation in an integrated manner. This framework, composed by three lines of action, provides the basis for the emergence of new scenarios in which innovation in Colombia has any chance of reaching an international level in the mid term. This approach can be a step toward building a policy and strategy model, applicable to all Latin American countries.

Findings and Discussion

Some efforts made to reinforce the process of entrepreneurship and the generation of knowledge have been made by private and government organizations. Foreign models of successful clusters had been imported to Latin America to try to build up local environments where the transfer of knowledge and synergic work make the entrepreneurs' efforts more viable. Nevertheless, some "natural-born" local experiences of innovation adapted to the social reality are being developed in Latin America with interesting results. These kinds of clusters can be named Vertical Integrative Innovation. One example of this is the ParqueSoft initiative in Cali, Colombia.

Cali is the third biggest city in Colombia. With 2 million people, Cali has experienced hard times in the last two decades, when the lack of right economic conditions and the emergence of an underground illicit economy based on drug traffic degraded the social layer required to motivate people to search for opportunities in new and established businesses. Once the illusion of having easy ways to improve one's personal economic conditions has faded, some leaders had figured out how to take advantage of the creative talent available. In 1999, Orlando Rincon, who traveled to Ireland and India to learn about their expanding software industry, founded ParqueSoft, a small cluster having only three firms and 20 people employed. Today ParqueSoft, as a national network of Software Technological Clusters called ParqueSoft Nation, has more than 300 firms with more than 1,000 employees and nine R&D labs. Its solutions are running in 43 countries. As an example, a ParqueSoft company developed the legal information system for Panama at a cost of US$1 million, granted by the European Union.

ParqueSoft is a successful cluster experience. What's more, ParqueSoft is not only strengthening its business, but is also working on the reinforcement of the social layer of the region as a key for future growth. In their own words: "turn ParqueSoft into a space of convergence of diverse social groups oriented towards the generation of social capital."[7] Its *Semillero* program, on a rotation basis, let 900 students from ninth grade to first year of university interact annually with entrepreneurs of ParqueSoft to promote the birth of a whole new vision of the future for them. Most of the youngsters come from the most marginal neighborhoods. The *Semillero* participants became a community working online on projects as the "Open software club." Other innovative programs reinforcing the generation of human capabilities for creativity, entrepreneurship and business strategy are the "PIS Preparatoria para la Industria del Software" (Software Industry preparation program) and Human Talent Empowerment.

The knowledge transfer dynamic is one of the most interesting characteristics of ParqueSoft. People from different companies share their ideas freely in the informal work

---

7   Available at: www.parquesoft.com.

environment of the facilities. An example of the way they share creativity is how Felipe Cardona, owner of 4GP, a ParqueSoft entrepreneurship, got the idea for his Toronto's Mobifest winner short-movie. He took the idea from another ParqueSoft entrepreneur who was working on concepts for an iPod video. Another typical behavior of the informal culture is that written contracts are not common between companies in ParqueSoft. Verbal agreements are the usual way. Trust is the key.

The result of this strategy is more than simply the growth of the software business in the region. ParqueSoft initiative is building a network of people based on clearly identified values. This network has the capability of supporting the future needs for sustainable economic development. They are coming to believe more and more in their own innovation capabilities and in hard work as differentiating factors in global markets. Vertical Integrative Innovation initiatives are creating a new dream that, as one ParqueSoft entrepreneur said, is: "giving us the satisfaction of knowing that for some reason, via a CAOTIC organizational universal model, it will become a reality."[8] ParqueSoft has taught us how innovation can actively include social sectors usually left behind in the regional cluster policies.

POLICIES THAT STRENGTHEN VERTICAL INTEGRATION IN INNOVATION

The ParqueSoft model proposes productive and creative integration, through entrepreneurship focused on the development of differentiated products and services and based on an entirely new type of organization. However, one question remains: could this same model be applied to the integration of these people in the structures of existing businesses? Integrating marginalized sectors of the population is a difficult task for any company. Several barriers are presented to those who intend to open doors of companies to candidates from marginalized sectors.

Perhaps the main barrier is the mistrust that companies feel about the behavior that might be expected from these new partners. Taking into account the efforts that most companies do to build a consistent organizational culture, it is expected that one of the concerns when attempting to incorporate people whose training and life history do not match the corporate standard is the possibility that the process of identification with the current values and practices might be difficult. A traditional organization may fear that a person whose origin and academic background is not the usual may have behaviors and attitudes that do not correspond to those that characterize the formal culture. This fear provides the company with reasons to opt for traditional profile candidates during the recruitment process. Although most organizations have mechanisms that allow the integration of employees with diverse profiles, the scope of these mechanisms is limited. The organization lacks many of the specific human management knowledge required for succeed in this enterprise.

From the innovation point of view, integration will not only allow the entry of these new participants as labor but as purveyors of ideas and innovative solutions. This new role, much more integrated than the simple allocation of operational tasks, involves far greater challenges. The organization must ensure these new employees training and knowledge required to enable them to make valuable contributions to processes improvement and product design. It is here where social transformation is connected

---

8   Sarmiento Arias 2008.

with economic development. The new participants of the production processes acquire responsibilities traditionally banned for them. New things are expected from them, such as the generation of innovative solutions, the contribution in design or a strategic vision to complement the current one of the company.

A reasonable alternative is to find ways of relying on third parties for the integration tasks of this productive force. Perhaps one of the most interesting mediation experiences between the companies and the innovative capacity of the population with limited access to education is Tecnoparque, an innovation network established by the SENA (National Apprenticeship Service) in Colombia. For years, the SENA has been a real alternative of education for a big part of the Colombian population without financial capacity to access formal higher education. Founded in 1957, the SENA is specialized in providing technological programs. During its time of operation, the SENA has acquired extensive experience in managing people from all sectors of society. For the SENA it is not strange to work with people who are not usually candidates for selection processes, in research projects in companies. Many people refer to SENA as "The University of the Poor." This course has provided the SENA with the knowledge required to operate as a bridge between the research capabilities of its students and the real needs of the companies. The Bank of Requirements, administered by the SENA is a link between the needs of the market and innovation capabilities of the people who are part of the different programs offered by the institution. The Bank of Requirements is a database that stores the descriptions of real companies' needs, which can be converted into R&D projects for students.

For companies, the use of the Bank of Requirements has several benefits:

- Responsibility for human resource management involved in innovation processes is assumed by the SENA, reducing concerns about adaptability of people with organizational policies and practices.
- Most of the technology required for the R&D process is provided by the SENA.
- The SENA provides access to additional financial resources when required for the development of industry-related solutions.
- The SENA provides tools for monitoring and assessing the impact that developments have on the economic performance of the companies.
- The company has visibility over the human team involved in the project and can hire directly the researchers who demonstrate the appropriate skills.

TECNOPARQUE

Tecnoparque is one of the initiatives of the SENA that is having more impact in including young people in processes of innovation. It is a network of nodes in different cities that drives activities for technological development innovation and entrepreneurship. Since its establishment in 2006, the main fronts of action for each Tecnoparque have been the raising of awareness, reinforcement of skills and building an effective network of innovators.

In order to accomplish this objective the Tecnoparque uses lectures, presentations and activities aimed at reach people who have not had previous contact with innovation activities. The learning and training activities includes transfer of knowledge through workshops, courses and practical seminars, provided free of charge by the institution.

The network of innovation projects uses the Bank of Requirements. The aim is to connect students with the business sector needs through productive projects. Similarly, a Bank of Projects is available, which organizes ideas proposed by participants who wish to find support for their innovative projects. None of these services have a fee for the users. Any Colombian person can register on the website of the network (see http://www.tecnoparquecolombia.org).

The Tecnoparques are having a major impact on marginalized sectors of the population. A good example is the new node of Tecnoparque opened in Soacha in 2009. Soacha is one of the most densely populated sectors in the savannah of Bogotá. After being, during the first half of the twentieth century, one of the smallest municipalities surrounding the capital, Soacha became subsequently one of the fastest growths in population in Latin America, reaching rates of 12.5 percent annually. The number of inhabitants in Soacha has not been measured accurately. The DANE (National Statistics department), an institute responsible for population censuses, says Soacha has a little over 300,000 inhabitants, but the figures the government department (Cundinamarca) mentions are very different. The regional government estimates that Soacha has over 1 million people.

The inhabitants of Soacha are mostly of low or very low socioeconomic strata (levels 1 and 2) and it is home to a big part of the displaced people arriving daily to Bogotá. Many of the displaced people come from other regions of the country escaping from violent situations. Soacha shows one of the most complex socioeconomic structures in Colombia. The municipality is highly industrialized thanks to big companies that have established their manufacturing plants there, taking advantage of its proximity to Bogotá and cheap labor. Much of the population derives its income in the informal economy activities carried out in Bogota. The crime rates are high and education is very low quality. The above elements help us to understand the context in which the SENA opens its Tecnoparque in Soacha.

An estimated 180,000 people will benefit from the programs offered by Tecnoparque Soacha. Students will have the opportunity to participate in processes of research and technology development. They will be able to be in contact with projects developed in other Tecnoparques that besides Soacha include Bogotá, Medellín, Pereira, Rionegro, Neiva and Bucaramanga. In all these cities, the model of the Tecnoparque has been successful in getting people with limited means to generate innovative projects with high impact.

AN INTERMEDIATION ALTERNATIVE

The role of SENA as a mediator[9] between employers and the population that has traditionally been excluded is presented as a solution to overcome the barriers in the process of inclusion. In a model in which the SENA works as a representative for both parties or as an intermediate stage of adaptation, companies do not need to expand their capacity to manage human resources beyond what they do now. The search for talent for innovation projects for companies is provided by the SENA.

The return produced by the innovation projects belongs to the productive sector, meaning the companies. The dynamics of new capabilities for R&D of technologies that

---

9   In the sense of being an actor that helps to level knowledge and value structures to allow people to integrate appropriately into the different corporate cultures.

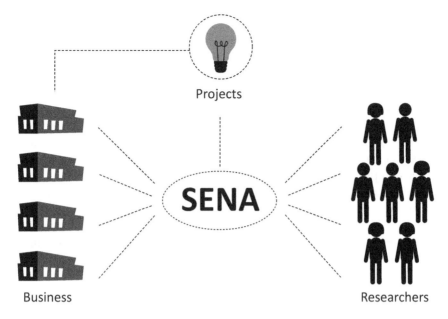

Projects

Business

SENA

Researchers

Figure 9.1 Intermediation model

students acquire drives the emergence of enterprises with high potential. This working model makes viable the integration of marginalized populations in innovation processes. At the same time it assures that innovative efforts correspond to market needs identified by the companies and it guarantees its future diffusion and use. The connection to the productive sector can also provide meaning and direction to the training. As expressed by DABS researchers "training processes must be linked to productive output, otherwise it increases the frustration of the citizenry …".[10]

Challenges for Making the Vertical Integration of Innovation Viable

COMPREHENSIVE APPROACH TO POLICIES AND INCENTIVES

The first change required is related to the perception about the producers of knowledge in society. In the case of Colombia, Colciencias has used a model of knowledge based on a producer-consumer pair as a base for the design of the policies of science, technology and innovation. In the view of Colciencias, producers of knowledge are the research centers, mostly associated with universities. Moreover, the consumers of knowledge are the companies, usually the larger ones, which have product development departments. In this model there is no room for socially excluded groups. Therefore small businesses or entrepreneurs who have developed on their own any kind of innovation have problems accessing the benefits of institutional support.

---

10   DABS 2003.

To participate in open support programs from Colciencias, you must be a recognized research center. Companies can participate only if they have a joint project which involves at least one of the "authorized" investigation centers.

Other options for getting support, closer to those who are not part of the university research community, such as competitions and grants intended to promote innovative ideas, have focused their attention on participants who have a very well-structured innovative project. Indeed, the soundness of the approach, the market research behind it, and maturity of the technology involved, tend to be important parameters in deciding the winners. The Destapa Futuro grant, from the firm Bavaria, or the Ventures grant are examples of such programs[11] in Colombia.

Although the role that these contests play to stimulate innovation activities of small and medium enterprises is undisputable, it is clear that those who can participate are precisely those who already have a strong interest in technology and academic training that enables them to formalize convincingly all the components of their project. There is still a link in the chain missing. It is still necessary to find a way to include a large proportion of the population that feels that its language and structure of thought is not that expected of a participant in these competitions.

A change in the way in which participation in innovation projects is encouraged in Colombia is urgent. It should start by considering as main actors all the Colombian people who may have creative capacity to contribute to innovation processes. And this includes those whose academic training is minimal. But do the Colombian people want to be included in these participatory strategies?

Do Colombian People Want to Participate?

A survey conducted in 2007 by the Colombian Observatory of Science and Technology called "Survey on public perception of science and technology in Bogotá" (hereafter called as perception survey) gives us some clues about how society perceives the science and innovation activity. In one of its parts the survey asks how the thematic agenda of investment in science and technology for the country should be defined: 43.33 percent answered that it should be the result of an agreement among universities, scientists and government; at the other extreme, only 6.13 percent said that it should be made from the identification of community needs. A large percentage of the population understands that the distribution of resources and the definition of priorities in the research activity should be left to these three participants (universities, scientific community and government). If we consider that the vast majority of scientists work associated with one or more universities, we must conclude that are not actually three but two players, according to a large part of society, decide the country's scientific path: universities and government.

The perception survey is very interesting for our purpose if we take into account that almost half corresponds to a population with very limited access to higher education – 47.75 percent of respondents earn the minimum wage or less, and only two of the 1,110 respondents have a PhD. In an important way, the survey shows the view of people who belong to the "poorer" sectors. It represents what we might call "the people's voice."

---

11   You can access more information on the websites of each contest. Destapa Futuro. Available at: http://www.redemprendedoresbavaria.net/ Ventures: http://www.ventures.com.co.

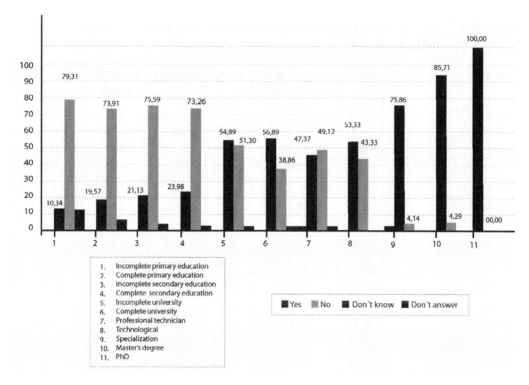

1. Incomplete primary education
2. Complete primary education
3. Incomplete secondary education
4. Complete secondary education
5. Incomplete university
6. Complete university
7. Professional technician
8. Technological
9. Specialization
10. Master's degree
11. PhD

■ Yes　■ No　■ Don't know　■ Don't answer

Figure 9.2　Percentage of people who prefer science section as first option by age

Much of the strategy of vertical integration requires that those sectors of society traditionally excluded perceive in a positive manner the science and technology activities. In the perception survey, mentioned before, participants were asked which sections of the newspaper they preferred. More than 24 percent replied that their first choice of reading is the political news section. Science ended up in eighth place out of 16, a post below the horoscope. Although it is a rather modest spot, the figures get interesting when you look at the preferences by age. Among those who responded that their first choice were the news on science, most are young. Figure 9.2 shows this situation. Of the total number of people who prefer science news, 42 percent are between 16 and 24 years.

If you think of a change of attitude from society, it will be important that both those who control the mechanisms of science and those who wish to integrate have the right attitude. A good positioning of the science and technology subject among youth will benefit, certainly, the process of integration. The favorable image that scientists have in general in the city also contributes to these processes. These were the big winners, along with medical doctors, in the results of appreciation for the various professions. The appreciation of science as a profession is a constant in all age ranges and virtually all economic strata. Only the locality of Bosa, whose inhabitants are almost all strata 1 and 2 (in a measure in which the higher strata of income and economic level is 6) showed little appreciation for scientific activity. It will be important to discover the reasons for this perception. In comparison, Usme, a locality with similar socioeconomic composition, was quite in line with the replies of the other localities.

Table 9.1   Percentage of appreciation of science as a profession by neighborhood

Locality	Much	Not much or not little	Little	Nothing	Does not know	Does not answer
Antonio Nariño	77.77	11.11	0.60	5.55	0.00	0.00
Barrios Unidos	44.44	44.44	5.55	2,77	2.77	0.00
Bosa	66.66	26.66	1.66	50.00	0.00	0.00
Candelaria	50.00	88.88	0.00	16.66	0.00	0.00
Chapinero	61.11	86.11	2.77	0.00	0.00	0.00
Ciudad Bolívar	44.04	88.88	10.71	5.95	2.88	8.57
Engativá	72.46	14.49	7.24	4.84	0.00	0.72
Fontibón	55.55	25.00	18.88	5.55	0.00	0.00
Kennedy	64.46	21.48	7.48	4.95	0.80	0.80
Mártires	61.11	27.77	11.11	0.00	0.00	0.00
Puente Aranda	79.62	14.81	5.55	0.00	0.00	0.00
Rafael Uribe	66.66	16.66	11.90	4.76	0.00	0.00
San Cristobal	75.55	10.00	10.00	8.88	1.11	0.00
Santafé	70.88	20.88	8.88	0.00	0.00	0.00
Suba	60.41	25.00	11.80	1.88	1.88	0.00
Teusaquillo	50.00	50.00	0.00	0.00	0.00	0.00
Tunjuelito	66.66	16.66	16.66	0.00	0.00	0.00
Usaquén	81.60	8.80	7.20	1.60	0.80	0.00
Usme	68.51	7.40	12.96	1.11	0.00	0.00

Table 9.1 shows the consolidated responses. Probably, the reasons for the answers obtained in Bosa should be looked at beyond the income and economic level. However, for our purpose, it is clear that inclusive actions should take into account cultural differences at the neighborhood level to increase the chances of success.

One set of answers that draws attention is the one which concerns to the level of attraction that young people of different strata show towards the scientific activity. When asked "How attractive to young people is the profession of scientist?", young people of lower socioeconomic strata found the scientific profession more attractive than those of upper strata as shown in Figure 9.3.

These responses provide an encouraging picture for innovation policies and strategies that seek to integrate marginalized sectors. Young people from lower socioeconomic strata want to be scientists. Another topic of discussion is whether they believe that this profession is within their reach, or on the contrary, it is an aspiration nearly impossible. It is likely that the people who design policies can use the knowledge gained from perception surveys to find combined strategies to increase participation in innovation activities of young people from marginalized sectors.

As a first step, these strategies should involve communication actions that change the perception about science and innovation that the poorer sectors have.

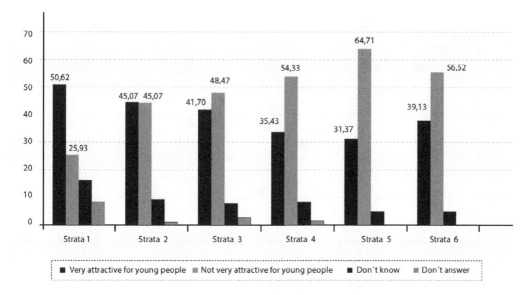

Figure 9.3 **Level of attraction of young people towards scientific activity by strata**

The Challenge of Measuring

The second radical change required is about measuring the effectiveness of integration efforts undertaken by entities such as the SENA or Colciencias. Those in charge of innovation policy design should refine their methodologies for measuring the success of these policies. As stated by *The Open Book of Social Innovation*: "In the market the simple and generally unambiguous measures are scale, market share and profit. In the social field the very measures of success may be contested as well as the tools for achieving results."[12]

It is necessary to design indicators that have the potential to simultaneously show the progress in technological development and improvements in skills and attitudes of the population

The Vertical Integrative Innovation Frame

Parquesoft and similar experiences allow us to understand an important way in which the components of a national strategy should be for promoting innovation that integrates non-traditional sectors. Here we review these components that can be integrated under the concept of Vertical Integrative Innovation.

EDUCATION FOR INCLUSION

The literature on national innovation systems puts education in a privileged place among the factors that influence more the innovative level of a country. In the case of Colombia

---

12   Murray et al. 2010.

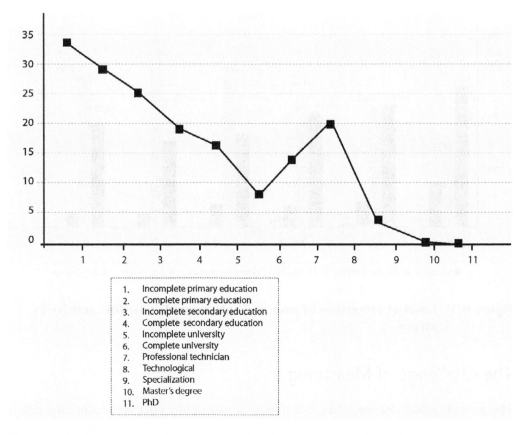

1. Incomplete primary education
2. Complete primary education
3. Incomplete secondary education
4. Complete secondary education
5. Incomplete university
6. Complete university
7. Professional technician
8. Technological
9. Specialization
10. Master's degree
11. PhD

Figure 9.4   Interest in science and technology by educational level

where a large proportion of the population have not completed their secondary education, it's clear that efforts to increase coverage of education will have great impact on including marginalized sectors in innovation activities. The educational level is directly related not only with the ability that people have to generate and take advantage of knowledge but also with the interest that these same people develop towards issues of science and technology. In the perception survey, the results of the questions regarding interest in science and technology issues discriminated by educational level show this situation clearly, as seen in Figure 9.4.

The people who showed little or no interest in science and technology issues were mostly people with low educational levels. The increase in access to schooling and university studies will help to improve social inclusion in innovation. However, although the study is very clear in showing the direct results that the educational level has on the personal interest in these issues, what we might call "viral effect" still remains to be validated. With the viral effect, it is possible that people near other people who have been interested in issues of science and technology will also increase their interest in these issues. Experiences such as ParqueSoft show that the new participants are increasing their interest in large part due to feedback that occurs in this type of environment. A young man who enters ParqueSoft finds a reality that differs from the one known in his neighborhood. The scale of values is different. The aspirations are different too. He finds in his new partners – colleagues – a benchmark for lifestyle that encourages him to change his behavior and to develop interest in the work based on knowledge.

State Support for Education

Both the Ministry of National Education and the departmental Secretaries of Education and municipalities forward programs to expand educational coverage. One example is the Plan Primavera, from the Secretary of Education of Cundinamarca, which aims to subsidize the university tuition of about 10,000 students. The Plan Primavera is aimed at young people in 1, 2 and 3 strata who have shown high academic performance and who wish to enter university.

In the case of basic primary and secondary education, the Ministry of Education has announced its interest in working on the issue of the quality of education. The need to improve the quality of education is evident when analyzing the results of state tests (ICFES exam) measuring the average knowledge of students finishing high school. In this test, the score of 0–30 is considered low, the scores of 31–70 middle, and higher scores are considered high. In the 2003 tests, the percentage of students nationwide who scored a grade below 50 points was 82.8 percent. That is, the vast majority of Colombian students have a level of knowledge that is considered medium-low or low. If we analyze the performance in mathematics, the situation is very worrying: 94.4 percent of the students in the country obtained scores below 50 points. The measurement of English proficiency, as required language to be inserted in the global culture of knowledge, shows a similar situation: 92 percent of participants at the national level scored less than 50 points.

Traditional programs to subsidize education seek to reduce the gap of education coverage that Colombia has in front of developed economies. However, it is clear that they are not sufficient and that another kind of approach is necessary. This is where the SENA model can have a significant impact in generating scientific and technological capabilities in a country with limited resources but with a population that has the capacity and a necessity to build innovative projects. This model could be replicated by many educational institutions in Colombia and Latin America. The words of Robert Schank, education expert, support this view: "The training provided by the SENA is in the correct line, because trainees, through the development of productive projects – which put into practice its ideas and knowledge – learn to think and find directly their own and true answers. It would be nice that the SENA could lead that to universities and other professional centers. That would have a great impact."[13]

The Atlántida Project

One of the most interesting studies developed in Colombia was conducted by the Atlántida project, where among other things it sought to know whether school contributes effectively to encourage young people in the development of knowledge, science, and technology. The project, conducted between 1994 and 1996, was supported by the FES

---

13   Schank 2010.

Foundation (Foundation for the Education and Social Development) and supported by the National Ministry of Education and UNESCO.

One of the most interesting contributions of the Atlántida project was the inclusion of university students and school teenagers as researchers at all stages of the project. It had more than 600 researchers participating in 10 cities in the country. In addition to discovering the key elements to improve the quality of education, included in five publications, a movement of interest was generated on the need to involve the research activity within the process of educational training.

The Atlántida project has received much recognition, including an Honorable Mention to the Scientific Research from the Alejandro Ángel Foundation.

The research approach, with a high qualitative component, produced more than 10,000 pages of views from the participants in the project on teenagers' lives.

One of the main findings of the research carried out by the Atlántida project is the poor performance of the basic schools in Colombia. In the words of Francisco Cajiao, one of the project directors: "the school focused its role in the distribution of information, putting aside pedagogical processes aimed at processing new information coming from multiple sources and the creation of new knowledge, annihilating thus its essence, turning it into a socially inefficient institution."[14]

The result of the Atlántida project experience has led to several institutions of basic, secondary and university education changing their pedagogical methodologies to include research as a fundamental pillar in the generation of knowledge culture. The project calls on the academy to go beyond the classrooms and facilitate the participation of their students in groups linked to municipal and regional development. The project stresses the importance of active youth participation in the analysis of the problems in their localities, leaving the school a key role in their stimulation.

Another discovery of the Atlántida project is about building models of life that teenagers can follow. The research found that it is common that those adults who are in close contact with young people do not appear to them as role models worth imitating. In the case of the best-known scientists, their image is presented to teenagers as idealized, which highlights the achievements and acknowledgments, but the effort path that has led them to those is not shown. There is a gap between the ideal model of adult incorporated into productive society and the models that surround the teenager, often far removed from that society. For young people, the way to become a citizen included in the culture of knowledge doesn't appear clear. In this respect, the school must help to draw the path for each student. Educational institutions in which the students peer into a reality different from their more intimate setting, have the ability to provide visions of the future and routes to reach them. The work of school as a guide in building life plans that focused on knowledge is often been hampered by the limitations of the teachers in their relationship with technology. Many of them have less knowledge of information and communications technologies than their students. Only a few are part of Internet-based social networks and even fewer perceive the potential of communications technology in the collective construction of knowledge. This situation is so evident in many educational institutions that it is possible to find inverse projects, in which the students teach their teachers to take advantage of technological tools. The "al reves" (upside down) project developed in a school in Sahagun, department of Cordoba in northern Colombia, in

---

14 Cajiao Restrepo 1999.

which students teach the use of new technologies to their teachers, was recognized as one of the best in the II Latin American Forum of Innovative Teachers celebrated in 2009 in Buenos Aires, Argentina.[15]

Education Even for State Officials

In addition to making a strategic decision to support the vertical integrative initiatives of innovation, the government must learn to recognize those who have the greatest potential and what specific actions should be taken to ensure their success. Officials must learn to manage risk, optimize the transmission of knowledge and proper allocation of scarce resources. As suggested by researchers from *The Open Book of Social Innovation* (Murray, Caulier-Grice and Mulgan 2010), it is important to include "Formation and training to integrate innovation into personal development, training, and culture. Some need to become specialists in spotting, developing and growing ideas. Others, particularly gatekeepers, need to know how to recognize the conditions for innovation. More generally, innovation, including a licence to take appropriate risks, should be part of personal development plans."

COMMUNICATION FOR INCLUSION

A communication campaign should use the appropriate communication channels to ensure a high impact. In the survey of perception, the reason most frequently used by those people who said they were poorly informed about science and technology was "Little were we informed about the issue." This suggests a deficiency of communication strategies that "sell" the subject of science and technology in the Colombian population.

But how should that communication be? The perception survey shows the main channels through which people often access scientific and technological information, as seen in Table 9.2.

Table 9.2   Percentage of use of each channel for accessing scientific and technological information

Question	Yes, frequently	Yes, from time to time	No, never	Does not know	Does not answer
Do you watch programs or documentaries on television about science, technology or nature?	29.73	48.02	21.95	0.18	0.09
Do you read scientific news published on newspapers?	15.65	34.14	49.73	0.27	0.09
Do you use Internet to find scientific information?	15.32	23.60	59.64	0.63	0.27
Do you talk with your friends about subjects related to science, technology or the environment?	13.15	37.21	49.19	0.27	0.15

15   You can see information about this project on its blog. [Online]. Available at: http://proyectoalreves.blogspot.com.

Table 9.2   Continued

Question	Yes, frequently	Yes, from time to time	No, never	Does not know	Does not answer
Do you visit museums, centers, exhibits about science and technology?	9.01	37.21	52.70	0.54	0.15
Do you read scientific magazines?	7.39	21.44	70.34	0.36	0.27
Do you listen to radio programs about science and technology?	7.21	18,29		0.34	0.36
Do you read books about science?	3.95	15.95	77.21	0.36	0.36
Do you take part or have you ever taken part in any action related to science, technology, or environmental subjects such as demonstrations or protests, letters to newspapers, taking part in debate forums, signing manifestos, referendums, etc.?	5.23	11.26	52.34	0.34	0.45

Table 9.3   Percentage of reasons for not knowing about science and technology

Reason	%
I'm not in the field	85.42
I have different priorities	18.55
Lack of will	40.00
It is not valued in Colombia	20.00
It is not especific	24.00
I'm not that environment	22.00
There is not an approach	20.00
There is not assertive coverage	43.00
There is not motivation in society	25.00
I did not learn them in school	19.00
I don't know about that	71.00
I don't have most of the studies to understand	46.00
They don't provide the necessary information	48.00
Because it is impossible to completely be informed	87.00
There is not coverage	44.00
Because I don't like to read, or boring programs	17.00
I just have general information on the subject	29.00
All the above	24.00

However, although the means included in the survey were found to be effective to convey scientific information, this does not mean that they are effective in promoting interest in the subject. Those who are already looking for scientific information or who are used to receiving it are not the priority segment that should run a communications campaign that seeks to increase social interest in science and technology. This campaign should target those who just do not usually seek information on these topics.

The people in charge of designing the communication campaign should deepen in the reasons why many people stay away from issues of science and technology. The answers received to the question about the reasons why people are poorly informed about science and technology provide information of more interest for communicators as shown in Table 9.3 on the page opposite.

In the survey, the reasons mentioned by more than 40 percent of participants to justify their lack of information on the subject of science and technology are, in order from highest to lowest frequency:

1. I do not know about that.
2. We were poorly informed on the subject.
3. I have not most of the studies to understand.
4. There is no pertinent disclosure.
5. Because there is no disclosure.

The second and the last two reasons reflect the lack of communication on the subject or at least their lack of effectiveness. The first and third are related to education.

A graph (Figure 9.5) that shows the relationship between education level and approach to issues of science and research is the one that represents the distribution of answers to the question: "Do you know any institution dedicated to scientific research?"

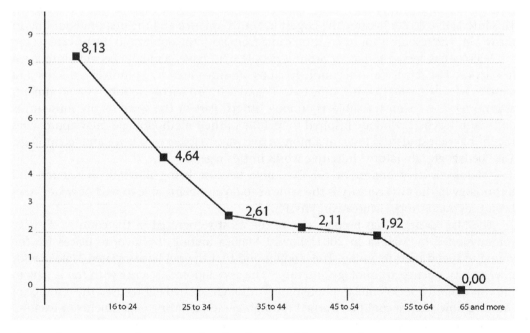

Figure 9.5   Do you know any institution working on science and technology? By level of education

The answers show a clear inverse relationship between level of education and knowledge of institutions working in research in the country. It is hoped that an increase in the level of education of the population improves knowledge about the institutions that work in research as well as other topics related to science. The knowledge of the scientific world, including its principal actors, helps people to perceive it as closer, more attainable. By contrast, the widespread ignorance about the functioning of the structures of science and technology in the country helps to foster a climate of apathy and contributes to the positioning of innovation as an elitist activity.

But the institutions themselves must communicate the importance of science and technology. Among the institutions that respondents in the perception survey say they associate with science, technology and innovation, in the second place is a very special one – Maloka. Apparently, the work Maloka has been doing to bring science closer to the population is changing significantly the scientific culture in Colombia.

Maloka

Maloka is a museum of science and technology similar to the City of Science and Industry in Paris, the Exploratorium in San Francisco or Papalote Museum in Mexico City. The center was conceived as a two-phase project, the first of which has been in operation since 1998 and includes the Cine Domo, first theater with giant format in South America, and the Interactive Center. The second phase will include the creation of the Cerebrarium, additional interactive rooms, labs and innovation centers for learning and creativity. The Interactive Center consists of nine rooms: Boys and Girls, City, Universe, Technology, Human Being, Life, Electricity and Magnetism, Molecules in motion and Biodiversity. This interactive center became the largest in South America and the first underground in the world. The resources for its creation came from both the public and the private sector.

Maloka has served to gather around people who have gradually become interested in science. The science and technology clubs are integrated by volunteer students and families who dedicate their free time to work and learn on energy, robotics, environment, astronomy and chemistry subjects, among others. Part of the work of the museum is done with teachers, who are inspired to include in their methodologies new approaches that bring their students closer, in a more active way, to issues of science and technology. The "pedagogic laboratory" initiative works in this regard.

"Maloka is very important for Colombia because being illiterate in science and technology in the next century is the same as today not being able to read or write," says Leon Lederman, Nobel Laureate in Physics.

The Maloka brand has become one of the most recognized in the country. A study commissioned by Maloka in 2001 showed Maloka among the favorite places for the young to spend their free time. The study found that the public associated Maloka with interactivity, science, technology and fun.[16] The association of science with fun is new to the vast majority of Colombian population. Although isolated efforts used the resource of showing how science could be learned through games, amazing experiments or exciting stories, none had had the impact that Maloka has had. Only a tiny minority had had contact with a museum of such "forbidden not to touch" kind. For the average people, fun

---

16   Echeverri Cañas 2010.

was not associated with science. Maloka has been successful in changing that perception. In the first 10 years of operation (1998–2008), about 16.5 million children, young people, teachers, parents and all kinds of people without prior scientific training participated in the Maloka activities. Visits to the Interactive Center added up to 4,602,309 in this period.

The impact of Maloka on the perception that the general population has about science and technology is clear. However, perhaps the most valuable contribution is its presence in sectors that have traditionally been away from these subjects: lower socioeconomic strata. Maloka has a policy of subsidies that enables free access to vulnerable groups such as communitarian mothers, children and youth homes, foundations, and participants in re-insertion programs, among others. According to Maloka's report, the number of subsidized visitors reaches 50 percent, of which the majority (approximately 70 percent) is at 1 and 2 strata. Maloka's action is not limited to Bogotá. In its first 10 years of operation the traveling Maloka program has visited about 50 towns throughout Colombia, with visits of over 1 million people. Its contribution was also helpful for creating Neomundo, a similar museum in Bucaramanga.

Maloka teaches us that communication can be made through channels that go beyond traditional media. Speaking well of science and presenting it as an interesting activity may be the way to get more Colombians to change their perception and attitude towards it.

NETWORKS FOR INCLUSION

One of the most interesting effects of the working methods of Parquesoft and Tecnoparque is the ability to generate networks that nourish in participants their interest in innovation. The opportunity to interact with young peers who have similar social situations and interests offers participants the opportunity to build social references based on knowledge.

From the point of view of vertical integration, the benefits of networks are not only the ability they have to move knowledge efficiently. This is, perhaps, the main argument used by those who analyze the value of knowledge networks offered to those interested in innovation. It is clear that in a society where knowledge is dispersed and people want to interact with others based on common interests, networks allow the cooperative and open construction of knowledge. In the case of Colombia, the networks offer an additional benefit: they can generate social cohesion around a lifestyle that has a different horizon than the one many young people find in their neighborhood. Such networks serve the purpose of generating social fabric while achieving technological developments. Social networks occur in physical spaces (this is the case of ParqueSoft), as well as in virtual environments.

One of the results of the Atlántida project is the Red Camaleón (Chameleon Network). The Chameleon project began in 1994 with the aim of providing a means of communication for the Atlántida project. The Chameleon project was organized in 25 committees spread throughout the country. These committees were formed by young people with different levels of schooling, some with only basic primary level. The project ran successfully for several years publishing a print magazine. It has now migrated to digital format and has become the Red Camaleón, with a website at www.redcamaleon.com.

The model of the editorial committees motivated young people, in addition to their work as part of the magazine, to participate more actively in their communities. Camaleón Barrancabermeja, for example, a committee that worked in an area with high social inequality in the department of Santander, was linked to the process of Peace

Laboratories in the Magdalena Medio. The Red Camaleón portal enables young people to keep contact and discuss issues of general interest. The Red Camaleón network also gave rise to the Access Code initiative of the *El Tiempo* newspaper, which offers children and young people from different cities the possibility of collaborating with notes and news.

In its moment of momentum, the Camaleón project served as a national network that genuinely involved young people from all socioeconomic strata around research in education. The keys to success can be found in the pedagogical model developed by the Atlántida program. This approach, which comes from a real and deep interest to integrate the marginalized sectors and provide participation-oriented education and research, can be a model for creating new projects that generate channels of communication and discussion among the nation's youth.

The Tecnoparques of SENA also use their network structure to generate dynamics that motivate the development of technology. Their association with the Fórmula SENA project, in which single-seater automobiles for competition, developed in different departments of Colombia, meet up to compete on the Tocancipá racing circuit, is a good example of the use of the network structure. The emotion experienced by those involved in the development of each car is amplified by the interest in competing. The common dream encourages creativity and generates the interest of companies linked as sponsors. Research efforts are multiplied. Young people begin to see technology as something closer.

Conclusion

The special situation in Colombia, where economic growth and international competitiveness are limited by the low participation of the population in activities linked to innovation, requires prompt action by those who decide national policies. The causes of low participation are concentrated in a high level of apathy for R&D activities (the result of very particular historical and socioeconomic conditions) and quality issues in education.

Some successful experiences of participatory innovation show a path Colombia can follow to increase its level of innovation and, simultaneously, strengthen the research culture in the country. A framework that involves three bases – education, communication and networks – is proposed as a starting point for the development of initiatives and the approach of national innovation policies. This framework, which will be called Integrative Vertical Innovation, brings together the elements that have made possible, despite economic and structural constraints, the emerging of cases of high-level innovation.

The educational methodology must be much more participatory. Students should participate from the beginning to the end and at all times in research processes that use the principle of "Learning by doing" and that promote the view that research is available for everyone.

The communication should focus on promoting interest in science. The state must "sell" the scientific activity as a viable dignifying and profitable alternative for those involved. A great creative work is required to design messages to position science as something close and attractive. A campaign is needed to help generate a sense of national challenge towards the strengthening of local science. It is vital to get the "translation" of the knowledge produced by academia, by Colciencias and other innovation actors in Colombia, to reach a wider audience.

Finally, networks, as a source of autonomous innovation spaces, are the third key for innovation to be truly participatory, open networks enabling real flow of knowledge, allowing people to quickly contact the experts and helping the formulation and implementation of innovation projects.

Actions that integrate in a strategic and coordinated way the three bases of this model will significantly enhance the country's innovative capacities.

Annex

INTERVIEW WITH PAOLA ANGEL (EXPERT IN CREATIVE PROCESSES IN ORGANIZATIONS AND EXPERIENCED IN WORKING WITH RE-INSERTED PEOPLE)

1. Do these people that are trying to integrate socially have the capacity required to join in innovation processes in companies?

PA *I think so, but they need training. They need to be trained and need a lot of coaching to be an actual productive component of a company and hold positions at higher levels. The society has cut their wings and they have not had the opportunities to continue studying. The educational and cultural level is low.*

It is also necessary to work from the psychology because they are mentally affected. They have been abused, maltreated; they have been in war and that makes them vulnerable. Recently a friend found one of them; he is working for Save the Children. He is helping in processes of re-insertion homes. He had completed his re-insertion process in a satisfactory way.

2. Is it possible that these people do not fit into the culture of the organization?

PA *I think that it happens. In my opinion, they have a scale of values different from ours. Starting from their familiar culture. That is why psycology work is needed.*

3. What is your prediction on the outcome of an experiment in which a company decides to incorporate people who come from processes of social re-insertion into its team?

PA *I think that the person, as any other, would adapt. If the person is happy, if the person is valued, if is respected, taught and if the person starts to watch other people, other behaviors more positive, I think they would manage to make that change. They will, sooner than later, be part of the corporate culture.*

What I do believe is that if conditions are good the person stays and does a good job, a good work. If all their basic needs are satisfied to self-realization, the person can reincorporate and be satisfied.

4. Are there prejudices or discrimination towards these people in the companies, in general?

PA *Yes, I think there is. There are these kinds of prejudices. If there are prejudices with the secretary, with people in the warehouse ... And many feel discriminated against and feel that the company is better with people with higher education levels. For example, they believe in their experience, that no other than salespeople are who warrant the success of the company.*

5. Would it be different a process of creative skills development for these people, from those traditionally designed for people already in the companies?

PA *I obviously would look at capacities and skills. Capacity for communicating new ideas. I think I would reinforce it a bit. I would think of doing something much deeper, more developed. If people who have been successful in corporate environments have so many fears when expressing their ideas and when time comes to generate ideas they freeze, people who have not had opportunity to read, experiment, move in different context, will experiment hard times.*

QUESTIONS

The following are questions proposed in order to motivate further development of the elements included in the Vertical Integrative Innovation model:

1. What teaching elements could the education system use to invite students to use research as the main way of approaching science?
2. At what stage of education should students be allowed to work as researchers in innovation projects?
3. How can people be recruited for a scientific activity?
4. What communication channels are appropriate to promote the culture of science?
5. What makes a network of scientists from a Latin American country different of an international network of the same kind?
6. Which could be the sources of funding for projects working simultaneously to improve education, communication and networks for innovation?
7. Who should perform each of the actions of a vertical integration model of innovation?
8. What would be the appropriate time to implement each of the actions in education, communication and networks?
9. How long and what kind of results should be expected?
10. What changes does a model such as the Vertical Integrative Innovation require to be implemented in other Latin American countries?
11. And, to be implemented in other emerging economies in the world?

References

Aldana, E., Chaparro, L., García Márquez, G., Llinás, R., Patarrollo, M.E. et al. 1995. *Colombia al filo de la oportunidad* [Colombia, at the Edge of Opportunity]. Bogotá: Tercer Mundo.

Cajiao Restrepo, F. 1999. 'Atlántida, approach to the Colombian school teenager'. *Nomadas Magazine*, April, Universidad Central, Bogotá.

Chamber of Commerce of Bogotá. 2005. Plan económico para la competitividad de Soacha [Economic plan for the competitiveness of Soacha]. Bogotá. Available at: http://camara.ccb.org.co/documentos/656_2005_9_14_9_13_25_PLAN_SOACHA_DEF.pdf.

Chingaté Hernández, Ius Nathalie. 2009. 'Mecanismos participativos para la democratización del conocimiento científico tecnológico' [Participative mechanisms for the democratization of scientific technological knowledge], unpublished thesis, Pontificia Universidad Javeriana, Bogotá.

Colciencias. 2006. *75 Ways to Generate Knowledge in Colombia*. Bogotá.

Colombian Observatory of Science and Technology. 2008. Encuesta de percepción pública sobre ciencia y tecnología [Public perception survey of science and technology], Bogotá 2007. Bogotá.

DABS (Departamento Administrativo de Bienestar Social). 2003. Experiencias innovadoras [Innovative experiences]. Bogotá.

Daza, S. and Arboleda, T. 2007. 'Comunicación pública de ciencia y tecnología en Colombia' [Public communication of science and technology in Colombia]. Policies for knowledge democratization? *Signo y Pensamiento Magazine* [Bogotá], June.

Echeverri Cañas, Lina Maria. 2010. *Maloka, Inspiración e innovación empresarial en una sola palabra* [Maloka, inspiration and business innovation in only one word]. Bogotá: CESA.

Education Secretary of Cundinamarca. 2009. *Annual Report*. Available at Government of Cundinamarca's website. Available at: http://www1.cundinamarca.gov.co/gobernacion/Link Click.aspx?fileticket=iVsTyZKfAmE%3D&tabid=87&mid=870.

El Espectador. 2009. 'Tecnoparque, nuevo motor de Soacha' [Tecnoparque, Soacha's new engine], November 11. Available at: http://www.elespectador.com/impreso/vivir/articuloimpreso171710-tecnoparque-el-nuevo-motor-de-soacha.

Hernández, I., Alemán, F. and Taborda, J. 2006. Parquesoft: Un estudio de emprendimiento social en cluster de la industria del software en Cali, Colombia [ParqueSoft: A study of social entrepreneurship in software industry cluster in Cali, Colombia]. *Economic Sciences Magazine*, 14(2) (Nueva Granada University, Bogotá).

Maloka's website. Available at: www.maloka.org.

Marcovitch, J. 2002. *La universidad (im)posible* [The (im)possible university]. Madrid: Cambridge University Press.

Murray, R., Caulier-Grice, J. and Mulgan, G. 2010. *The Open Book of Social Innovation: Ways to Design, Develop and Grow Social Innovation*. London: NESTA.

PNUD. 2008. *Reporte Final* [Final Report]. Local development and peace program with IV community of Soacha. Social Action from Presidency of Republic of Colombia – AECI and Spanish agency of international cooperation for development (AECID).

Red Camaleón. Case study. Published by Glocalyouth.com. Available at: http://www.glocalyouth.net/ita/stampa.php?id_studio=61.

Sarmiento Arias, C.A. 2008. Parquesoft, Orgullo emprendedor de Colombia [Parquesoft, proud entrepreneur from Colombia]. [Online]. Available at: http://emprendiendoavivir.com/category/emprender/page/5/.

Sen, A. 2000. *Social Exclusion: Concept, Application and Scrutiny*. Manila: Office of Environment and Social Development Asian Development Bank.

Schank, R. 2010. Interview in the Third International Congress Colombia e-Learning 2010, held in Bogotá, July 1st and 2nd. Published in the SENA's press release, July 6th, 2010. [Online]. Available at: http://www.sena.edu.co/downloads/2010/boletines/julio/Expertos%20reafirman%20calidad %20de%20la%20formaci%C3%B3n%20virtual%20del%20SENA.pdf.

SIPOD, RUPD. 2008. Base de datos unificada de la población desplazada [Displaced population unified database]. Presidential agency for social action and international cooperation. Available at: http://www.accionsocial.gov.co.

Valladares, L. La educación científica intercultural y el enfoque de las capacidades. *Revista CTS*, 6(16). Available at: http://www.revistacts.net/files/Volumen%206%20-%20N%C3%BAmero%2016/valladares_edit.pdf.

Salcedo, C. 2004. 'Buenas ideas + acción = innovación: estudio del caso ParqueSoft' [Good ideas + action = Innovation: Study of ParqueSoft's case], Management graduate thesis, Los Andes University, Bogotá.

Conclusion

In summary, these chapters provide an insight into innovation thinking and practice, particularly in Latin America. Originally drawing on a series of papers delivered at the Kickstart Conference the authors supply evidence that innovation offers Latin American countries an economic, social and political path to sustainable development. Critics argue that the region has lagged behind other parts of the world, in part because innovation has been neglected and maybe because its rich natural resources were easily exploited. The concern is that this pattern of development continues to this day, yet many believe these countries possess the potential to develop more vibrant economies, if government, business and academe collaborate more effectively to encourage innovation.

The writers demonstrate that innovation can flourish in Latin America, if societies are willing to adopt certain thinking and practices. Their evidence suggests that this thinking and practice transcends national boundaries, irrespective of each Latin American country's individual experience. Common themes emerge from the writers' thinking and research, notably the benefits that arise from shared knowledge, the positive impact of government spending on education and research, and the need to create a robust legal framework that protects intellectual property rights. These factors have been cited elsewhere in innovation literature and indicate that Latin America may be implementing a series of measures that bode well for the future.

The first two chapters focus on the idea that innovation although influenced by a variety of forces has to be framed in order to understand what binds together the 'management of and for innovation'. This framework offers practitioners, policy makers and academics alike a tool to understand how innovation evolves and can be shaped. The authors, Edgar et al. and Smith et al., critically identify the role communication plays in building relationships as a precursor to creating knowledge exchange networks, a process Meagher identifies as labour intensive, but essential in underpinning innovation. This theme of knowledge exchange is developed further in Gottwald et al. and Solano Fuentes' chapters who respectively explore innovation within the energy sector and Colombia. Their contention, like that of Diamantini et al., is that participation and cooperation stimulate innovation, a feature Diamantini et al. contend training can encourage. Other mechanisms offered include information communication technology. Rivera Leon believes ICT can not only connect 'actors', but can increase absorption capacities.

Regardless whether learning is delivered informally through networks or more formally through schools and universities, all the authors see learning as critical in building skills and knowledge. The argument is that encouraging learning provides a platform to stimulate research. A number of the chapters' authors identify government as occupying a key role in supporting research directly through the creation of appropriate legal frameworks to ensure robust intellectual property rights (Leal Gonzalez et al., Mayr et al.) or stimulating universities and trade bodies (Leal Gonzalez et al., Solano Fuentes). The argument is that government's role is about creating an environment that encourages innovation, one which arguably stretches wider to encompass business, support agencies and the education sector; in effect, these developments suggest Etzkowitz's Triple Helix model, a model supporters believe offers a more sustainable pattern of economic growth and by extension socio-political development.

Index

Note: Figures and tables indexed in bold.

For Product Safety Concerns and Information please contact our EU
representative GPSR@taylorandfrancis.com Taylor & Francis Verlag GmbH,
Kaufingerstraße 24, 80331 München, Germany

Printed and bound by CPI Group (UK) Ltd, Croydon, CR0 4YY

01/05/2025

01858348-0004